Furniture Restorat

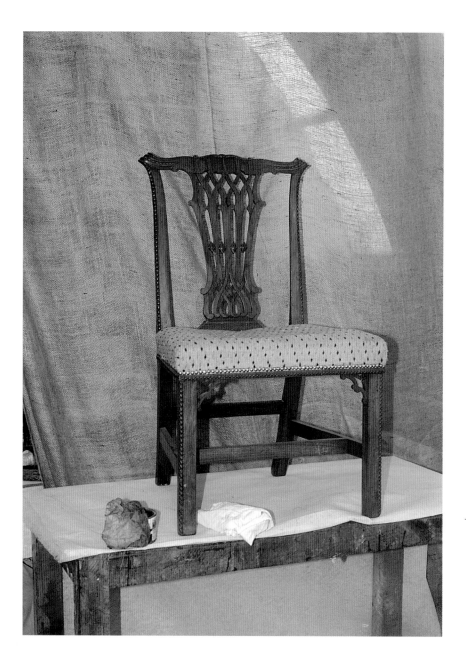

Furniture Restoration

Graham Usher

The Crowood Press

First Published in 1997 by
The Crowood Press Ltd
Ramsbury, Marlborough
Wiltshire SN8 2HR

British Library Cataloguing-in-Publication Data

A catalogue reference for this book is available from the British Library.

ISBN 1 85223 905 0

Line illustrations by David Fisher.

Photographs by the author.

Acknowledgements
To Bill Willis, one of my very first students, who encouraged me to write articles, which led to this book.
    To all my students, because through teaching them I extended my own knowledge.
    Many, many thanks to my long-suffering editors at The Crowood Press.
    And lastly, to my wife Jackie, without whom this book would never have been written.

Photograph previous page: a chair ready for waxing.

Typefaces used: text, New Baskerville and Garamond; headings, Optima Bold.

Typeset and designed by
D & N Publishing
Membury Business Park, Lambourn Woodlands
Hungerford, Berkshire.

Printed and bound by Paramount Printing Ltd, Hong Kong.

CONTENTS

Introduction 6

TOOLS: SELECTION AND CARE 9

2 WOOD: TYPES AND PROPERTIES 15

3 ASSESSMENT OF PIECES 19

4 DISMANTLING PROCEDURES 21

5 CLEANING 36

6 REPAIRING JOINTS 44

7 GLUING AND CRAMPING 60

8 MAKING UP MISSING PIECES 76

9 REPAIRING SPLITS 90

10 REPAIRING AND REPLACING TURNINGS 99

11 VENEERS I: SELECTING, STORING AND LAYING 112

12 VENEERS II: PATCHING AND REPAIRING 122

13 VENEERS III: INLAYS AND STRINGINGS,
   PARQUETRY AND MARQUETRY 141

14 PREPARATION FOR FINISHING 152

15 FINISHING: STAINING AND COLOURING 167

16 FINISHING: POLISHING 183

17 FIXTURES AND FITTINGS 204

Appendix: Furniture Period Chart 211

Glossary 212

Index 223

INTRODUCTION

When I started out on this book I had several strong ideas as to how it was to be written. Over the years that I have been practising and teaching I have read a good number of works on restoring, and have come to the conclusion that although many were sound in their instruction, there were areas where most fell down. The main reason was that projects were really too ambitious for a beginner or for persons with only a small amount of knowledge and experience. I firmly believe that high-quality period furniture should not be used as a learning ground in using tools: only when the practitioner is skilful in the techniques required to repair them should he tackle these pieces. Furthermore, he should have a good overall knowledge of antiques; their setting, and the history of furniture making, otherwise a repair might be out of context with the vintage and as a result its worth destroyed.

On the whole this book is for the beginner or for the person on the first rung of the restoring ladder; however, this is not to exclude the more experienced craftsperson, and in fact I still pick up restoring books as there may be a new approach that I can test. I will take you step by step through typical problems encountered in restoring a very badly damaged piece from start to finish. It is rarely that you will encounter every one of these in one piece; but most will present themselves from time to time. The frame of mind in which a task is undertaken is as important as technique; so we will cover many of the usual problems and more besides, starting with easy ones and building up to more complicated work, and hopefully providing you, the reader, with a sound catalogue of experiences.

My last criticism is that many books cover peripheral skills, which the majority of all-round restorers rarely use, and which would take chapters to explain clearly; this sometimes confuses the issue, and distracts the apprentice from those he really does need.

How to use the book? If you are like me, you will jump straight to your project: all right, but do read the beginning chapters because they are relevant to everything in the book. Forewarned is forearmed! Thorough assessment to devise a work plan saves time and error later on. Think of the course this book describes as a journey, for this is exactly what it is – and it would be silly to try and start a car journey without opening the garage doors first! Think of the initial chapters as putting your luggage in the boot: if you leave them out you will only have to come back later to pick them up.

Each chapter is divided into various project sections, and each can be followed through to its end before the next one is started – just like a day trip on your journey. And when you have finished the whole book, it can still be used easily for reference because it stands on its own, containing all the information needed for that particular step in the restorer's tool kit.

You may find this a very personal book, and indeed I hope you do because this is how I like to teach. I will often use anecdotes, and can do no better than relate to you one of my favourites, the words of a craftsman from whom I learned a great deal. His explanation as to why he liked to work on antiques: placing his hand on a late eighteenth-century chest, he said 'This chest was made by hand: you can turn it upside down and inside out, and the evidence is everywhere – the man who made it left behind a part of himself in the making, and that part is still there. If you listen carefully and with patience it will speak to you; through the piece he will tell you why he did this here and that there, and in this way he will tell you how it should be repaired.'

Too imaginative? Perhaps – but if you don't study the piece you are about to restore, you won't be 'at one' with it, and doing anything at arm's length is always more difficult. Also you will be imposing your personality on it, when it has plenty of its own – it doesn't need yours to mask it.

Well, enough preaching: enjoy your journey!

CHAPTER one

TOOLS: SELECTION AND CARE

There can be no more logical start than to discuss the tools you will use, because after your hands, tools are of next importance. They are very personal possessions: in time, a well balanced tool will fit your hand just as a well worn shoe fits your foot, and will become a friend – not something to do battle with! Some you will have to make, and instructions for this will be found throughout the book; this gives you a chance to become acquainted with their uses.

When buying new tools always try and purchase the best you can afford, and never cheap imports, particularly in the cutting line, as generally these are made of inferior steel. And always be cautious of 'the bargain': remember, you usually get what you pay for. There are, however, many warehouse shops that sell brand-name tools at below recommended prices, and these can be relied upon. Such outlets are now having tools manufactured under their own names and although usually imported, these are sound even if rather more bulky and not as well finished as the home brands.

What about Japanese tools? These are different altogether from the usual imports: they are in a class of their own. By all means buy them, although they can be rather expensive. I don't have any myself, but several of my colleagues do and report good results. For those who acquire a Japanese saw, be sure to read up about it because technically they're not the same as others, and they may need to be used differently; this is also the case when sharpening their chisels. Japanese saws cut on a draw stroke, and not a push stroke, and the thinner blades make

a narrower kerf. Ultimately, the choice is yours, though I believe their popularity is due to fashion as much as to quality.

SECONDHAND TOOLS

Secondhand stalls at flea markets, car-boot sales and auctions provide good hunting grounds for picking up the odd well looked-after tool, and indeed are the only places to look for tools no longer manufactured. But even so, beware! I went to an auction that was selling off a workshop full of tools from an old cabinet-maker. The old, rare items made good prices, but what did surprise me was that tools one could buy new and of the same quality went for the same or even more money than they would have cost 'off the shelf'! This I can only put down to auction hysteria, or people thinking that because they were old they must have been better!

There are now many traders in secondhand tools at flea markets who clean and repair their stock for re-sale. Again, beware. Always check tools out, and if they are not straight or of they are warped – as in the bed of a plane, chisel edges and plane blades that have been ground on a carborundum wheel – then don't buy, unless you have the skill to put them right. The old-fashioned grinder has ruined more chisels and plane blades than anything else, the reason being that when grinding with a carborundum wheel it is difficult not to overheat the blade and take out the temper.

SELECTING TOOLS

CHISELS

When buying a chisel, always hold it gently but firmly by the handle and try to gauge its balance and feel. If it is not comfortable, lay it aside: it is no use trying to accommodate it; because your tool must be your partner; if it is not, you will find it harder to work with. It is important always to feel comfortable when you work, then you will find it easier to concentrate.

Should you choose plastic handles, or wooden ones? It is really to do with what you are used to. I don't possess a plastic-handled chisel: to me, wooden handles seem to have a 'life' that plastic handles don't, and a comfortable warmth, but without making your hand sweaty as plastic ones do. Man has not yet made a product that has all the virtues of wood, from shock absorption onwards. The only thing you can't do with a wood handle is hit it with a hammer and not damage it.

The most common types of chisel are these: firmer; bevelled; mortice; and long-handled or crankhandled paring chisel. Also a firmer gouge, and a scribing gouge. There are several more, but these are the most usual. To help you get started and so as not to over-stretch your budget, buy a set of five or six bevelled chisels and only purchase more when you can afford or need them. The sizes to get are 6mm, 9mm, 12mm, 18mm, 25mm and 36mm.

PLANES

The most frequent question asked by my students is whether metal planes are better than wooden ones and the answer is somewhat contradictory. For a beginner with little experience I would recommend the metal plane with its adjustable mechanism. The reason is that although the blades of wooden planes are thicker and less likely to chatter, and the steel seems to hold its edge better, even so they need more care and attention, and also it is more difficult to adjust them.

The wooden one has another drawback: it is susceptible to climatic change and needs to be constantly checked, even though beech is the wood used, as a rule, which is very stable. Nevertheless, I have a 40in (100cm) wooden try plane, and it is a remarkable creature. The blade keeps like a razor even when I have not sharpened it for some time, and it makes a wonderful sound as it knifes off the wood.

However, initially it may be best to choose a metal plane, as it needs less skill to master, and on the whole you will get a better performance out of it without the disadvantages typical of the wooden ones. Make sure you buy one that has an

Work for Boxing Day

The old fellow who taught me twenty years ago was nearing seventy, and had served a seven-year apprenticeship. According to him, Boxing Day was always used by craftsmen to true up and condition their tools, and no other work was done on that day. Whether all companies did this, or whether it was peculiar to his, I don't know – but once Christmas Day was over, all the mens' planes were brought out and the bases trued. In the course of a year a plane covers a huge mileage going backwards and forwards over wood, and inevitably this creates a certain amount of wear.

Different Planes

(1) Smoothing plane (2) Jack plane
(3) Fore plane (4) Jointer plane
(5) Block plane – a must for the restorer

Rebate Planes

(1) Bull-nose plane (2) Plough plane
(3) Shoulder plane (4) Hand router
(5) Carriage rebate plane

Spokeshaves, etc.

(1) Spokeshaves (2) Draw knife
(3) Adze – dangerous tool
   in inexperienced hands

adjustable mechanism, and do check even a new one. First turn it upside-down, and sight along its base to see if it is true: if the sole is not flat, then you will never get a true surface when you plane. This can be corrected, but there isn't much metal to play with. Now check the underside around the mouth: hairline cracks are most significant, especially on the back end of the mouth, and such planes are almost guaranteed irreparable; obviously secondhand ones will be more liable to this. However, drop it and it will crack, also as a result of a badly adjusted frog, because this causes too much pressure from the blade on the back lip of the mouth, which is fairly thin here. Next, check that the adjusting mechanism is working properly by taking the blade out

and looking for bad alignment or wear; then check the blade and back-iron.

Tackling Problems
If the plane judders and leaves a rough or torn surface then it may be for one or more of these reasons:

- The lever cap is not tight. Solution: tighten the lever cap screw.
- There is dust between the blade and the frog. Solution: remove the dust.
- The back iron does not sit properly on the blade. Solution: the curl edge of the back iron needs to sit along all its edge; if this is uneven, you must hone it until it does.
- You are planing against the grain. Solution: turn the wood around.
- The grain of the wood is going every which way. Solution: adjust the back iron closer to the end of the blade and take a finer cut. If this fails to stop the problem completely, try planing with the plane set at an angle across the wood, creating more of a knifing action. Is it still there? Then adjust the frog so the gap in the mouth is narrower. You can also hone a sharper angle on your blade, though don't go below 25°, as your edge will be weakened.

There are several different types of plane, but there is no need to get them all; I would suggest the block plane, the smoothing plane, the bull-nose plane, and the flat-faced spokeshave.

SAWS

When buying saws, again make sure of comfort: the saw must not bunch your hand up. Try to buy one that uses bolts to hold the handle to the blade; the reason behind this is that if you use a saw doctor he may want to remove the handle. If you do get one that is riveted, make sure it is

Types of Tooth Shapes and Saw Shapes

(1) Rip saw   (2) Cross-cut saw
(3) Panel saw   (4) Dovetail saw
(5) Bead saw   (6) Razor saw
(7) Tenon saw   (8) Coping saw
(9) Crank-handled veneer saw
(10) Fretsaw

tight – there is nothing worse than a rocking blade when you saw.

Before purchasing, hold it edge-up to your eye and sight along it. Do this to both edges: if there is a bend, kink or twist in the blade, reject it.

DRAWING INSTRUMENTS

As well as working tools, you will need drawing instruments to measure and draw straight lines and accurate curves. Besides the ubiquitous pencil, you might purchase a marking knife and a straight-edge, and the following selection of tools:

- **Try square** A medium-sized one for boards and large joints, and a small, 1½in (38mm) engineer's square for small work.
- **Sliding bevel** For marking odd angles. Next to this on my shelf I have a good quality protractor, for adjusting the bevel.
- **Steel rules and French curves** It is useful to have 6in (15cm), 12in (30cm), 24in (60cm) and 36in (90cm) rules.
- **Compass.**
- **Rule** Made for both metric and imperial measurements.

- **Moulding template** It enables you to take a section of a moulding.
- **Cutting gauge** Also known as a knife gauge. It is used for marking and cutting any direction of grain.
- **Dovetail template** This looks like a butterfly with a bar through the middle, though the angle on one wing will be different from the other wing: 5° for hardwoods, 8° for softwoods. These are used to scribe your dovetails.

HAMMERS AND MALLETS

What can be said about a hammer? It, too, is a personal thing – I have used other people's hammers and I assure you that it is not always a pleasant experience. So, find yourself a sound, well balanced hammer, and not a cheap one, either, because the head will soon show blemishes from hammering; and trying to put a nail in straight with a blemished head can be tiresome.

Choose a light one for light work, a heavy one for heavier work, and a pin hammer; also a wooden mallet for your chisels' sake, and lastly a set of rubber hammers for knocking things apart. Purchase a couple of various-sized nail punches.

Remember, the purpose of a hammer is to drive things home, not to smash things up.

PLIERS, PINCERS AND SCREWDRIVERS

Buy a selection of screwdrivers, from a small electrical one to a large cabinetmaker's; you will be surprised how handy they will be.

I would also suggest that you collect a selection of pliers, over and above the normal carpenter's pincers. I would recommend three types: blunt-nosed, long-nosed, and a pair of electrician's side cutters. Grind the face flat on the latter, and make it into a sharper point; these I find invaluable for getting out stubborn nails that are close to the surface of the wood.

MISCELLANEOUS TOOLS AND ITEMS

There are so many other things I could suggest; nevertheless, I have tried to keep to a few handy objects:

- A good set of high speed drills, and a medium wheel brace if you do not own a power drill.
- Several paint scrapers, a putty knife, and search out a long kitchen palette knife (only don't pinch your wife's because she will get mad!).
- G-cramps, as many as you can afford; a pair of 4ft (120cm) sash cramps, and a band cramp.
- A cabinet scraper: one of the most useful pieces of kit – also the hardest to learn to sharpen and use (see chapter on Finishing for method).
- Last but not least: a honing stone.

To buy all these tools at one go would be a considerable investment, so be choosy to start with; purchase only what you really require and get the rest when needed. So which ones to choose? Several years ago I lived in America; when I decided to come back I found that I would be without my tools for some considerable time because I only had room for a briefcase. I therefore loaded it with these essentials:

A set of chisels (five) and a ⅝in (16mm) paring chisel
Medium claw hammer; a mallet
Tenon saw, a gent saw and a coping saw
Rule; 6in (15cm) and 12in (30cm)
Scalpel knife; a marking knife
Mortice gauge and a knife gauge
Set of drills and a wheel brace
Try square, and a sliding bevel
Side cutters
Several screwdrivers
Block plane, smoothing plane, bull-nose, and a spokeshave
Nail punch

Cabinet scraper
Double-grade India honing stone

SHARPENING AND CARE OF TOOLS

There are several reasons for keeping your tools sharp. In particular, is the fact that a blunt tool is a dangerous tool, especially when it comes to chisels; you need to put much more pressure behind it to do the work. This pressure is less controllable, and an out-of-control tool is dangerous.

A new chisel or plane will need honing: this describes the means whereby a cutting edge is put on a blade, and should not be confused with grinding: the tool will already have been ground to the correct angle, which is 25°. The honed edge for most work is 30°. The reasons for these two edges are as follows:

- Cutting bevel 30°: the cutting angle gives a little more strength to the edge, and should be between ½in (0.07mm) and ⅟₁₆in (1mm); any longer than this will create an interference and cause difficulty in cutting. If you are working on pine where the fibres tend to buckle under the pressure of the blade before it actually cuts, lessen the cutting angle from 30° to 25°.
- Grinding bevel 25°: it is important that the clearance, or grinding angle should always be 5° less than the cutting angle. When working in softwoods change the grinding angle to 20°.

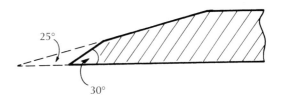

Chisel angles.

13

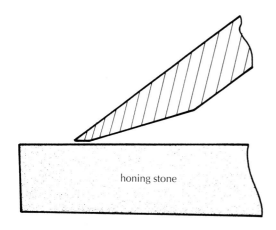

Honing edge to 30°.

GRINDING STONES

After a lot of honing you will need to grind a new clearance angle. This is done on a grinding wheel, preferably a water bath wheel as a normal wheel can overheat your blade. The angle should be 25°. Always square up the edge before grinding.

There are many types of honing stones, but they fall into three main categories: oil stones, water stones and diamond stones.

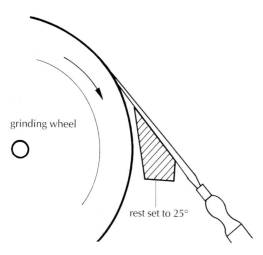

Grinding to 25°.

ANGLES: HOW TO ATTAIN AND KEEP THEM

Watching an old craftsman sharpen his chisels is one thing, copying him is another. I can't stress this enough, and suggest that it may be best to go out and buy a honing guide: it will give you a good edge every time, whereas doing it freehand takes a lot of practice. Admittedly, freehand is quicker, but there is nothing more frustrating than not being able to get a good edge. Sharpen your tools regularly – and you will be surprised how few that is; because most of us always tend to reach for a favourite. So hone little but often, and use the whole of the stone or you will wear it unevenly.

THE FIRST POWER TOOLS

The most useful hand-power tool is the drill. Out of several different sizes, the most useful is a 9.5-volt battery drill. They are so handy and you have no trailing leads to trip over.

Many of my students ask me what stationary power tool they should buy first. The answer is always a bandsaw, and the reason for it is quite straightforward: versatility. You can cut straight lines as well as shapes, at right angles or through to 45°. The bandsaw is an investment, so try and buy the best you can afford, and do some research; most woodworking magazines report on most machines. Look for a two-wheel machine with two speeds, at least a 12in (30cm) throat and a depth of cut of at least 6in (15cm); it should take a blade as small as ⅛in–½in (3mm–13mm). The blade should run against a thrust bearing, not a metal plate, and the guides should be able to support most of the width of the blade. A book on this machine will help maintenance.

This is a basic overview of essential tools. I recommend that you buy a comprehensive book on tools and their care.

two

WOOD: TYPES AND PROPERTIES

A restorer's wood stock is somewhat different from that of other craftsmen who work with wood, being predominantly old bits and pieces of broken furniture. This does not mean that a restorer never uses new wood, but if there is a chance to choose, most will prefer old wood every time.

Reclaimed wood is becoming increasingly rare because furniture that would once have been scrapped is today fetching very high prices, and is now often considered worthwhile to restore. For instance, I have a late Georgian bureau that is in a very bad state of repair with large portions missing; twenty years ago I would have been tempted to use the wood on another worthy piece, but now would not even contemplate such a thing.

So why is old wood preferred? Because the quality of the wood in antique furniture pieces is far better than most wood you can get today. For instance, it is nearly impossible to get new Cuban mahogany, which is a higher grade than Brazilian mahogany; furthermore I believe there is an import ban on it.

This does not mean that new wood is out of the question: it is just second best. However, new wood of the same species must be used rather than old wood of a different kind.

When breaking up a piece for its wood, proceed as gently as possible. Don't smash it apart. Veneers can be reclaimed too, but I leave them on their substrata until I need them, because the process of lifting them from their base wood can leave them brittle and thus harder to store without damage.

TYPES OF WOOD

One can safely say that wood comes in two main categories: softwoods and hardwoods. This categorization is not an indication of how hard or soft a wood is, nor of its strength and weight, although in a great many cases this does hold true and helps us recognize what it is. For example, one of the softest woods in the world and the lightest known is a hardwood, balsa; and yew is a fairly hard softwood. The definitive way of distinguishing between the two is that the hardwoods are from broad-leaf trees which shed their leaves and stand bare in temperate winters, and are known as deciduous; and softwoods are from coniferous or cone-bearing trees. This terminology is mainly botanical.

Recognizing different species is a far harder matter and comes with experience, yet even experts can sometimes be fooled or left in a quandary. I always remember one old auctioneer who, when he didn't know what wood a piece was made of, would catalogue it as tree-wood. Don't be afraid to admit that you are not certain about a wood. There are one or two books on recognition with plates in which colour is very true – but a warning! These plates depict new wood, new wood can vary enormously from that in a piece which has aged and changed in colour through exposure to sunlight. Another factor to help you get to know your woods is that there are general rules of thumb concerning the types of wood which would be used in furniture of a particular type and period – although this is not foolproof, and can sometimes be misleading. Nevertheless, a good knowledge of furniture will certainly help.

The one good thing about restoring antiques is that the list of different woods used in furniture until the twentieth century is small. They can be separated into three main categories: softwoods (pine, yew and so on); European hardwoods (oak, walnut, beech, fruit woods and so on); and exotic hardwoods (mahogany, rosewood, satinwood and so on).

SOFTWOODS

Softwood can be seen in pine or country furniture and yew pieces; it is also used for carcases, drawers and substrates. However, throughout all periods of furniture, better quality pieces may have their carcases, drawers and substrates made of oak or mahogany. Pine comes from temperate climates, as do the European deciduous hardwoods. Yew is different in that it is used as a decorative wood. Although early yew furniture is always solid, later periods may be veneer.

EUROPEAN HARDWOODS

Oak, elm, walnut and ash are not restricted to just early furniture. Even so, except for walnut, they are always thought of as being woods used in early periods and country furniture; it was only from the William 1V and Victorian period that oak became favoured for more sophisticated pieces. Oak was also used for carcase and substrate work because of its innate stability. Beech and birch were used mainly for frame work and in chairs.

Walnut was the major wood from the mid-1600s to the early 1700s for both solid and veneered pieces. It became increasingly unpopular from the 1740s onwards – not, as some stories have it, because there was a walnut tree disease, but because of

import commerce and the wider availability of mahogany which had better working properties. (*See* Appendix for a chart mapping the corresponding periods, woods, and monarchies.)

EXOTIC WOODS

This appellation would seem to imply woods that are only rare or of a particularly unique nature, but this is not so. Exotics include subtropical and tropical woods which are, on the whole, hardwoods; so South America, Africa, the Middle and Far East, and Australasia are in this category, and exotic woods range from mahogany to camphorwood, and teak to rosewood, whether used in the solid or as veneers.

WHY VENEERS?

There are two reasons for the popularity of veneers: first, the wood was extremely expensive or rare; second, it was sought after when the figuring in a piece needed to be matched for decorative purposes. It was also needed when decoration was in a form such as marquetry or parquetry; this was much easier to create from veneers than from solid wood. Veneer also facilitated the mixing of woods, again for the purposes of decoration.

CARING FOR WOODS AND VENEERS

Woods should be stored in a stable atmosphere, for example, if the storage area is of a different humidity to the workshop, then the wood to be used should be brought into the workshop for a few weeks or months to acclimatize.

The planks and uncut logs should be sealed, leaving them to breathe through their sides; otherwise splits will occur in

Wood Count

This list does not include every single wood used in antiques; nevertheless it is fairly comprehensive. 'C' indicates where it is used as carcase; 'D' indicates woods used mainly as decorative embellishments. 'EH' means European and North American hardwoods; 'E' exotic hardwoods, not veneered; and 'F' means framework. 'S' indicates softwood; a small 's' under *Use* indicates solid, and 'V' veneers.

Wood	Type	Use	Origin
Apple	EH	s	Europe
Ash	EH	s	Europe
Beech	EH	C/F/s	Europe
Birch	EH	C/F/s	Europe
Boxwood	EH	D	Europe
Cedar	EH	C	Eastern Mediterranean
Cherry	EH	C/s/V	Europe & N. America
Chestnut	EH	C/s	Europe
Ebony	E	D/V	S. India/Burma/Ceylon
Ebony (macassar)	E	D/s/V	Indonesia (also known as Coromandel)
Elm	EH	C/s	Europe
Holly	EH	D	Europe
Jarrah	E	V/D	Australia
Laburnum	EH	D/s/V	Europe
Lignum Vitae	E	D	W. Indies & S. America
Lime	EH	Carving	Europe
Mahogany	E	s/C/V/D	Cuba/S. America/Africa
Maple	EH	C/D/s/V	Europe/N. America
Oak	EH	C/D/s/V	Europe/N. America
Olive	EH	D/s/V	Mediterranean
Padauk	E	D/s/V	Burma
Pear	EH	C/s	Europe
Pine	S	C/s	Europe
Plane	EH	D	Europe
Rosewood	E	D/s/V	S. America & E. Indies
Satinwood	E	D/s/V	Ceylon/India/Burma
Spruce	S	C/s	Europe & N. America
Sycamore	EH	s/V	Europe
Teak	E	C/s	Burma & India
Walnut	EH	D/s/V	Europe & N. America
Yew	S	D/s/V	Europe

logs as they season, and in cut planks too if temperature and humidity fluctuate too much. Planks and logs should be laid flat on battens 4ft–5ft (1.2m–1.5m) apart and off the ground; where a number of planks are laid, battens should be employed to separate them, enabling an air flow between them which will prevent the risk of moisture gathering and rot occurring.

The best time to cut down a tree is in late autumn when the sap has stopped rising. Lay the cut log on battens, and put a cover over it to prevent too much weather penetrating or lying on it in a thick layer.

Seal the ends. Leave it for six months to a year, and then debark, roughly thick-plank it and lay it down again with battens and a cover, ensuring a good air flow between the planks, for another three to four years at least; then bring it inside for a minimum of another year. Try to keep the planks in sequence; this will help if you need to match.

Veneers are usually cut when green, and as they dry may tend to buckle. When storing veneers lay them flat and out of the damp. Drips from leaking roofs will stain and ruin them.

Various types of timber.

CHAPTER three

ASSESSMENT OF PIECES

It surprises me how many books on restoration do not even mention 'assessment' in any detail; I can only assume that the writer knows his business so well that he makes his assessment automatically and does not really consider it to be a subject of importance.

Restoration is not magic – although many in the profession would have you think so – but the application of many skills. Looking back on my training it seems that I was not taught how to assess the problems to be tackled, nor what to do first, but learned through osmosis.

The obvious doesn't always come first, the inclination being rather to follow your nose through the work to the end. However, you are more likely to get into trouble if you take this course of action, without prior thought.

So, where to start? I feel that restoration is lost or won at this moment. So many young (and not so young) restorers don't ask the question 'What is this?' By that I don't just mean identifying whether it is a table, or a chair, but what period of manufacture. The matter of period is important, as furniture did not just appear but evolved over many centuries. The way things are made, the materials used and the tools that made them, all these play a part. It is always abundantly clear to me when looking at a bad restoration (although the actual standard of work may be of good quality) that these factors have not been taken into consideration.

It simply is not practicable to devote five years to studying furniture and its whys and wherefores before you start restoring. So, when approaching a piece find out as much about it as possible, and if your local library or dealers can't help, write to the Victoria & Albert Museum; I have always found them of great help.

To illustrate this point, let's take an example. The finish on a chair is totally destroyed: how does one re-finish it?

Question: Materials to be used? Oil? Wax? Shellac(French polish)?

Question: What period? It will not be Shellac before 1780–1800 because the technique and materials were not introduced into this country before then.

Answer: It is 19th century.

Question: What manner is it? There are many answers to this question: first, is it country or town? Was it made in an unsophisticated manner by a country carpenter, or by a cabinetmaker?

Answer: Not sure.

Question: What wood and finish is it? If it is one of the broad-leaf English woods the answer is possibly wax: even in the Arts & Crafts movement at the turn of this century some workshops only used wax or oil, even on walnut. Shellac was used only on Victorian mass-produced oak and walnut, and of course the foreign hardwoods. Of course, there will always be one joker, but on the whole this is a fair rule.

From this little example I hope you can appreciate the need for caution.

Within the chapters which follow, many clues will be set down. Below is a check-list on how to approach the problems within a piece. This formula should not be regarded as set in stone, but I feel that this system may help you.

ACTION LIST

Treat restoring like making a new piece, even though with a new project one starts with the design and plan; with an antique of course this is already done for you – the piece is already there. For this action list, let us take a hypothetically damaged piece: a table, which is rocky, has a broken leg and a badly marked finish.

1. Take apart.
2. Gently clean all pieces.
3. Clean all joints and check them for probable repair.
4. Make repairs to each piece one by one
5. Re-assemble and glue.
6. Repair finish.
7. Assemble completely. Where a table is concerned it may be easier to complete the finish to the top and base separately, and only then put the bits together to make the whole.

The Checklist (work sheet)

- Type of furniture? . . . .
- Period?. . . . .
- Style? . . . . (Chippendale, Sheraton, etc.)
- Manner? . . . . (Country, Town)
- Solid or veneered? . . . .
- What decorative woods? . . . . (such as inlays)
- The carcass is made from. . . . .

Problem questions:
- Treatment for worm?. . . . .
- What is the state of the finish?. . . . .
- Are the joints loose?. . . . .
- Are there broken pieces? . . . .
- Are there missing pieces? . . . .

four

DISMANTLING PROCEDURES

Before you start any work on a piece, it is wise to remove all 'furniture' (brass handles, locks and so on), the simple reason being that the easier you can make the work to be undertaken the better. For example, when polishing a drawer front, remove the handles, even wooden ones that are glued in. The fewer obstacles in the way the better.

Removing these can be harder than you think, especially rusted-in screws. I would also suggest that you use your own discretion if you come up against a hinge or a piece of furniture you cannot remove without damaging either it, the wood or the screws; if you can manage to do the job without removing them, albeit a little awkwardly, then admit defeat.

REMOVING SCREWS

Because a screw is such a familiar object, one's first instinct is to pick up a screwdriver that seems to fit, jam it into the slot

Old and modern screws.

and turn. However, let's be a little scientific about this and have a closer look at what we are dealing with; the screw did not get there by chance, so don't leave removing it to chance now. The first screws were handmade and the threads were quite irregular, with a head that could be thin in relation to the body, and the slot wide but not very deep in comparison to the machine-made ones. The early ones did not have the benefit of the precision engineering that we take for granted when we use one made today.

Wherever possible it is desirable not to replace new for old: the original screw is part of your antique, so great care should be taken in its removal. There are many ways that a screw can thwart you, and not least yourself. Remember that a screwdriver is of harder metal than the screw, so you are likely to damage the screw, from rounding the slot to snapping off the head.

HOW TO DO IT

1. Take a bradawl or a hard, sharpish instrument; I have an old carving chisel that I broke and so rendered useless, about ⅛in (3mm) square. This I ground to a point, then blunted by gently tapping the point with a hammer, which has left a burr. Use your tool to scrape the slot clean of old hard wax and dirt. If the slot is not very deep, or someone has been there before you and rounded the slot, then don't attempt to unscrew it yet. Instead use the tool you cleaned the slot with to scrape it deeper.

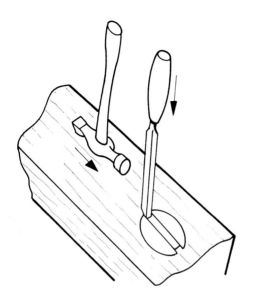

Cleaning out a screw slot.

2. Place the tool in the slot at the end furthest away from you, leaning the handle
towards you so that it is at an angle of

Cleaning out a screw slot.

about 70°. If you are right-handed hold
it in your left hand with a firm downward
pressure. In your right hand take a pin
hammer and tap the side of the blade
near to the point gently, moving the tool
towards you. If you hit it too hard it will
come out of the slot and damage the surrounding area. After several goes, you
will find the slot should be deeper. If it is
not, then the screw is much too hard for
this tool – but we are not beaten yet. Get
a fine-toothed hacksaw blade (new) and
snap off the end where there are no
teeth, at an angle of 30°–40°. Keep it
short; it will be less likely to bend. Wrap
a rag around the other end, then place
the pointed end in the slot and draw it
backwards and forwards until the slot is
deeper. This can take a little time.

3. Once you have a deep enough slot,
select a screwdriver that fits snugly.
Don't use a driver that is too small,
because it can twist in the slot, damaging it, and will then ride out. Now tap
the top sharply with a mallet, which
does two things: it makes sure the driver
is bedded properly, and it drives the
screw in slightly and so loosens its grip.
If the screw is rusted the shock will
loosen the rust, as this forms a brittle

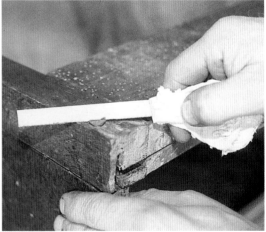

Deepening slot to take a screwdriver.

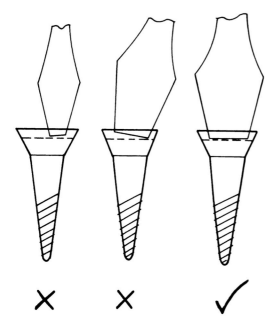

How and how not to use a screwdriver.

Heating screw with a soldering iron.

shell. With a firm downward pressure, twist the driver slightly clockwise, as though you are screwing it further in. Now twist the other way – most screws will start to move. If this does not occur, try several times. However, it is most important not to destroy the slot.

4. If the above method fails, heat a large soldering iron and place this on the head of the screw. This will heat the screw and make it expand, forcing it to enlarge the hole. If this fails you can use a 'sprung' screwdriver, holding it in the slot and giving a sharp, hard clout with a hammer. This generally moves most of the very stubborn screws. However, there are two drawbacks to this method: you cannot use it on fragile pieces for fear of damage; and the sharpness of the twist can either shear off the head, or the screwdriver will just ride out of the slot, damaging it in the process.

5. The last method will actually destroy the head altogether, and that is to use a centre punch and tap the screw round.

If the head shears, use a tool that you can make yourself. Select a piece of mild steel tube, the same size as the diameter of the screw, and file teeth around its edge – four or five will do. Tap this over the broken screw, then fit to the chuck of a drill, and drill down to the depth you believe the screw to be. If you have guessed right the screw will come out as you withdraw the tube. This is also used for nails and pins.

REMOVING NAILS

Let us first concentrate on those which hold things together in a proper manner, and not those used in bodged repairs.

Back panels on a chest of drawers (and similar items): Because of their position the wood is normally very dry and liable to split.

HOW TO DO IT

1. Lay the chest on its front and start from the base, where there is easy access to the end of the panels. Start at a joint in

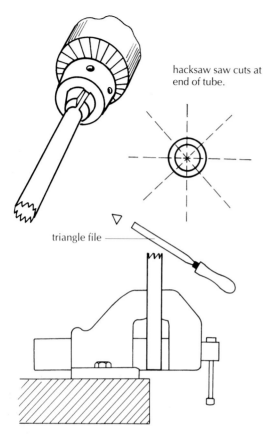

hacksaw saw cuts at
end of tube.

triangle file

Tube nail drill.

A drill tube.

Easing a panel without splitting.

the panels as centrally in the piece as
possible. With a paint-scraper, tap it
under the panel until it touches the nail.
With the nail midway along the blade,
take another scraper and place it on top
of the first scraper. Tap this one into
position as well.

2. Now, push a medium-sized screwdriver
between the two blades until it reaches the
nail, and then gently twist. This will prise
the panel away from what it is nailed to,
but don't lift the panel away too far or you
will split the wood around the nails next to
it. Do this methodically around the panel,
easing it up gently until you return to the
first nail. Repeat the prising and lifting

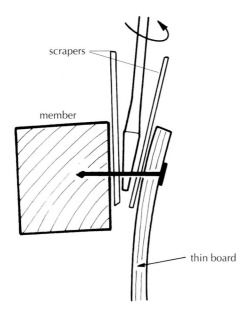

Easing up panels with scrapers and a screwdriver.

until the whole panel is released.

This method should be used as normal practice with most nailed objects, and it has two major advantages:

- You should rarely, if ever, split anything.
- You will never leave tell-tale screwdriver

Damage done by screwdrivers.

marks which look unsightly and disfigure and devalue the piece.

Loose joints held together by nails: This practice is unfortunately all too common, and occurs in the belief that a loose joint will become firm if a nail is driven through the joint. To release the joint, the nail must first be extracted. Neglect this and the joint is forced apart, invariably damaging the joint itself and worse, splitting off the female part of the joint.

HOW TO DO IT

1. Sometimes the nail has been punched below the surface and covered over with a wax or plaster stopper, be sure to check your joints before opening them. Tell-tale signs are a lighter or darker patch, or a sunken area. In this case, gently dig it out with a pointed instrument; the best way is

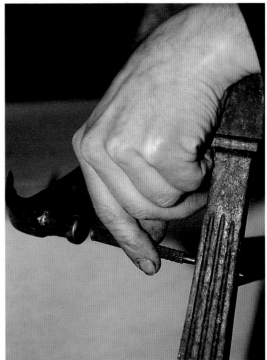

Punching through a nail.

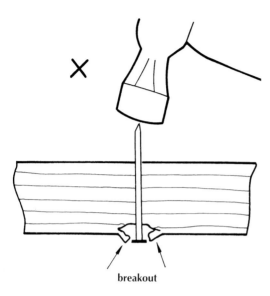

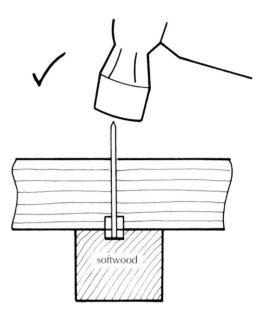

Controlling nail breakout.

to use a small nail-punch, and drive it on through until the point just appears.

2. Blunt the point with a hammer and drive it back through the wood. It is a good idea to place that part of the piece on a bit of scrap softwood so the nail head is then driven into the softwood; this will prevent it splintering out any wood

surrounding the hole as it emerges from the piece.

3. When the head is far enough out, use a pair of pincers or electricians' side-cutters to pull it out the rest of the way. Remember to lay a scraper blade on the wood abutting the nail before you use the pincers or cutters, otherwise you will

Using sidecutters.

leave indentations in it. My preference would normally be side-cutters for this job, mainly because you will not need to drive the pin so far out of the wood, and so will lessen the risk of splitting the wood with the nail-punch.

4. If the nail has a flat round head and is on the surface of the wood and cannot be pulled out without digging into the wood, centre-punch the head and drill the head out, then use the method described in Extracting Pins below.

The nail that can't be driven through: This happens when the nail is shorter than the member it is driven into and the use of a nail-punch will split the wood before it clears the joint. The hollow drill (mentioned in the section on extracting screws) is about the only safe way to get over this problem; although it will leave a large hole, it will be less unsightly than digging it out.

Although you will find the nail botch mainly in conjunction with the mortice and tenon, don't be fooled. Always check, as I have found them going through dowelled joints, and even through dovetails (both ways). The chair is the main culprit, but I have found them in all forms of furniture where nails were not intended. My latest find was an oak gateleg table where a couple of 6in (15cm) nails were firming up a joint.

EXTRACTING PINS

Other kinds of pin can be found: for example, early oak and walnut furniture had wooden pins through the joint, and this method is still used in some furniture today. Unfortunately in later furniture the pin generally does not go all the way through the member.

HOW TO DO IT

1. The only way is to drill it out. Start by centre-punching the hole – this will stop the drill from wandering – and use a slightly smaller drill bit. The shim of wood left will pull away from the wall of the hole by using a sharp instrument, and can then be extracted quite easily with the long-nosed pliers. To make sure you drill to the end of the pin, put tape round the drill that will just stop short of going through the member.

Table leg with a nail in it.

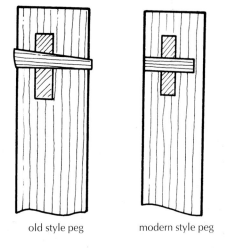

old style peg   modern style peg

Two ways of pinning a tenon joint.

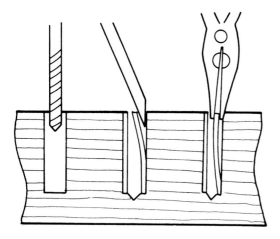

Extracting a pin.

2. With earlier furniture the pins quite often went right through the member. If this is the case, drive them back through with a small metal bar; generally a ³⁄₁₆in (4mm) bar is just right. Save the pins and mark which hole they came from, because each will vary in size and shape; as a rule they were slightly rounded, square, tapered pins forced into round holes, and over the years they take on a character of their own.

Teak and Indo furniture also have their joints pinned, and there are several reasons for this. Much Far-Eastern furniture was held together not by using glue, but by staggering the holes and using tapered pins. This was because many Far-Eastern species of wood will not bond well other than with the most modern hi-tech glues, because of their oil content. Teak is a typical example.

WITHDRAWING JOINTS

This can sometimes be easier said than done, even with the loosest joints. As you take the piece apart, mark the joints, especially if the members look similar.

Hand-made objects may seem the same, but a fraction of difference can put the whole piece out of kilter. I mark my joints by using a ¼in (6mm) chisel, and make Roman numeral marks of the same value on each female and male joint.

Always use a rubber mallet, or a wooden mallet with a piece of waste wood that is softer than the wood of the construction, and use short sharp taps. Never lay into the task with more force than you can control – that way lies disaster.

Although a joint may feel loose and can be wiggled quite freely, it may not want to part. So first check that there is no pin holding it, and check thoroughly. The reason is possibly that when the joint was made, the female part (the hole) was cut tapered, the hole widening towards the bottom; the male part (the tenon), still having a layer of old glue on it, forms a wedge. This will be the case if the joint becomes firm as it is partially withdrawn.

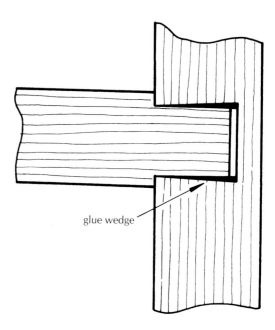

glue wedge

Tenon with glue attached.

28

HOW TO DO IT

1. Sometimes several sharp taps will free the joint, because as glue ages it will crystallize, especially thick animal glue; the sharp taps are likely to shatter it, leaving the component parts separate.
2. If this does not work, drill a fine hole underneath the tenon until you reach the bottom. Inject near-boiling water into the joint, then wiggle it about to make the water circulate; this may have to be done several times, but slowly the glue will melt and release its hold. Try and chat up a friendly vet, because the type of syringe and needle you need is the sort they use on large animals.
3. Sometimes a joint appears to be loose, but is still stubborn to withdraw: this situation arises when a tenon crosses the path of another entering from an adjacent side, for example in a chair leg. The end of the tenon may have a lump

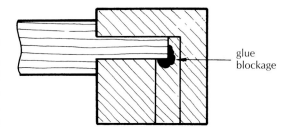

Tenon with glue attached.

of glue attached to it where the adjacent mortice comes into contact. This can be a problem when that joint has to be removed first, and if it refuses to shatter, then the hot water method must be used. If, however, the other joint can be removed first, then it is simply a task of breaking away the glue with a small chisel, via the other mortice.

DISMANTLING A CHAIR

When dismantling a chair, do it in a methodical manner, trying not to stretch the joints too much, as this can crack the other joints. Slowly ease one joint a little, then work on the opposite side, drawing them both apart evenly. Sometimes only one joint is loose, and the others are so firm you are likely to damage them if you do try to prise them too far apart.

HOW TO DO IT

1. This being the case, open the joint gently. Most chairs have the flexibility to stretch, but stop before you break anything. It is virtually impossible to gauge how far to go by tapping the joint apart, so I use a joint-spreader which is easy to make: it is simply two blocks of wood that open up as you turn a threaded bar, gently forcing the joint out of its socket. This method is not foolproof, however,

Steaming a joint to loosen it.

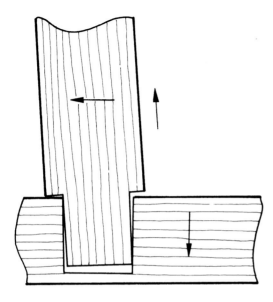

A trapped tenon.

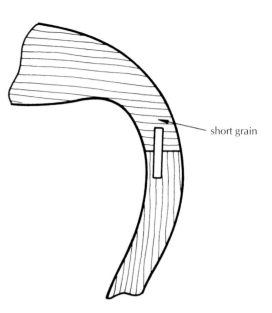

short grain

A joint with short grain.

and needs a little experience, so practise on something of no value.

2. When opening a joint one tends to tap it on one side which will make it lock up as the angle changes; so do it on both sides, as the force must be in the direction of the joint. Many joints are damaged because of this fact alone.

Removing the head or top rail: The Queen Anne type and the spoon- or hoop-back, can present a problem because of the nature of the joint and where it is in relation to the grain of the wood. The chair is notoriously weak in this area as the joint has a lot of short grain around it, and so it will not take a lot of sharp tapping. It would not be surprising to find that many of these chairs have repairs in this area already.

What is short grain? This is where the design has dictated that the grain is running contrary to its real structural strength. For example, on a spoonback chair, the top rail is semicircular, and it is cut out of a solid plank, so that instead of the grain

running round the circumference, it normally goes straight ; this means that the ends of the semicircle cut across the grain, leaving little strength. When tapped too vigorously the grain will split, especially on old, dried-out wood.

HOW TO DO IT

1. Make up a small block of softwood that corresponds to the inside contours of the rail. Holding it firmly underneath the rail, tap gently, first to one side, then the other. Don't open up the joint on one side too much, without easing the other side, otherwise it may be enough to crack that area. Make the block large enough in order to spread the shock of the tap and prevent the wood from breaking.

2. Another type of fixing which may fox you is that found on Regency chairs, although many periods have it. The rail is 4in–5in (10cm–13cm) deep, and is curved. It is attached to the back uprights by a dovetail, and must be tapped upwards to remove it.

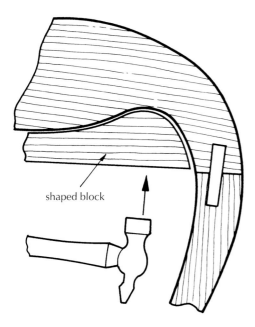

Correct position of a cramping block.

Because of the nature of the joint and the shortness of the grain, this too is an area of weakness, and many chairs of this design will be found to have

repairs. Most commonly, this was by the addition of screws, and the splitting out of the wood either in or around the joint. The real reason for this damage is not because things have been bashed against the piece, but because of the way in which it has been handled: one should lift a chair by holding the seat, whereas most people lift it by the top rail, one of its weaker areas.

DISMANTLING DOWEL AND DOVETAIL JOINTS

Dowel joints are found mostly in later chairs and furniture. When these break people find some difficulty in replacing them properly, and particularly in keeping in the same position without a jig (this will be covered in the chapter dealing with repair of joints). To dismantle these joints, use the same method as explained for the mortice and tenon – remember to check for nails! Even in small-diameter dowels I have found them.

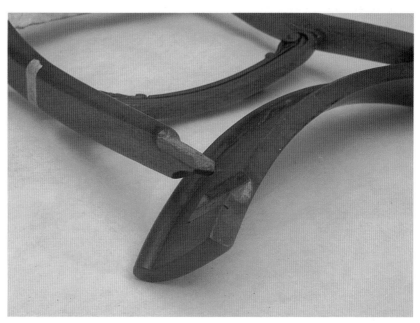

Dovetail joint for chair back.

Dovetails are used in several places in furniture, most commonly in drawers, and in the carcases of chests and wardrobes of all types.

HOW TO DO IT

1   Dismantle by placing a length of scrap wood along the whole of the jointed area, then gently tap the joint out. Move the head of the mallet along the scrap of wood with each tap to prevent any splitting of the wood.
2. Dovetail joints are also found in the runners of chests-of-drawers, and should be extracted by sliding them out from the

Opening up dovetails.

back; also hidden dovetails that look like mitres until you try to get them apart. The only way to find out which way they come apart is to look behind them and find out which piece has the pin. It is the pin piece that needs to slide out.

3. Carver chairs sometimes have dovetails to hold the base of the arm support, and are also screwed from the inside of the seat rail for extra strength, especially on quality chairs. The support slides down into the joint cut into the side seat rail.
4. Pedestal tables with cantilevered legs also use tapered dovetails to hold the legs to the base, plus a metal spider for extra support. Always replace the spider. There are two reasons for using a tapered dovetail:
    (i) Because the legs are to the side of the column and not underneath, a leverage pressure is set up which will try and pull the bottom part of the joint out of its socket. With a dovetail, the more pressure exerted in this area, the more the joint tightens up.
    (ii) The taper acts in a similar way. The downward pressure of the column will push the taper tighter into the joint.

The spider acts as support, for the reason given in (i), so before the joint can be

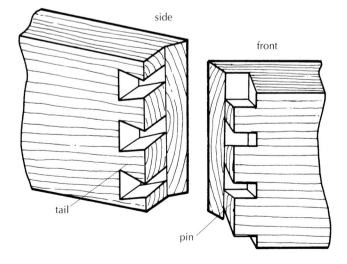

Mitred dovetail.

separated it is necessary to remove the spider. This is usually held on by old forged nails: try and save these if possible. Remove each leg by a sharp downward tap on its top end, and as near the joint as possible. As soon as it is loosened it should slide out.

LOCATING SCREW FIXINGS

As I have mentioned before, screws have been used in furniture for a long time, and over the years many ingenious ways have been used to conceal them. This section will help you to find them and to know when a joint is using them. There is nothing so frustrating as trying to open a joint which should come apart, but doesn't. And when finally it does, you might well have done a great deal of damage.

Locating screws in chairs: There are certain areas on most chairs where it is usual to find hidden screws. For example, the arms of carver chairs generally have a screw fixing the back of the arm to the back upright.

The arm is notched into the upright in a bird's-beak joint and is glued, but this is not enough and a screw is used as added support, introduced into the back of the upright and passing right through it and into the arm. This screw is hidden by a core plug, and has to be removed by drilling it out with a slightly smaller drill bit.

A core plug is a circular piece of wood of the same type as the chair. It is unlike a dowel inasmuch as the grain runs across the plug, and not down its length. It is not always easy to spot core plugs; the best thing to do in this case is to align your eye with the middle of the arm – the screw goes through the upright slightly diagonally so that it passes into the strongest part of the arm.

The other place to locate hidden screws is around the seat area on late Victorian and Edwardian bedroom chairs. The same method is used as described above.

Removing hinges: There is a type of hinge used on cupboards and wardrobe doors that can be difficult if you are unacquainted with it. These hinges are situated at the top and bottom of the door in recesses, and not on its side. Access to the

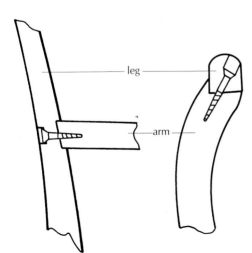

Location of screw for holding an arm rest.

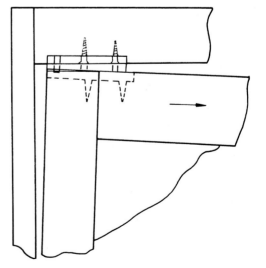

Pivot hinge being removed (1).

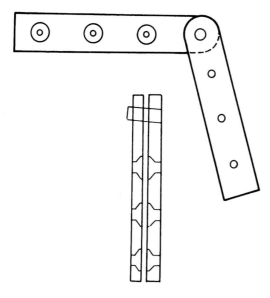

Pivot hinge being removed (2).

door, so release the screws from the bottom plate of the top hinge and reverse the process.

Recessed screws on tables: The most common hidden screws on tables are the expanding type, situated in a recessed pocket between the runners that let the table expand, and the only way to get at these is to open it fully. It is wise to turn it over on its top for easier access; also, when you have released the tops from the frame, if the runners are worn it can fall apart. These tables can be very heavy, and with legs and frames going every whichway you risk damage not only to the table but yourself as well. A 2ft 6in (75cm) square piece of mahogany on the end of a frame is no joke when it lands on your foot: it hurts!

screws is difficult and there seems to be no way for the hinge to come out.

HOW TO DO IT

1. The top hinge is the one to work on. The hinge is made up of two thin plates, one having a pivot pin, the other a hole for the pin to turn on. Each plate has two or three screw holes. Unscrew the screws in the top plate attached to the carcase.

2. Using an electrical screwdriver, put it into the furthest hole away from the pivot, and wiggle it free from its recess. It should drop down onto the lower plate leaving just enough room for you to pull the freed top corner out of its frame.

3. When free of the frame, just lift the door and the bottom hinge pivot-pin should slide free of the plate attached to its frame.

4. Sometimes these hinges are put upside-down. If this is the case, the pivot pin will stop you from withdrawing the

TEN GOLDEN RULES

1. When working either on the bench or the floor, put down a piece of clean carpet. It is amazing how any piece will slide around and pick up dents and scratches.

2. Always study the piece before you start work, and map out in your mind what must come off first.

3. Take off doors and mirrors first, and put the latter safely away; protect them by putting them behind a board. I'm not superstitious, but I hate to tempt providence!

4. Lay out all the tools you will need so they are to hand before you start. There is nothing more irritating than to find you need a tool which is out of reach, but you can't let go of the piece you're working on.

5. Have a container ready for the bits and pieces. Don't throw anything away. And be sure to put even a bent nail into the container, even if you know you are going to replace it. Make this a habit.

(Early in my training I did not do this and let a nail fall to the ground; when I had finished, the top of the piece was scratched. Learn from my bitter experience!)

6. When tapping things apart, always use a piece of scrap wood as a buffer; this should be softer than the wood of the piece being worked on, and if the surface is polished, glue a felt pad to the end.

7. Never wallop the piece; use controlled sharp taps.

8. If you break something, retain it and do not touch the broken edges. There is a chance you can glue back and not see the break. (*See* following chapters.)

9. Always mark the pieces so that they will go back in the same place. Have a piece of chalk handy – a roll of masking tape too, because you can write on it and number the screws; this is particularly relevant when dealing with tops when a screw from another place in the top may go right through.

10. Look after the slot in the screw; lose this, and it could mean a great deal more work.

Some Useful Tools for Removing Various Fixtures and for Dismantling

- Assorted screwdrivers

- A medium screwdriver with a centre section ground down (to remove slotted nuts that retain drawer handles)

- Assorted sizes of mild steel tubes

- Pin and centre-punch

- Large kitchen palette knife

- Couple of old paint scrapers

- Pincers

- Electrician's side-cutters

- Hammer

- Rubber and wooden mallets

- Large syringe and needle

- Bradawl

- Oak wedges (assorted)

five

CLEANING

It might seem more logical for a chapter on cleaning to come just before the one on finishing. However, if a chair is already in pieces it will be much easier to clean like this, or even to strip if the finish is beyond repair. Also, if you have to replace an area of wood or veneer then it is very important to know what the original wood looks like and not guess what it should be through a veil of dirt or crazed polish. Moreover when joints are dismantled it must be supposed that there is old glue still on them, and this must be cleaned off if regluing is going to be a success.

Tools and Materials You Will Need

Tools

Assorted sizes of chisels, cabinet-scrapers, paint-scrapers

Drill and bits

Various bristle toothbrushes of different sizes

Small stiff shoe brush, brass suede brush

Wedges made from a hardwood such as mahogany

A pointed instrument

Modelling knife

Paint brushes (1in/25mm and 2in/50mm)

Materials

Steel wool (0, 00 and 000); methylated spirits; proprietary brand of stripper; cleaner, plenty of old rags, hot water.

CLEANING JOINTS

People make the mistake of thinking that cleaning joints is a simple affair. In one way it is, but the operation needs thought, especially if the glue is not an animal glue. It is not a matter of simply chiselling the old glue off, because that way you will surely remove some wood as well, and make a sloppy joint. Therefore we will look at a number of different glues, and the easiest and safest means of cleaning them.

ANIMAL GLUE

Scotch pearl glue, rabbit skin glue and hoof and horn glue are generally known as animal glues, and are termed hot water glues – also called stinky glues by many who remember the glue corner in the school workshop. These glues will be extremely hard and will blunt your chisels very quickly, but there are several ways to cope with them.

HOW TO DO IT

1. Put the joint in a vice if you can. It is important to use a vice, or to cramp the piece firmly to the bench, especially when using a sharp instrument, thus leaving both your hands free and preventing you from maiming yourself.

2. Lumps of glue are very often found on the ends of joints and at their bottoms, but these will readily chip off with a sharp chisel. And if, after removing the large bits, you find yourself cutting away the wood – stop! A cabinet scraper should be used to remove the thin coating. Some people prefer to use the chisel to scrape this off: okay, but remember a chisel is for cutting, and scraping can damage it.

3. The proper tool is the cabinet scraper, but it is one of the harder tools for a beginner to sharpen and master (*see* Chapter 14). If you feel more comfortable with a chisel, then use the bevelled and not the flat face to scrape with, as the scraping action will leave the chisel with a bevel on its edge, making it necessary to regrind it.

4. Another way of removing the glue is to use hot water brushed on after you have removed the large lumps. Leave it for a minute or two, then repeat several times. Now take a chisel and the glue will literally slide off. The trouble with this method is that the joint must be thoroughly dry before you can reglue (*see* Chapter 7 on Gluing); furthermore if you use steam, especially where polish is near, it will destroy the finish. This method is harder to contain to the area that needs to be cleaned unless you use a fine jet to apply it.

5. Former breaks where old glue has shattered apart, or where the mend was badly aligned, are difficult. For example, a chair leg that has been broken down the grain: it was repaired, but was misaligned. To break this joint, first mask with masking tape close to the joint all round, and then hold over a jet of steam, like a kettle spout; keep moving it around the whole joint. After a few minutes start to flex the leg; this will allow the joint to open slowly and admit more steam into the joint. This is slow work, so be patient!

6. The next operation is the same as for cleaning a joint, except for one detail:

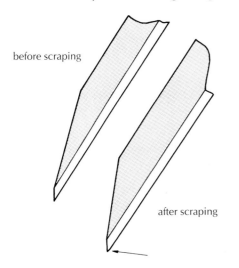

The flat face of a chisel bevelled by scraping.

before scraping

after scraping

An old break showing misalignment.

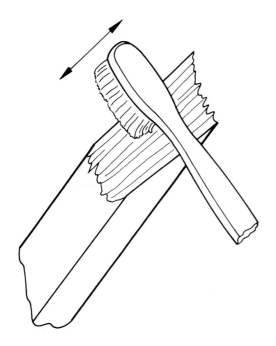

Washing old glue out of the grain.

when a piece of wood breaks with the grain it will not break in a flat surface but in ridges and valleys; also you will find loose splinters pulled out and hanging. The glue will be filling this unevenness. Take a small stiff shoe brush; if the joint is small use a *bristle* toothbrush. Brush hot water onto the glue; the action must go with the grain.

7. Gently wash away the glue with the brush, leaving only the most stubborn lumps. Pat dry with a rag, never wipe.

8. Take a sharp modelling knife or chisel and cut the remaining lumps away, always remembering to follow the direction of the grain of the wood. Inspect closely; you are quite likely to find some glue remaining in the valleys of the grain. Remove this by using a sharp pointed instrument, again running with the grain. It is now nearly ready to glue. Leave to dry. It is important to make absolutely sure of this, before recommencing

PVA GLUES

These are generally white glues out of a tube, the most well known being Evo-Stick 'W' resin. They will break down after a time if left soaking in methylated spirits, but this is usually highly impractical as the spirits will destroy the finish. So the only recourse is to use the chisel and scraper, and again, with broken pieces the glue will have to be cut away.

IMPACT GLUES

These will dissolve and soften if you apply cellulose thinners. (Make sure you ventilate the workshop.) Brush it on and wait a few minutes; if it is not too thick it will peel or roll off when rubbed with your thumb. These glues stay elastic and tend to jam up a scraper, and unless your chisel is very sharp it will stretch the glue rather than cut it.

CASEIN GLUES

The best known of these is 'Cascamite'. This type of glue sets like concrete: methylated spirits is supposed to soften them but it is a very long process. The larger lumps will chip off, but on the whole you will need to take a thin layer of wood off, to clean the joint. Not a happy situation – just grit your teeth and be careful.

Cleaning off softened glue.

EPOXY GLUES

The same applies to these glues as with Cascamite.

AEROLITE GLUES

These will dissolve with cellulose thinners, but take a long time. I recommend you use the same method as the last two glues.

There are a few other glues, but it is rare to come across them. If you can identify them, find out what the manufacturers recommend.

THE CLEANING AND REMOVAL OF FINISHES

It is worth spending a few minutes identifying and understanding the condition of a finish before you undertake the task of cleaning.

RECOGNIZING THE FINISH

The following tests are not totally foolproof, but they constitute a good guide.

Testing a finish.

Always use an area out of the way, such as underneath the seat member of the back leg out of the line of sight. Give the chemicals a minute or so to work, and do it in the order laid down below.

(a) Test with turpentine. If this moves or removes the surface, then it is an oil varnish, or wax.
(b) Test with meths. If it moves or removes the surface then it is French polish, or a shellac varnish.
(c) If neither of these tests moves the surface then it is either a synthetic varnish or a cellulose lacquer finish.

CLEANING A FINISH

Unless you are experienced at recognizing the state of a particular finish I would always recommend that you start with the least damaging process; it will soon be apparent whether cleaning (with for example, the recipe below) is sufficient. You should be left with a bright, clear sheen on the finish. I prefer the following cleaner recipe as it is fairly gentle, even though there are several others that you can use:

40 per cent vinegar
20 per cent meths
40 per cent linseed oil

HOW IT WORKS

The vinegar degreases the surface and cuts into the dirt (such as fly spots). The methylated spirits also cuts through grease and dirt, and also dissolves a layer of the polish. (French polish is made up of many coats and this should not normally remove all the finish, unless it is already damaged.)

The linseed oil has two jobs to do:

• It acts as a lubricant to the meths so that it neither takes off too much polish nor leaves the surface rough.

• It also rejuvenates the finish, and brings colour back into a faded area. (Not only does the wood fade, but the finish can as well, turning to a cloudy, buttery colour.)

1. Shake well, as the mixture separates quite quickly. Never leave the top off the container even when in use, as the meths will evaporate and leave it unbalanced. A good container to use is a squeezy soap bottle. Use with 000 steel wool, and wipe each area clean with rag as you do it. Leave on for a few moments before working, as it will loosen the dirt and make the task less arduous, but never let it dry before wiping. Always work with the grain.

2. Check the surface beforehand for bare patches in the finish. These should be protected by first cleaning with dry 000 steel wool, then a couple of layers of shellac polish should be brushed on; alternatively, keep away from the bad area altogether when cleaning. The reason for this is that a chemical reaction will take place between the vinegar and the steel wool, and this will stain the bare wood black. This should be thought of as more annoying than distressing, and can be remedied easily by using oxalic acid (*see* Chapter 14 on Preparation for Finishing).

3. Sometimes the surface is so good that waxing is all that is needed. However, as a rule, more attention needs to be taken (*see* Finishing chapters).

Cutting back the surface with methylated spirit: If the cleaner does not work, try cutting back with meths. This does not mean you have to strip to the wood, although you can. It is slower than stripping with the stripper, but faster in the long run because it leaves the polish in the grain and therefore cuts out the long process of grain-filling with polish. It also leaves some of the patina in the wood. This is a good method

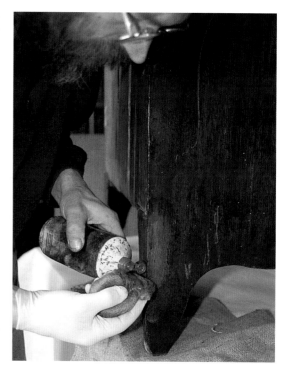

Cleaning a surface.

when the polish is not perished, only crazed. Stop when the surface looks even, and wipe clean and dry with a lint-free cloth, rub smooth with 400 paper when hard. The drying takes a good hour.

STRIPPING

This process is always the last resort as it will destroy all the patina, and it cannot be reversed. Therefore be sure a piece really needs to be stripped. If it is painted then there is no other way, but if it is polished it may be rescued. The following points may help you to arrive at the right decision:

(a) If the finish is cloudy and flaky – strip.
(b) If when you run the back of your thumbnail firmly across the finish it leaves a buttery or white line, it means the finish is perished – strip.

(c) If the surface has been renewed badly at some time leaving brushmarks or bad staining – strip.

Use a proprietary brand, water-washable stripper; these are generally thicker which makes it easier when doing the sides of chests and suchlike. I have often heard people exclaim how messy and time-consuming stripping can be, but this is not the case if you use stripper properly, even on the most stubborn of finishes.

HOW TO DO IT

1. Spread the stripper onto the surface, being careful not to tackle too large an area at a time – 3ft × 3ft (0.9m × 0.9m) is enough. Leave it covered thickly; do not spread it too thinly as this will decrease its effectiveness. The beginner makes this mistake all the time, and in the long run if you are too mean with it, it will take you longer to do and also cost you more in stripper. When just applied, it will look very shiny. It will dull, and go either bubbly or crinkly as the chemical cuts into the finish. (This takes a minute or so.)

2. Apply a second coat without removing the first, but this time you will not need to use so much. Use the brush to agitate the surface, and watch to see if the finish moves. It should. Wait until this coat goes dull before using a paint scraper.

3. I only use the scraper to remove the first thick top coat, and then only when the wood surface is in good repair, especially when the surface is veneered. Watch out for bubbles or loose cracks in the veneer. NOTE: that the scraper itself has been modified by rounding the scraper edge on fine emery cloth.

4. With the modified scraper, with the 'x' upwards, remove the stripper, scraping it off on the edge of a stiff cardboard box. If the surface wood is delicate, use a hardwood wedge, which also should have its edge rounded. The reason I first use the scraper is because it is more flexible and it is easier to scoop up the mess. On the steps and flats of mouldings, use wood wedges, but not on any convex areas.

5. When the area is scraped clean, apply another coat and wait for that to dull; you should now be close to the surface of the wood unless it was a thick-painted surface to begin with. Use the wooden wedge this time, as the gunge should be much thinner and less gooey.

6. Once all is removed, take a sizeable pad of 0 steel wool, enough to ball up and cover the palm of your hand; fill it with meths generously until it drips, and hold it over the piece you are stripping. Then wipe over the surface, going with the grain – you are basically washing the surface.

Why use meths when the stripper is water-washable? The water-washable types are always thicker, and meths will still neutralize the stripper but it will go on

---

Materials and Tools Needed

Cheap paintbrush, stripper

0 and 00 steel wool, paint scraper

Wooden wedges, stiff cardboard box

Rag, rubber gloves

Methylated spirits

Be aware that both the stripper and the meths are toxic and give off a certain amount of fumes. Only work with plenty of ventilation and a mask.

Modifying a Scraper

You will find when you buy a new scraper that it has been punched out of a sheet of steel, and all except the most expensive types have sharp edges. However, the edges must be rounded and blunt, and also the ends – don't leave the corner ends sharp.

Lastly, put your thumbs in the centre on the scraping edge, and holding the corners, bend slightly: when you release the blade it should be evenly but slightly concaved. Then carve an 'x' on that side of the handle, so when holding the flat of the blade on the wood, the 'x' is facing up and the blade corners are raised away from the wood surface.

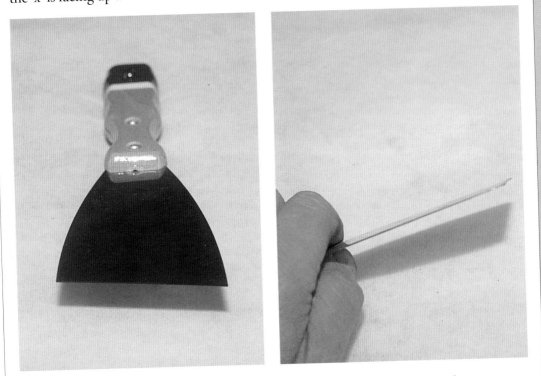

A new scraper.   *The scraper blade slightly bowed.*

softening any area where the finish is a little thicker, except for cellulose finishes. It also takes just a minute or two to dry, and then you can go on to the next stage.

NOTE: When dealing with veneered pieces it is unwise to use water because if this penetrates down to the glue-line it can soften the glue and expand the veneer, creating bubbles. Lastly – and this is sheer luck – water-washable strippers are generally cheaper.

7. The steel wool will absorb most of the remaining gunge, but it will leave the surface swimming with meths. Wipe it over with a rag. Now make another ball of steel wool, but this time 00, and again fill it with meths and wash over the surface. Finally dry off with a clean dry rag.

Balling up the steel wool.

STRIPPING WITH CAUSTIC SODA

I do not approve of this method of stripping: it kills the wood, burning out the natural oils and removing its innate colours, and unless it is properly neutralized (which is difficult) it eats the animal glue that holds the joints together. The method of bath immersion causes the wood to be thoroughly soaked so that when drying out without its natural oils to protect it, it will distort and split. It may help you to understand how much damage it can do by telling you that it is one of the processes of turning wood into paper pulp. On hardwoods it discolours by means of chemical reaction with the tannic acids within the wood. This is virtually impossible to reverse, and leaves it looking grey. Furthermore I have always found it most difficult to prepare properly for the final finish, because the surface is horribly hairy and stays that way.

I do believe that even when a tree is chopped down, its wood goes on living as a piece of furniture. It dies when treated with caustic soda.

Never plane a surface to remove the finish, even if there are gouges and digs; usually there is a way to save it. Similarly, do not use sand-blasting: the results are horrible.

six

REPAIRING JOINTS

SELECTING REPLACEMENT WOOD

Selecting new replacement wood to match in with the old wood of the piece to be repaired is an area of the restorer's skills that can make or break a job. However much old wood one collects there is never enough choice, simply because each tree is unique: no two trees are the same, and so no two planks are the same. Moreover as we have said, the different types of wood suitable for the restorer is not large, although the collection of veneers has to be more extensive. Most carcase wood is pine, oak, mahogany or walnut, and a wood used on the sides of Victorian chests that can be mistaken for mahogany, called Spanish cedar.

Matching is therefore difficult and often wasteful; it always seems that the best match is in the centre of a large plank! And so often when at last you find a piece that matches, the grain is going the wrong way – that is, the figuring may match and look right, but the direction of the grain along the length of the wood is different. This has a significant effect on the way light is reflected by a piece: when light changes, and also when you look at a piece of wood from a different aspect, the wood will seem different, the dark areas becoming light, and the light becoming dark. This is most pronounced in a wavy-grained wood such as fiddleback sycamore (so named because it is used to make the backs of violins): from one direction the 'figure' has tones of dark, light, dark, light, but turn it around and in the same position it changes to

The reflective change in wood.

light, dark, light, dark. This is solely because of the way the light reflects off the grain, which is either coming out of the wood, or going in.

So the problem is not only finding a wood with similar figuring structure, it also needs to have the grain running in the same direction. This is compounded by the fact that colour balance and tonation also need to be similar, although this problem can be overcome to a certain extent by clever bleaching and colouring (staining) in the finishing stage. Let us take one step at a time.

HOW TO DO IT

1. Identify the wood. (A word of caution regarding book illustrations: the wood pictured will probably be new, and this sometimes looks a little different from a piece of wood cut and polished a hundred years ago.)
2. Check your stock for the most likely in that species.
3. Bring it out into the natural daylight and find possible matches.
4. Within the area of damage, decide which way the grain is running: this will narrow down selection even more. The easiest method is to use a small chisel in the damaged area, and try and shave off a little bit of wood. If it cuts easily you are cutting with the grain, and the grain is coming out of the wood in that direction; if it cuts raggedly, then the reverse is true.
5. Now do the same with the selected woods. Say you have found several pieces that appear to match quite closely, but the grain direction only corresponds with two. Of these, one is slightly darker than the piece you are trying to match, and one is lighter. Choose the one that is slightly lighter because it is always easier to control the darkening of wood, than the bleaching to lighten it.

You only need to try and match the appearance of the grain when these parts of the repaired joints are visible, although the grain should run in the same direction to attain the best gluing strength.

Study the piece you are about to repair. The problem may in fact appear more serious than it is, being that you are probably looking not just at one problem but many small ones added together. The first thing to do is to find the possible causes for damage; it is important to know 'how and why' because it helps when reconstructing the damaged area.

REPAIRING A TENON

Let us start with a broken tenon, that is, the male part of a mortice and tenon; it has sheered off directly before the shoulder, the joint being part of the seat rail of a chair. Why should this joint break? Knowing why is important, as there may be other faults in the chair that caused this to happen, and if

Broken tenon.

these are not corrected then the joint is likely to break again.

- It may be worm damage, in which case the whole chair must be treated.
- It may have failed because the whole chair is loose and wobbly; however, this will be rectified when you reglue the chair. (This is one of the main reasons why joints break.)
- An old repair may have weakened.
- The chair may have suffered an accidental fall.

For now, we will settle on the fact that the whole chair is shaky.

HOW TO DO IT

1. First check the seat-rail: if this is in fair condition, the rail can be re-used. Only remake a rail or other part if it is beyond recovery; keep as much of the original as possible.
2. The mortice (hole) needs to be checked as well, because if the joint was loose it could have worn and now be misshapen; normally, however, if the

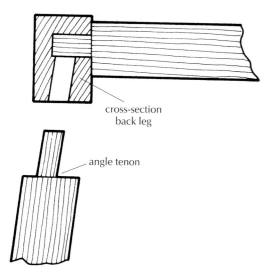

cross-section
back leg

angle tenon

Position and angles of joints of a chair.

joint is broken the tenon will still be in place. This broken tenon must be drilled out, using a drill bit that is slightly smaller, then digging the rest out with a chisel. Do this before starting on the replacement tenon, as measurements need to be taken from the mortice. (Take into consideration the angle at which the rail is fixed to the leg, especially at the back, because the tenon may not run parallel to the sides.)

3. Decide what the wood is. If the seat-rail is covered with upholstery this will normally be beech or birch; seat-rails left uncovered will be of the same wood as the whole chair.
4. (Use a vice.) Mark out where the replacement tenon is to go; it has to be double-ended, as a housing must be made in the seat-rail. Using a mortice gauge, take the measurements from the mortice, also taking into consideration that not all seat-rails will be flush with the side of the leg, especially those that are upholstered. Mark the end and underneath of the seat-rail with the gauge, the underneath about four times the depth of the mortice in length. Most tenons on the back legs of chairs are the full height of the seat-rail. To give the false tenon strength, the housing is not cut fully to the top of the rail, but is staggered (called a saddle housing), making it necessary to have a step in the tenon; when glued in place the rail sits on this step.
5. The mortice is open on the base side, and as mentioned is cut back four times the length that is needed for the mortice in the leg. The false tenon is fitted and glued into the rail and left to set. I prefer to use the same glue that was originally used on the chair; this is normally animal glue.
6. When the glue is set, clean up the tenon and dry fit it to the leg, to make sure it fits properly. If this was the only repair then the chair is ready to glue up.

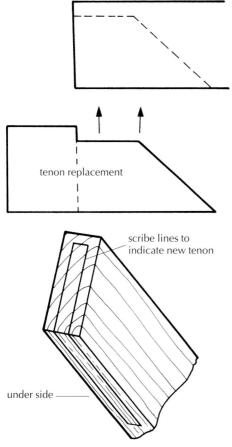

tenon replacement

scribe lines to indicate new tenon

under side

Seat rail.

Replacement tenon ready to fit.

Broken mortice.

REPAIRING A MORTICE

A broken mortice occurs less frequently than a tenon, and it usually involves the front legs. Let us take as a working example a joint that has been shattered into several pieces; to compound the problem, someone has put a large nail into the side to secure the tenon, and a screw into the front of the leg to pull the joint tight. First, however, let us establish why this joint should have broken.

- It could be for the reason above: a loose joint that someone has bodged.
- It may have failed because of wood-worm, especially in legs that are made of beech or birch.
- If the chair has been re-upholstered several times the holes created by the tacks can weaken the wood, leaving it perforated like a postage stamp.
- A loose joint or joints in the chair will weaken and crack it, and in this state being sat on improperly or heavily will be enough to cause failure.

HOW TO DO IT

We will assume that the broken pieces are so badly damaged a new part has to be made. The mortice comes within 1in (25mm) of the top, making the task easier; but you must remember that another mortice

47

Repair to a mortice block.

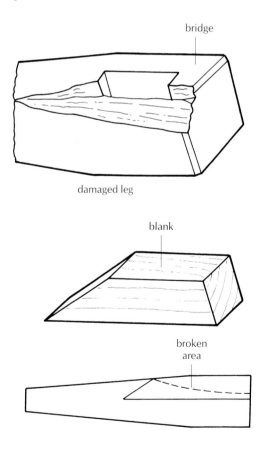

Repairing a mortice joint.

comes in from the adjacent side, so part of the first one may need to be recut.

1. Clean up and inspect, then using a pencil, roughly draw on the sound wood where you propose to cut. As the bridge over the top of the mortice is normally damaged, mark beyond this point.

2. Find a piece that matches with plenty to spare; it is always better to have extra than trying to cut it tight. Also, remember that the joint may not all be covered by upholstery. The piece to be inserted we will call the blank.

3. Plane the face of the blank that is to be glued. From this face make an upwards 45° mitre on the bottom end, to be spliced into the leg beneath the mortice; this is so the blank can be wedged down into the leg, which will support the repair from lateral stress; it is also easier to mask the repair when finishing.

4. Mark the cut line just beyond the old mortice line with a marking line, and square off all round the leg. (Use a vice.) Using a fine tenon saw, cut down the line to where the end of the splice is going to fit.

5. Place the planed face of the blank up against the sawn line, with the point of the splice finishing at the end of the saw cut. With the marking knife, line up the face of the blank accurately, and scribe the 45° splice onto the leg, then square up on the adjacent face. *A little trick to help you cut this mitre that will stop the saw from sliding and cutting past the line*: lay the leg flat, so that the side face is uppermost. Scribe the line several more times, then using a chisel, cut a trough on the waste side of the line. Put the saw blade into the trough and saw down to about $\frac{1}{32}$in (0.8mm) then running the saw backwards and forwards without any cutting pressure, lay it over to the required angle to cut the splice.

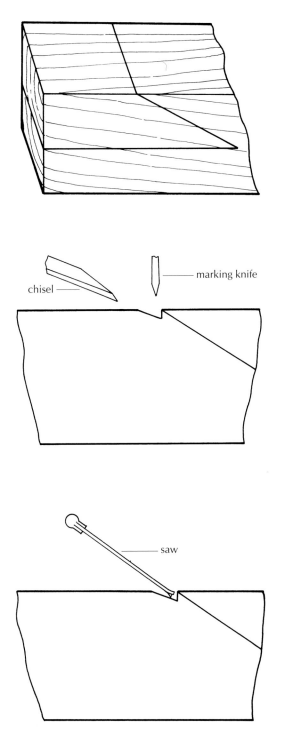

chisel —   marking knife

saw

Cutting an accurate line with a saw.

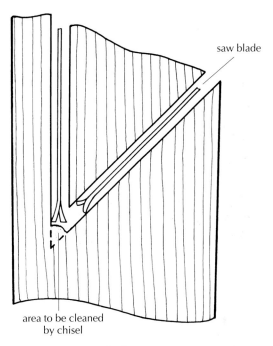

saw blade

area to be cleaned
by chisel

The blunt area created where two saw-cuts meet.

When the saw is nearing the cut line, slow down and make sure the length of the blade cuts through evenly. The point of the splice should be knife-edge; at this moment it will not be, because of what is called the kerf (the thickness of the blade plus the set of the teeth).

This is the point where a novice often comes unstuck. Using the widest chisel you have, and as sharp as you can make it, lay the flat face of the chisel onto the splice face, with the edge of the blade in the point of the splice. Run the blade backwards and forwards whilst pushing firmly down, across the leg. Because the bevel angle on your chisel should be no more than 30°, it should leave you with a sharp point to the splice mitre. I actually have a wide chisel with only one angle of a little less than 25°.

6. This leaves the flat upright face on the leg to clean up, and unless you have a very fine-set saw indeed you will need to attend to this surface. Again use a

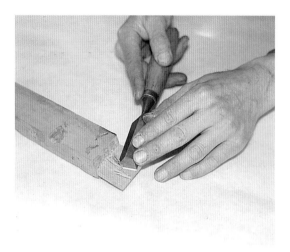

Paring face of tenon.

and mark round them, then cut away the waste before gluing.

8. Glue together, using a small sash-cramp initially to push the splice down hard into the joint, then use a couple of G-cramps to hold the flat faces together. Leave to set for at least twelve hours.
9. When set, release the cramps and plane back to the original size.
10. Using a mortice gauge, mark out the new mortice. Because the joint is still quite fresh, support it by recramping before you chisel out new mortice(s).
11. Leave for another day with the G-cramps on, then glue the chair back together.

wide chisel, and with fingers pressing the blade flat onto the face, use a circular motion to clean it. Beware of coming onto the edge; only come off, using the flat face of the chisel like a plane. All you are trying to do is cut a whisper of shaving off.

7. Try a dry run and see how it fits, and keep adjusting until you are happy. Hold the two pieces tightly together

DOWELS

The dowel is normally of birch, beech or if modern, ramin. These woods are prone to worm attack, so if there is any sign of worm in the area of the joint there is a high possibility that loose joints have resulted. The other type of failure is when the hole becomes enlarged. Filling it full of glue and sawdust is not going to

Cramping a spliced tenon (note the various directions of the cramps).

solve the problem: to me, this method is a make-do bodge.

WORM-DAMAGED DOWEL

Squared-off dowels also apply, as the procedures are identical. The method is simply to drill out the old dowels, but doing it without misaligning the holes.

HOW TO DO IT

1. Cut the dowels flush with the face.
2. Centre-punch the dowel as accurately as possible.
3. In steps, drill down through the dowel, increasing the size of the drill until you are nearly touching the wall of the hole.
4. Using a gouge slightly smaller in radius than the dowel, place it on the glue line around the dowel and ease the dowel away from the wall of the hole. Continue this operation until the whole dowel has been peeled away.
5. Extract the bits of dowel with long-nosed pliers, then using a drill bit the size of the hole, clean out any old glue.

NOTE: Most shop-bought bits of dowels are now metric, and not imperial as the old

dowel would have been. One can, of course, enlarge both holes with a metric bit, but there is no guarantee that the holes won't be misaligned. I have had a scraper drilled with varied imperial holes for the purpose of drawing a metric dowel down to size. This is the surest way. When sizing down a dowel, always push it through the hole in both directions.

ENLARGED HOLES

One way to overcome this problem, you might suppose you would find a dowel to fit the enlarged hole. However, don't do it! First, a dowel should be no larger than half the width of the piece it is tapped into, and a little less is best. Second, there is no way of knowing how far out of alignment the hole has become, and the bigger the hole, the more the differential in misalignment increases between the two holes.

HOW TO DO IT

1. Use a dowel that covers the hole and a little more. Drill out the hole and glue the dowel in place, cutting it flush with the surface.
2. Normally the dowel will still be in place

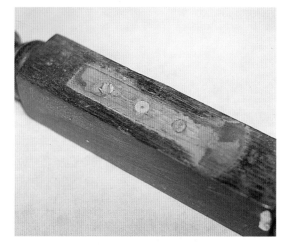

Centre dowel ready to drill.

Enlarged hole around dowel.

Enlarged hole filled.

Pin head being cut off prior to marking.

in the partner joint. Cut this flush with the surface.

3. Tap a panel pin into the dead-centre of the old dowel. With side-cutters, cut off the head, leaving it no more than ⅛in (3mm) above the dowel's face. If you have one perfect dowel left, simply put the joint together and (making sure the piece is squarely aligned) press together. Then pull apart: a pinprick hole will have been left by the panel pin, exactly locating the centre of each hole.

4. If both dowels are missing, set up a simple jig to ensure the two faces come together in perfect alignment.

One More Note of Caution

The new dowels should be a tight fit: this being the case, cut glue-run channels on both sides of the dowel, simply done with a chisel. It is amazing how much pressure can be built up with even a ⅜in (9mm) dowel when it is pulled together with a sash-cramp with nowhere for the glue to escape. Fluid does not compress like air, and will therefore find the weakest part of the wood and split it, sometimes with devastating results.

Making the glue run on the side of the dowel.

5. I have a set of centre-point drill bits that I keep specifically for this job. Drill the new holes using this type of bit. If using a hand-held drill, try and find someone to help you align it; otherwise use tally sticks to keep the drill aligned: these are thin sticks put in place before the piece is put in the vice, to show you the angle at which the hole must be drilled. Line up the sticks with the bit and slowly drill the hole, checking constantly.

DOVETAIL JOINTS

The dovetail is an ingenious little joint, as well as being quite decorative, a feature used to great effect by the Arts and Crafts movement. Good craftsmanship is established when you find well proportioned dovetails on the sides of drawers; it is a pleasure to appreciate the skill entailed in making these. The narrow pins disappear to a knife-blade point, and the tails are cut in such a way that the saw must have been exceptionally thin – no mean feat. The tail is made by cutting away triangular holes to accept the pins in the end of the other piece of wood to be joined, the triangular holes having their pointed ends to the end of the wood. These holes leave a series of tails similar to a fantailed dove, hence the name.

Both pin and tail can become damaged, and the only way to repair these is to cut in a fillet of wood and recut. Usually the pins break off, but the short grain on the tails may split away as well, especially where the joint has been loose for a long time and the movement has been ignored. I remember when a student brought me a chest of drawers in which the whole carcase rocked from side to side so badly one could have mistaken it for a rocking horse. When we removed everything and turned it upside-down, we found 4in (100cm) nails going through the tails and up into the sides. These tails were not only split, but also the short-grain areas were missing and these had been filled with glue and toilet paper!

The function of the dovetail is to join corners together and stop them from spreading, especially where there is some stress to make them, such as drawers which are constantly being pulled; it is therefore desirable to make a joint that will actually tighten when the force is in that direction.

Damaged dovetail pins..

HOW TO DO IT

Repairing the Pin

1. (The blank.) Select some replacement wood as similar as possible to the piece and cut a triangle. The wood should be slightly thicker than the pin's depth and about four times its length. The base of the triangle should be about twice the width of the pin, the sides of equal length, and smooth and square.

2. Place the blank with the base of the triangle to the end of the wood and keep overhanging slightly. The blank must cover the pin, keeping it even. This is best attained by using a set-square and drawing a line down the centre of the

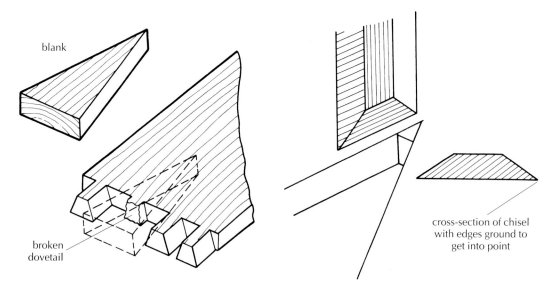

blank

broken
dovetail

cross-section of chisel
with edges ground to
get into point

Marking-out repair using a blank.

Chiselling-out waste.

pin and just past where the point of the blank will be.

3. Holding the blank firmly in position, mark around it with a marking knife.

4. With a fine saw, cut down on the waste side of both lines, until they meet.

5. With a small chisel, remove as much waste as possible. I have ground down a chisel to fit this shape, but the point is very weak and must be used with care. Once you have gone down below the saw cut, take a thin knife and re-scribe

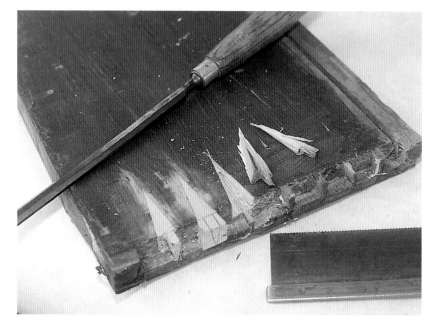

*Cleaning out wood
to take a blank.*

Marking out the pin.

the line several times, and again take out the waste. Repeat this until you have reached the depth of the pin, and this face is flat.

6. Before gluing do a dry run. If it fits tightly, glue and tap into place, then leave to dry.
7. Plane flush with the surface, and cut the overhanging end.
8. Place upright in a vice, then place the side piece with the tails on its end; you should be able to notch some of the pins in place, thus ensuring correct alignment. Take a marking knife and scribe through the tail that covers your blank; then square off down the length of the pin.
9. Using the fine saw, cut down both lines as far as you can. Again, chisel out the waste.
10. Before gluing do a dry run. If all is correct, glue and reassemble.

Repairing the Tail

Treat repairs to the tail in a similar way to the pin repairs. The best thing with this task is that most tails use the complete width of the wood, so accurate sawing with a fine saw may be all you need to do.

TAPERED DOVETAILS

These joints are often found at the base of pedestal tables. Normally the pins which are part of the leg are in good shape, unless someone has tried to repair the joint with nails and screws, and the trouble lies in the tail on the base. Because there is so much stress in this area, the sides of the tail will split out, and again many repairs may be found here. Unfortunately not all of these are satisfactory, the pieces either being out of alignment when they are glued back, or because nails have been put through this area into the tail causing it to split and shatter the joint completely. For the purpose of this working exercise we will assume that both parts of the joint are damaged.

HOW TO DO IT

Repairing the Pin

Because several screws have been drilled through the leg into the joint, and also nails have passed through the base into the pin, the pin has been weakened and has split and broken away; the parts left are so small that it would be wise to replace the lot. The method is similar to replacing a tenon.

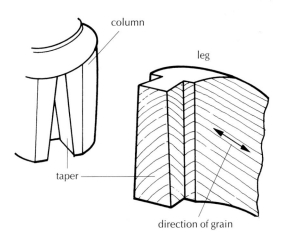

Tapered dovetail.

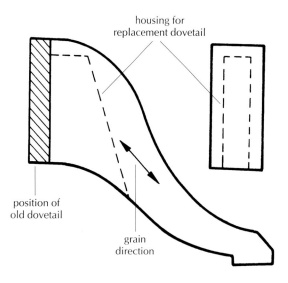

Direction of grain in a tripod leg.

1. Have a good look at the leg – the grain will be coming out diagonally.
2. Make a saddle housing, following the steps taken for a tenon. This time cut back 3in or 4in (75mm or 100mm) to give you more gluing surface. Take the saw cut up to a fraction under the top edge. Make the width of the housing the same size as the narrowest part of the pin. NOTE: When cutting the housing, make

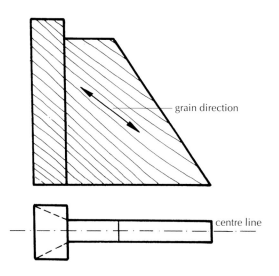

Cross-section of a tapered dovetail joint.

sure the top runs slightly across the grain and not true with the grain, as this will cause a weakness.
3. Cut the thickness of the blank to a little more than the width of the thickest part of the pin.
4. On every edge face of the blank, mark a line along the centre of its length; then divide the width of the housing in two and taking this measurement, measure out from the centre line on both sides.
5. Turn the blank on its side. The profile should be that of an elongated triangle, plus extra on the end to take the depth of the pin. Using a sliding bevel, place the shoulder of the tool on the shoulder of the leg and find the angle at which the housing passes through the leg.
6. With the bevel on the blank, mark out the angle at which the pin runs down the blank. There is no need at this time to mark out the depth of the pin on the blank.
7. Leaving the pin area alone, cut back the rest of the blank in width to the marked lines made from the centre line until the blank fits the housing snugly.
8. After a dry run, if it fits properly, glue. Do not shape the pin at this time, but work on the tail.

Marking dovetail with a sliding bevel.

Repairing the Tail

Both tails are damaged, one (*No. 1*) having been badly aligned and glued, the other (*No. 2*) totally shattered because of nails and screws.

No. 1

1. Steam the old glue joint apart, and clean as described in the previous chapter.
2. Test to see that it will fit back correctly (Don't glue yet); if it doesn't, and too much is missing, then a replacement piece will have to be made. (Follow directions for *No. 2* below.)

No. 2

1. Select a piece of wood to match the remaining sound area.
2. Take the back face of the joint, and mark a line defining the damaged area. Square this line up to the top of the joint where usually there is a masking collar; this will hide your joint line. Sometimes the split goes further than the collar and up into the turning itself. If this can't be rescued, take it up until it tapers out of the column.
3. Cut away the damaged area, cleaning up the face with a paring chisel or bull-nose plane if possible.
4. Mark out your blank, adding on enough to cover the tail area and a little more.
5. Dry fit, and if everything is all right, prepare to glue. However, before you glue, work out how you are going to cramp the pieces together.
6. Glue both pieces into place and cramp. If you find that they slide, tap a couple of veneer pins into the gluing faces and then cut off their heads just above the surface. Press the blanks exactly into place and then cramp; this will normally do the trick.
7. When the glue is set, clean up and shape up the outside faces; do not start on the joint itself.
8. Start with the barrel, getting the new piece to follow the circle.
9. Now the shoulders: this is the face that butts up to the joint, and it needs to be worked out carefully before actual cutting. Study the other two legs: the shoulder will be the width of the leg where it joins the column. If one of the shoulders remains, then there is no problem, just scribe across. Normally these shoulders are level with each other. If both shoulders, joint and all, need replacing, you will need to re-mark this area. To do this, proceed as follows:
   (a) Turn the column upside-down, and measure between the two remaining legs, from edge of shoulder to edge of shoulder. Mark a centre point between them to the column base. Sometimes the old turning centre remains; if not, find the centre.
   (b) Draw a line through the two marks and out to the edge where the new shoulders will be.
   (c) Open a pair of dividers to half the width of the leg, then with one point on the line, find where the other

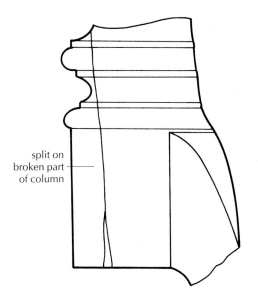

split on broken part of column

Possible damage to a column.

Cramping Columns

Because of the shape of most columns there is a difficulty in cramping. Here are two methods of getting over this problem:

(a) Find some old chair coil-springs, and with bolt-cutters cut them into rings; when flattened, they make perfect sprung ring-cramps.

(b) The tripod legs are placed at equal distances around the column, like an aeroplane propeller. Take two pieces of scrap wood, place them under the column between the two remaining legs, and mark out the shape. Cut out the shape so that each can sit firmly between two legs, and act as cramping pads.

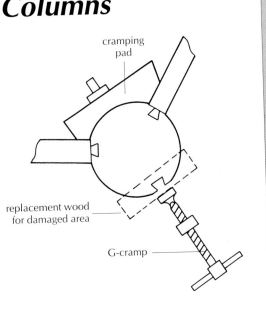

How to make proper cramping pads, and their position.

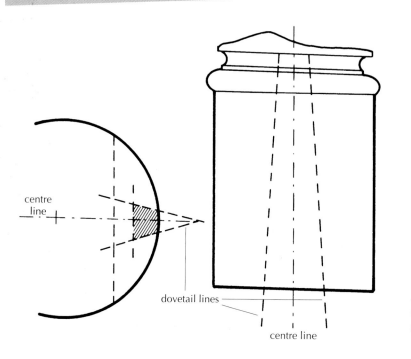

Layout and position of tripod joints, one to the other.

point breaks the circle. Remember to keep both of these points at right-angles with the line unless the other shoulders show to be different.

(d) Join up the marks. This should be the line of your shoulders.

10. Cut the new shoulders down to the line you have made.
11. These shoulders will be large enough to take a couple of screws to give the repair added support. Drill pilot holes first.

HOW TO CUT THE JOINTS

Now tackle the actual joints. It will be easier if one of the other legs can be detached.

Cutting the Pin
1. With this leg, make two cardboard templates of both ends of the pin.
2. With the templates, mark out the repair.
3. First cut the pin to depth size.
4. Cut down both sides of the pin, just leaving the marks showing.
5. Finish with a paring chisel.

Marking out the Tail
Use only one of the templates this time, this being on the bottom. If one shoulder remains, take the measurements from it. If the whole area is new, proceed as follows:

1. With the centre line made for assessing the shoulders, carry it up the column to the top of the joint.
2. Mark out the bottom with the template.
3. Using dividers, take the measurement of the narrow part of the pin from the top. Transpose this to the column.
4. Join up the lines.

Cutting the Joints
1. With a fine saw, cut both lines leaving the line just showing.
2. Chisel out waste wood.
3. Before cleaning up with a chisel, fit the joints together. This will give you an idea of how much needs to be removed.
4. Carefully remove more waste, then fit again, and carry on like this until the joints fit snugly. I must stress that the less one takes off between each fit the better, as taper joints can be deceiving: it can seem that there is much to be removed, when in fact there is not.
5. After a dry run, glue and knock together. If the joint is a proper fit no cramps will be needed.

Restored chairs with Cabriole legs and spoon backs, made from rosewood in 1850–60.

59

seven

GLUING AND CRAMPING

GLUE

The idea that one just slaps on glue without regard to the state of the wood or the joints being put together may seem so ludicrous that I should not even need to mention it. But sadly, after twenty-odd years in the profession, I know I do. Let us ask a few simple questions: thus, why do we use glue? Because it is an effective medium that bonds two surfaces together. How does it work? It fills the pores in the wood, thus creating a perfect surface between two imperfect surfaces. To explain this, imagine two sheets of perfectly lapped metal surfaces: put together, these would be difficult to separate without sliding them apart. This can never happen with wood because wood can never attain such a perfect surface: glue is the medium that fills in these imperfections.

And finally, how much does one need? As little as possible: the glue layer between two surfaces is called the glue-line, and its thickness is all-important in bonding them: most glues used for wood have no real shear strength, and will shatter quite easily if the glue-line is too thick – although the area to be glued must of course be adequately covered.

There are many glues on the market and some are made for specific purposes, but on the whole we will only need to concentrate on what may be termed general purpose glues. There are three main types you will ever need: gelatine, casein, and PVA.

Collection of glues.

GELATINE GLUES

These are made from animal proteins and are the same as the jelly that is formed in a stock pot, though purer and more concentrated. They have always been used in cabinet-making and are termed traditional glues. Many professionals share my opinion that when restoring furniture where such glues have been used, these should be used again and not replaced by another type, even though scientific analysis concerning the differing strengths of glues has proved that modern ones are more effective. I myself have no qualms in continuing to stay with tradition, and there are two arguments in favour of this decision: first, there are many pieces of period furniture with sound joints that have not been disturbed since they were glued; this proves to me the glue's worthiness. Second, protein glues are heated and use water to liquidize them; they can therefore be remelted, enabling one to undo anything that is not correct or if at a later date is thought to be a wrong method, without too much damage to the fabric of the piece. (This has already been covered in previous chapters.)

HOW TO MAKE AND USE ANIMAL GLUE

There are three common forms of this glue: cold **fish glue** that comes already prepared in a tube; **rabbit glue**, which is used mostly by gilders for gold leaf; and **Scotch pearl glue**, which could be classed as the general-purpose glue used in cabinet-making, veneering, and so on.

FISH GLUE

This is not a glue I use myself, and I don't know of anyone in the trade who uses it frequently. It can be safely assumed that the ready-to-use PVA glue has taken its place. Also, although all animal glues smell, fish glue is particularly revolting.

RABBIT GLUE

Traditionally this glue was obtained in broken sheets, though nowadays it comes more often in granule form. It is a light glue and, as mentioned above, is primarily used by gilders. To prepare it, cover with cold water overnight; it should absorb most of the water, but drain off any excess before heating in a double-jacket glue pot.

SCOTCH PEARL GLUE

This glue can be identified by its form of amber, pearl-like beads. Mix it as follows: take a standard size (420g) tin; half-fill this tin with the pearls and cover with cold water to about 1in (25mm) above the pearls; give it a stir, then leave for at least six hours and preferably overnight – the glue will swell which is why you should not fill it to the brim. After this time the pearls will have become milky, and always remind me of frogspawn. Any water left should be drained off. In fact I use a tapered plastic container for soaking, because the pearls stick together and will need digging out of a straight-sided can, whereas a sharp slap on the base of a tapered container will cause all to slide out.

Put the softened pearls into a double-jacket glue pot and bring the jacket-water to the boil; then turn down to a slow simmer. Never let the water pot go dry, as the glue will overheat and be rendered useless. Stir occasionally until it reverts to the former colour of the pearls. To test if it is ready, dip the glue brush into the glue and then lift out; it should run off in the consistency of thickish double cream, in an even stream. If it runs off in a lump, the mixture is too thick and should be diluted a bit. If it runs off in a liquid gush, then it is too thin, in which case take off the lid and leave for a while so that some of the water can evaporate. If when you try to spread it, it soon gels up, check the room temperature: 50°F (10°C) or a little more is about right.

Consistency of glue.

To check whether the glue is hot enough, test it with the tip of your index finger – but be careful, as scalding glue is like hot tar, and you don't want to leave your finger in for more than a few seconds; although in actual fact it should not scald. If it *does* scald you, this indicates that the glue is damaged, and it should be discarded because it will crystallize when set.

Gluing time is 8 to 12 hours within cramps; to cure is 24 to 48 hours, depending on atmosphere and temperature. This glue is hygroscopic, meaning it will absorb moisture, so a dry workshop is essential. It can go mouldy within a week if left uncured.

CASEIN GLUE

The most recognizable of this type of glue is 'Cascamite'. Casein glue is very strong and is not water-soluble once it is set; nevertheless it is very user-friendly, and is stocked almost anywhere. It is excellent as long as there is no need to reverse the gluing process and open the joint.

To make, simply mix with water, but do follow the mixing instructions on the side of the container carefully, as bad mixing can lead to a breakdown in the glue. It is applied cold. Setting time can vary according to the surrounding temperature. Refer to the manufacturer's instructions.

PVA GLUE

PVA must be one of the most used glues for wood, in the UK the most popular brand being Evo-Stik 'W' resin, recognizable by the green plastic container. There is no mixing involved, you simply squeeze the bottle and spread. Again, always consult the instructions on the container.

CRAMPING

Cramping things together is not that simple and is *not* just a question of tightening up a thread and saying 'Hey presto! Job done'– many a tortured chair has been left in a sorry state because of this attitude. A good quality cramp is a well engineered product, and more inventions are coming out each year. If you come across a cramp with a thread which has been damaged, or where the cramp itself has been distorted, then it has probably been used incorrectly.

The first consideration when cramping anything is to protect the wood which the cramping faces will be pressing against; protective pads will also spread the load. The second is to align the cramps so that they pull the joints at the same angle at which the joints were made. This is especially significant on open-framed structures such as chairs, because even a slightly different angle-pull will distort the frame, and when the glue is set will leave it twisted. If possible, always do a dry run to sort out any problems that may arise in the gluing operation. This will also mean that your cramps will be set to size and ready and waiting. This is important when using animal glue, which will only stay liquid for a short time before it starts to gel. And if it has been left to gel too long, clean it off and start again because it is questionable that a good bonding will be obtained.

TYPES OF CRAMP

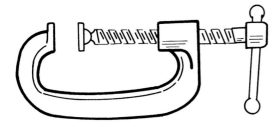

G-cramp: A G-shaped metal frame with a threaded bar at one end. These cramps come in sizes of 1in (25mm) to over 12in (30cm). They are used to hold pieces together, for example mouldings, battens and small joints, and can exert a tremendous amount of pressure.

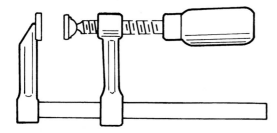

F-cramp: This cramp looks like the capital letter F; the inside strut with the screw-bar on it slides freely up and down the upright. When in a cramping position the lower strut crimps into the side of the upright, stopping it from sliding.

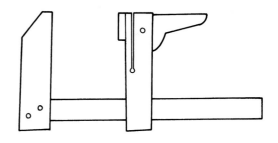

Speed cramp: This looks similar to the F-cramp, and works on the same principle except that instead of a screw-thread to tighten it, a lever with a cam is used.

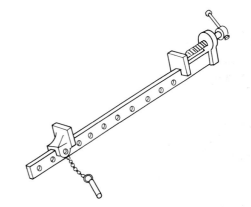

Sash cramp: This cramp is used for cramping wider areas, coming in sizes from 2ft (60cm) to 12ft (375cm), and used principally for frames and wide boards.

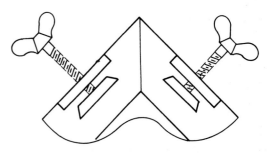

Mitre cramp: Generally used in pairs, or two pairs. These are essential when dealing with picture frames and suchlike.

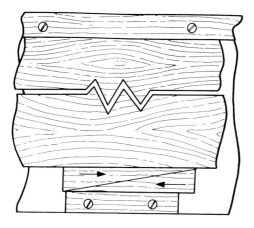

Wedge cramp: This is a home-made cramp, consisting of a length of batten with one fixed stop and one sliding stop. To tighten, a pair of folding wedges are used.

Band cramp: This is made with webbing and has four or more corners. The band is pulled and held together and either tightened using a screw-thread or a windlass. Used for picture frames, circles, octagons – all this family of shapes, or irregular-shaped objects.

CRAMPING CHAIRS

Because of their nature, chairs can be the most taxing of items to cramp. They will twist or go out of square when too much pressure is applied, and it can be difficult to find a 'purchase' because of their shapes. Most people experience difficulties for the following reasons:

- They fail to take into consideration the complexity of the structure.
- They fail to realize that one part relies on the other, and that some parts of the chair have to be done in correlation with others.

- The first pitfall is not having everything ready. It is not the first priority, but nevertheless, once you have started gluing, the motto is 'Wait for no man, and have three or four pairs of hands'.
- It is also important to realize that glue can change the final fit from the dry run if you are not prepared. There are two reasons for this: first, when two pieces of wood are glued together they may slide around initially and refuse to align because the glue acts like a grease. Second, when glue is added to a tight joint, the joint itself becomes like a hydraulic ram, and needs great pressure to close it, so if the wrong cramp is selected or the area of purchase is a little insecure, it will be impossible to draw the joint closed.
- Pieces within the chair may have warped or twisted because of their age and may be one of the reasons that the piece had become loose in the first place.

Simple Chair Frame

HOW TO DO IT

1. If it is possible, I always try and glue the front and back sections in separate operations. This cuts down on the cramps needed, as the piece can become very heavy. Also, one limits the problems arising at the time, thus making the whole task more manageable.
2. When gluing the front, have your sash cramps adjusted to the required size and your protection pads ready. *Always use a pad that is softer than the material to be glued.* If possible put one leg in the vice with the joint to be glued uppermost. Now apply the glue to the mortice first, and then to the tenon and by hand, quickly push the two parts together as far as they will go.
   NOTE: If there is a bottom stretcher this must be glued in now.

Using a vice when gluing.

3. With the leg still in the vice and the member(s) sticking upwards, apply glue to the next mortice and then the tenon. Fit these together by hand, and quickly release from the vice. The sash-cramp should be lying on a flat surface, so lay the legs between the jaws and place the pads in as well. Gently tighten up until the whole is clinched.

NOTE: In this position the pads will usually stay in place, but if you have difficulty, then tape them to the legs with masking tape. The pads are essential to protect the wood.

Cramping front legs together.

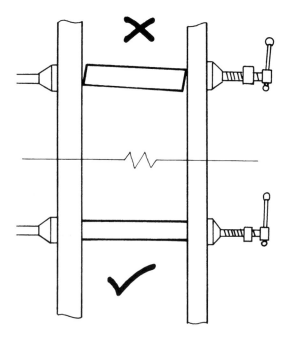

Correct alignment of cramps.

and if it slides into part of the joint, or into one side, the cramp is not aligned properly. Slacken the cramp and adjust it until the joint closes squarely.

If all your tries fail, check again that the shoulders are square with each other. If they are not, ease open the offending joint and fit a shim (very thin sliver) of veneer into the gap.

6. Now check for squareness. This can be easier said than done, when the legs are tapered or shaped. Measure from the bottom of the member on both legs equally and make a mark near the foot. Now measure the diagonal from the bottom of the member to the mark on the opposite leg. The measurement should be the same, or so close that it makes little difference (remember that a difference of ½in (13mm) means that the legs are only ¼in (6mm) out.

NOTE: Another reason why it may be out of alignment, especially when the joints are completely closed, is that the leg(s) are bowed. Sight along the legs to check this, and if it is found to be the cause then rely on the closeness of the joint as an indicator of it being all right. Leave overnight.

4. Once clinched, check that the cramp is in the correct position: this should be at the centre of the joints, making sure that the sash-bar runs parallel along the member. This is most important, otherwise the section will twist and not pull up evenly. Now tighten up the cramp, checking all the time for snagging and that the glue is escaping readily.

NOTE: It is important that the sash-bar does not touch the wood directly, so place a spacer between the member and the sash-bar. If the bar touches the wood around the area of the joint, the wet glue can rust the steel overnight leaving a black stain in these areas. If this happens, use oxalic acid immediately to remove the stain.

5. Use a damp rag – if using animal glue, have the rag hot – to clear off excess glue. Using a thin knife-blade, check round each joint: if the knife can slide between the joints, then it needs tightening more;

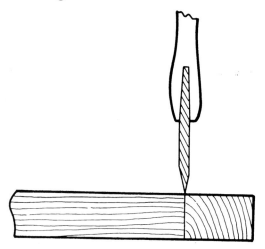

Testing the tightness of the joint with a knife-blade.

Shims

Shims are used regularly; many times I have found paper, card, or sandpaper as the filler along with veneer. However, my advice is, only use veneer, because paper and card will delaminate and weaken the joint. You could leave the joint filled with glue. Animal glue is a good filler, but it is not as strong as a wood veneer.

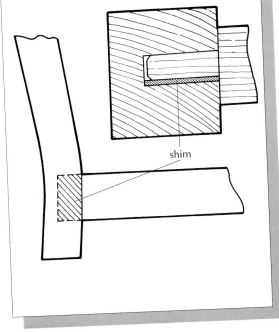

shim

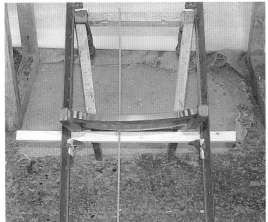

Using a cross member to assist in pulling the chair in straight.

insecure cramping positions. To overcome this problem use a 4in × 2in (10cm × 5cm) piece of wood that matches the front in length. Cramp this behind the back, level with the mortices, making sure that it overhangs evenly each side.

2. Lay the back flat on a bench. Place the members in position around the frame, close at hand. Have the sash-cramps already sized, and the pads also close by.

3. Apply the glue to one mortice and tenon, then fit and press together. Do this with the next, and stretchers if any. Now apply glue to all the mortices on the front section and to the corresponding tenons. Attach the front to

The back is done in a similar way except for the top rail which may fit on top of the legs and not between. (Later in this section we will discuss coping with different shaped tops.)

The Rest of the Chair

HOW TO DO IT

1. On almost all chairs the front is wider than the back, and this can lead to

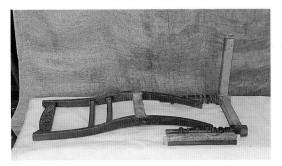

Chair ready to glue together.

Testing the tightness of a joint with the tip of a knife blade.

Using diagonals to check squareness.

the already assembled pieces. This may mean fitting one side in a little way but not fully home, and then easing the other side in. Once all the mortices and tenons are located, press home as far as you can by hand.

4. Stand the chair on its legs and fit one cramp on one side; tighten up, but not all the way. Then do the same on the other side. Once all the cramps are in position, tighten them all up a little at a time, until the joints are closed. Clean off the excess glue with a rag, and try the knife test.

5. Now check that the seat-frame is square by measuring across the diagonals from the left back leg to the front right leg, and vice-versa. If one diagonal is longer than the other, release the cramp on that side by half a screw-turn, and tighten the other side half a screw-turn. Measure again until the two measurements become equal.

6. Stand back and eye up the frame: the seat-frame should be level. To help, I have a line marked on the wall behind my glue table that is parallel with the table top; using this I can be fairly certain that the seat will be level when it is standing on the floor. Leave overnight.

DIFFERENT SHAPED CHAIRS

The Rounded Seat-frame (Queen Anne Style and Tub Seat)

These frames are semi- or fully circular and need special techniques when cramping. The main problem is that the leg runs flush with the shape of the chair, leaving no purchase for a cramp, and the joints are opposite to each other and not at right-angles to the leg. Further, the whole frame needs to be glued in one operation.

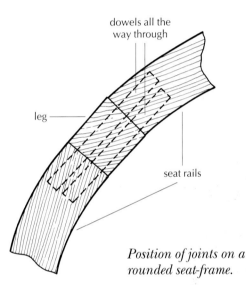

Position of joints on a rounded seat-frame.

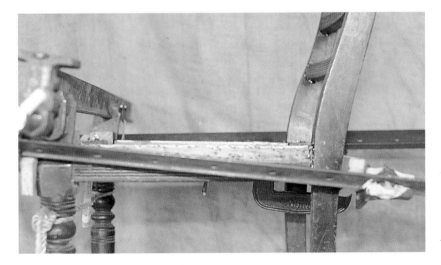

Lining up to ensure against twisting. The cramp is misaligned in this picture to give a better view.

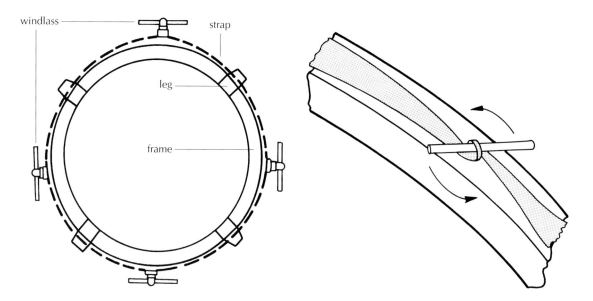

A windlass.

HOW TO DO IT

First Method: the band cramp. This method is the easiest, but is not always successful because the tool can exert only so much pressure; this can create a problem when the joints are tight, even before gluing. This type of cramp can be bought and works on a wind-up system to create the tension; the band is held in tension by a ratchet. A cheaper way is to get a length of upholstery webbing which is looped around the frame and tied tight. Then a stout dowel is inserted into the loop and twisted, causing the webbing to tighten. This is known as a windlass.

Second Method: this uses shaped wood that corresponds with the shape of parts of the frame externally, but has flat faces on its outside so that cramps can be used on semi-circular frames. It is not as successful on a completely circular one. The reason for this is because the pull is actually not going in the direction of the joint, and the joints tend to buckle before they are fully closed.

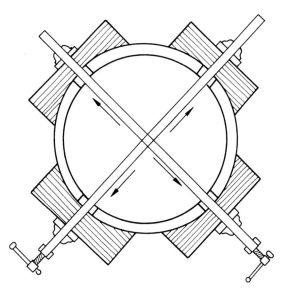

Pulling a joint together using formers and cramps.

Third Method: This method is far more complicated, but works where the others might fail:

1. For a semicircular frame you will need four blocks, and a circular frame eight blocks measuring 4in × 2in × 2in (10cm × 5cm × 5cm). These are cramped to the outside of the frame members, about 1in (25mm) away from the joint, with the 4in (10cm) at right angles to the length of the member. (If you can fit two cramps to each block, so much the better.)

2. Glue all joints and fit together, pressing them closed as far as you can by hand.

3. Taking two cramps, locate the top and bottom of the two blocks which are now sandwiching one leg. Tighten up together but do not completely close the joints yet. Do this to all the legs. Once all the cramps are in position, tighten each leg a little at a time, making sure to tighten both top and bottom cramps together.

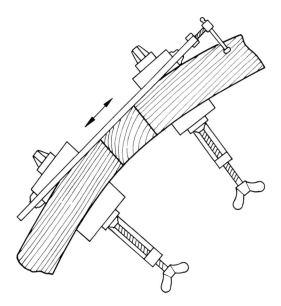

Drawing joints together using blocks and cramps.

TIP: Try and find someone to help if you can (although it is not impossible to do it on your own) because this operation needs speed before the glue gels. The chair will look like a porcupine and be extremely heavy; if you need to move it, use the utmost care in where you lift from, as it can be easily distorted.

Top Rails – Hoop Backs and Shaped Rails
These are handled in a similar way to the last technique, though the second method usually works the best in combination with the third method as it is sometimes difficult to keep the cramping direction aligned when using a long sash-cramp from top to bottom of the chair.

DOVETAIL DRAWER

Any wide area that is jointed with dovetails, such as drawers and carcases, should be held evenly under pressure.

HOW TO DO IT

Place a batten just under the joints on each side and cramp with at least two cramps – more if it is a wide plank. The reason it should be under the joint? Because of shrinkage, the pins may protrude slightly through the board; if this were the case and the batten were over the joint, the joint would not close up properly.

GLUING TOPS AND BOARDS

Where a top or a group of boards to make up a top or side has/have location dowels or a rebate and tongue, or is/are just butted together, the joints will need to be pulled tight and held in position until the glue has set. The best type of cramp for this is the sash-cramp. How many to use? I always have two on a short length, and for anything over 3ft (90cm) use one

Cramping sides of drawers using battens. Note the dovetail pins are not covered.

more, increasing the number after that by one more every 2ft (60cm). It is not wise to use just one on its own, even on a short length, because the boards will tend to twist.

JOINTS WITH DOWELS OR REBATES AND TONGUES

You need to be careful in aligning the joints, the rebate and the tongue, and the dowel joint takes care of this problem.

HOW TO DO IT

1. Set out the sash-cramps ready sized on a flat surface, with pads.
2. Also four battens long enough to cover the widths of the boards to be glued, and four cramps.
3. Apply glue to the edges and fit together; place in the cramps and tighten up until the boards are clinched. (Remember to put spacers between the sash-bar and the wood.)

Using battens to keep boards level.

4. Put two battens, one on each face of the boards at one end, and cramp into position. Do the same to the other end. Now tighten up the sash-cramps and wipe away any excess glue.

NOTE: The battens are to prevent the planks bowing when the sash-cramps are tightened.

BUTTED BOARDS

The difficulty with plain butt joints is getting the joint to be smooth: this is no problem at the ends because of the battens, but in the centre of the boards this is not so simple, especially where the boards are long, because when pressure is asserted by the cramps the boards can slide apart as a result of the glue, leaving a 'step'.

The problem is exacerbated when the boards have been apart for some time and have warped. These should be pinned with dowels if possible, although this cannot be done if the joint to be glued is a crack in a top, or a side that is sloped and not at right-angles to the face of the board. However, there are one or two methods that can be adopted to resolve this.

HOW TO DO IT

First Method: this is the simplest.

1. In one board, tap panel pins into the glue edge about every 6in (15cm) leaving half the pin showing. Cut off the pin-head with side-cutters.
2. Cramp one board to a flat surface. Next, place the other board on a flat surface and bring together the two faces to be glued. It is important to make sure the ends are flush, so cramp the batten to the end face of the board to act as a stop.
3. Release the boards, and uncramp the board from the flat surface. Lay paper (newspaper) onto the flat surface, and then cramp the board back onto the surface, and the end-stop.
4. Apply glue to the two faces; bring the two faces together, and fix the sash-cramps.
5. Cramp the battens to the ends to stop the centre bowing, then tighten the sash-cramps.

Using a stop to keep boards level.

board glued without bridging cramp

Method of keeping joint flush.

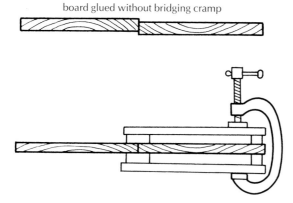

Second Method:

1. Lay the sash-cramps onto a flat surface. Follow the gluing method through to the cramping of the end battens.
2. Before tightening up the sash-cramps, take two battens that reach from the edge of the boards to just past the centre. With four blocks of the same thickness (about 2in (5cm) square), place one at the edge of the board and one straddling the glue-line dead opposite (lay paper under the block). Copy these positions under the boards with the two remaining blocks, and using a wide jaw cramp, tighten up the battens as far from the edge block as possible. (The battens will act as bridges, so that when squeezed together they will transmit half the pressure onto the centre blocks that straddle the glue-line.) Because the battens will bow when squeezed, chamfer the centre block to take up this shape. Now tighten up the sash-cramp.

CRAMPING BOARDS WITHOUT SASH-CRAMPS

One never seems to have enough cramps, and certainly not enough long sash-cramps for large pieces. This method is simplicity itself, as long as you have a sufficiently large flat surface – I've even used the floor itself at times.

HOW TO DO IT

1. Screw a batten the length of the boards into the flat surface. Screw blocks opposite the batten, leaving enough space between for the boards to lie flat and 1in (25mm) extra.
2. Apply glue, and place the boards into the space.
3. Cramp the battens to the end of the boards to stop these bowing.
4. Using two wedges to each block, tighten the boards by easing wedges between the blocks and boards, using the folding-wedge method (where the wedges are slid together making a double ramp). The wedges are tapped together from each end, forcing the two along each other and increasing the pressure between blocks and board.

BUTTERFLY

A butterfly is a double dovetail-shaped piece of wood used to stop joints and splits from spreading. This method of strengthening is acceptable in repairing splits and joints, and is used on the underneath of a surface. The joint is noticeable because the butterfly is inserted into the body of the wood at right-angles to the split or joint; it is made of a similar piece of wood to the piece being repaired, but the grain runs across the joint.

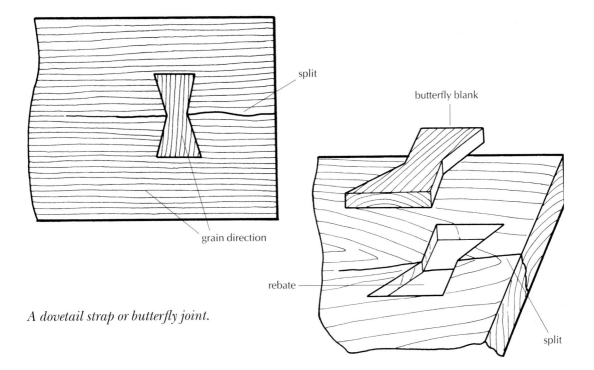

A dovetail strap or butterfly joint.

The butterfly or double-dovetail is aptly named because in shape it looks like the two wings of a butterfly or dickie bow.

HOW TO DO IT

1. Mark out the shape of one dovetail on a flat piece of wood, then reversing the dovetail shape, mark out another so the narrow ends of each dovetail join together.
2. Cut and clean up the edge with a wide chisel.
3. Place the butterfly across the joint to be strengthened, making sure that the narrow part of the neck is over the line of the joint. Scribe around the blank with a marking knife.
4. Chisel out the waste wood to the depth required; usually a third of the thickness of the wood is needed. (I use a router freehand to clear most of the waste away, leaving just a little margin of wood from the line. This saves having to use a mallet to chisel away waste and possibly breaking the joint.)
5. Clean up the edges of the hole, dry fit, then glue and tap home.

RUBBED JOINT

This is a method of gluing without using a clamp to hold the pieces together, or where just a light clamping such as masking tape is used. The process is quite simple to understand: using a glue block, cover the surface liberally with glue and press into position by hand; then while still applying pressure, the block is moved backwards and forwards to expel air and squeeze out the surplus glue. Sometimes a heavy piece will slide out of position; in this case use masking tape to hold it there until the glue has set.

eight

MAKING UP MISSING PIECES

Most furniture that comes into the workshop for repair has pieces that are missing, or damaged to the extent that they need replacing. This is apart from veneers that need attention (discussed in a later chapter). Here we will address what I describe as solid wooden pieces, as opposed to veneered. These solid bits can be as small as a splinter or as large as a chair leg, and will need specific selection of matching woods to blend with the remaining old wood.

In restoring practice there is a 'correct' way of doing things which should always be observed. Thus when replacing a section, such as inserting a piece into a moulding damaged in the middle of its length, it should be grafted in a certain way.

GOOD PRACTICE WHEN PATCHING

When patching it will be necessary to cut across the grain. For instance, a piece of wood is missing from the edge of a solid top, leaving a jagged hole. You could cover this with a square of wood, matching the grain quite adequately, except that the square blank will have straight ends that cut at right-angles across the grain, leaving a thin, dark glue-line which will be difficult to disguise. So when cutting across the grain it is better to do so obliquely; this will necessitate shaping the square blank into an elongated triangle. The resulting glue-line will still cut across the grain but at a shallower angle with the grain, and

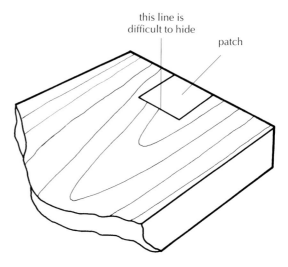

A square patch insertion.

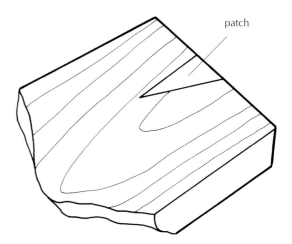

Using a triangular patch for insertion.

is therefore easier to lose into the grain structure. Also, when polishing and colouring this line can be further disguised.

MOULDINGS

Mouldings come in all shapes and sizes and are fitted to different areas of furniture, some flush, others as an integral part of the wood, or rebated in. This difference must be taken into consideration before commencing a repair, because otherwise damage can result.

FLUSH MOULDINGS

Flush mouldings are found on all periods of furniture. You may be lucky and find that this type of fixing is not glued, but either pinned through from the front or screwed through from the rear. Always check for this first. If the moulding is glued, this joint can usually be broken quite easily by using a broad paint-scraper. Place the blade along the joint and give the handle a sharp tap, forcing the blade into the joint. Once inserted, tap along the length of moulding until it springs apart.

HOW TO DO IT

1. Select replacement wood.
2. With a pencil, lightly mark out the area to be replaced. Never mark straight across the grain, but obliquely across.
   NOTE: If the damage occurs near to its end, then take this in as part of the area to be replaced. Several small repairs along a moulding's length is unsightly; it is preferable to have just one.
3. Prepare the wood, leaving it slightly oversized, with plenty of length to cover the damaged area. This piece will be called your blank.
4. Taking all measurements, transfer these to the blank; the ends will be cut in opposite directions. So they slope away from each other. (When fitted, the blank will be pressed into a tapering gap; this will help in producing a snug fit and a secure base whilst the

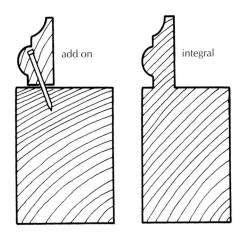

Different types of moulding.

glue is setting.) Cut the ends with a fine saw and then shoot them with a finely set block plane, or if the blank is small enough, pare the ends with a wide chisel.

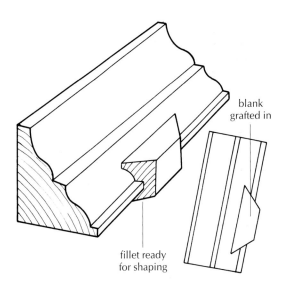

Working out the area needing repair on a moulding.

Ready to cut blank in to repair a moulding.

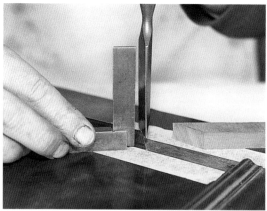

Using a square to align a chisel.

5. Place the blank over the damaged area and mark both ends with a marking knife. This can be difficult when the surface is not level, as in a moulding. To achieve this, cramp a straight piece of wood by the side of the moulding, to be used as a fence.

6. Cut along the inside of the marked lines with a fine saw, leaving the knife line just showing. Remove the waste as described above.

   NOTE: Always lay some masking tape on both sides of the moulding before you start cutting with the saw. As soon as the saw snags the tape, stop; this way you will never cut into the surrounding area. Use slow, measured strokes when sawing.

7. Pare the ends with a wide chisel – be sure that the chisel is not so wide as to overlap the ends and mark the surrounding wood.

   NOTE: Make sure when paring that the ends stay square. This can be achieved by using a small square held close to the chisel when cutting. If you have cut about a 1/64in (0.04cm) from the knife mark, you will feel the chisel locate into the knife groove, giving you an accurate cut.

8. When satisfied with the fit, glue and secure with tape.

9. When the glue has set, shape the moulding with chisels, and sand until your finger can't tell the difference between the two parts.

FURTHER TIPS AND TECHNIQUES

If the moulding is inset into a panel, then try and remove either the moulding or the panel itself. Mouldings already released must be supported as you do the repair – this is even more important when you come to gluing. For this I use a backing-board, and pin a batten to it, giving me a straight-edge.

The same method is used when repairing shaped mouldings, such as a scroll. In these

Finishing shaping the moulding.

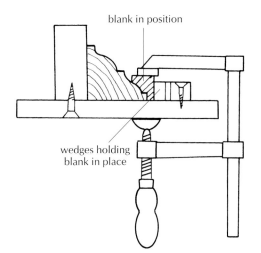

Using a backing-board to assist in repair of mouldings.

cases I fashion the batten to correspond to the shape being repaired or replaced, as when the moulding is shaped in a more three-dimensional fashion – and edge moulding to a chair that has a serpentine front, and is also scalloped, for instance. These can be tricky to repair off the piece, and are generally built up and shaped *in situ*. It can be done on a 'former', but I

would recommend the beginner not to use this method because so many directions have to be considered as the moulding is being restructured or reshaped. If it is built up in place, the piece itself will support the repair as the work is being done, and will also give guidance to its actual shape. With shaped mouldings the general tone is of movement, and it is easier to keep this feeling if you work *on* the piece rather than off.

COCKBEADING

Cockbeading is the raised, rounded moulding that surrounds the edges of drawers; it is principally thought to be a mid-Georgian ornamentation, although it has been carried on through many periods of fashion, disappearing and reappearing from time to time. These mouldings are in a very exposed position on the drawer, and so are protectors of the very edges they cover. However, they are ripped off by over-industrious dusting, and they also tend to split and chip.

They are easy to replace, although if there are only a few small chips I would rather mend these with a fillet of wood.

Drawer with damaged cockbeading and the replacement ready to fit.

For some reason if one drawer is damaged, you will find that all the others are in a similar condition. If possible, when replacing long lengths I endeavour to save whatever I can, and these pieces can be used again in the repairing and patching of smaller areas.

These mouldings are always mitred at the corners, so make a small mitre block to cut these. A stock of thin, narrow strips of mahogany can be stored ready for use, with the rounded edge already done. Because they seem to be an insignificant part of the piece, many would-be restorers use any old mahogany rather than wood of a better quality. However, it is better not to do this: as a feature, cockbeading is so noticeable, and this practice will compromise what would be classed as a good repair.

PREPARING THE BEADING

HOW TO DO IT

1. Cut the wood into strips of ⅛in × ¾in (3mm × 19mm).
2. Plane one side and edge. This edge is to be shaped.
3. Take a cabinet scraper and with a small 'rat-tail' file, make a notch in the narrow end of the scraper to match the thickness of the wood-strips.
4. Place the cabinet scraper in a vice with the notch uppermost. Keep the notch close to the jaws of the vice so the scraper will not vibrate too much.
5. Holding the strip of wood in both hands, draw the wood through the notch, holding your hands either side of the scraper.

When replacing, pin and glue into position, using veneer pins. When patching, use the same techniques as explained with the repairing of the other mouldings above. If the drawer needs to be refinished, then fit but do not fix, as it will make refinishing simpler.

RESTORING CARVED SECTIONS

FITTING AND CARVING REPLACEMENT SECTIONS

The extremities of any carving are the most vulnerable, especially on furniture that is moved regularly, like chairs, or carvings that are applied and can become unstuck (and go missing). The latter is the easiest to replace, and so I shall start with this type of repair first.

HOW TO DO IT

The carving is made and shaped *off* the piece, although it can have its finishing touches done *in situ*. For example, we will take a pierced floral design that is laid on top of a pediment of a Victorian wardrobe. These usually come in matching pairs or more; they are rarely single motifs.

1. If the missing piece's opposite number can be released without damage, then take it off because the easiest procedure is to trace around it and then to reverse the tracing. Otherwise take measurements and do a freehand sketch.
2. Next, take cross-section measurements with a moulding template. (This tool enables cross-sections of mouldings and carvings to be ascertained.) These cross-sections can be transferred to stiff card, then cut out and numbered in sequence.
3. Once the thickest part of the cross-section is known, a piece of wood can be prepared to size.
4. Trace the shape onto the flat surface of the wood, remembering to reverse the tracing.
5. Cut out the shape and any pierced areas with a coping saw or fretsaw, whichever is best for the size of the job.
6. Glue the cut-out shape to a block of wood that can be secured to a bench.

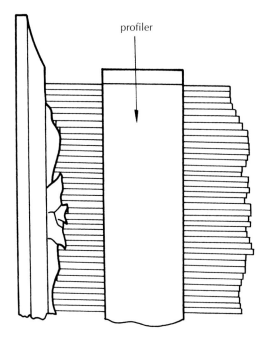

Making templates for carving.

profiler

Design ready for cutting.

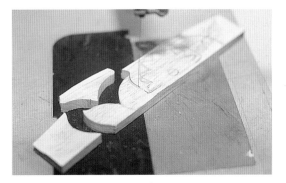

Cutting out design with a fretsaw.

NOTE: There are two methods of gluing that I know of:
(i) Using a PVA or animal glue: apply it to the back of the piece, then stick a sheet of paper to it. apply a second coat, and another piece of paper to that. apply a third coat, and place the piece onto a block of wood. Hold lightly in cramps until dry.
(ii) Using a hot glue gun: place blobs of glue onto the back in areas that will hold it securely. Press firmly onto the block of wood, but leave a thick glue-line. With this method you can start shaping straightaway.

7. This is not a carving book, so I will not embark upon how to carve – this would take up many chapters to do it justice. If you are not proficient at carving, either find someone who will do it for you, or buy a book and learn the many steps needed.

8. Once the carving is completed, remove it from the block of wood by slipping a thin-bladed paint-scraper into the glue-line. With the hot-gun glue you must actually cut through the glue with the blade, and then afterwards scrape off any glue that is left. With the other method, gently ease the blade in and lever it away from the base wood; the paper should tear and release the carving. Clean off the glue and paper before applying it to the furniture.

NOTE: If no further carving needs to be done, it is quite a good idea to leave it on the base wood, and colour and polish it before actually gluing it to the furniture.

REPAIRING SOLID CARVING

As a working example to demonstrate this technique I am taking the highly decorative back of a wooden-framed Victorian armchair. This type of chair sometimes has a small, carved, decorative flower motif on the top of the back frame, and this is often damaged by careless handling.

HOW TO DO IT

With this type of repair one has to make a decision on how much to replace and where to start. For instance, maybe only half a flower is broken, a bit of branch, a couple of leaves and a flower bud. Before deciding, I make a drawing of the whole carving, sketching in what I feel the missing area would look like, then mapping out the cross-sections of the areas that are there as well as those that are missing.

With all this information you can start to see the structure of the carving and its weak points, and how deep the blank will have to be set in to be structurally sound. Then go a step further and work out how

to hide the joints of the blank within the carving – that will help let the work flow. You may even have to cut out the good half of the flower to help hide the repair and to make a superior joint.

1. Make a blank that covers the area to be repaired, in height, width and length; be sure that the base of the blank is flat and true.
2. Mark out with the blank where it is to fit. This will be easier said than done, because there will be no flat surface to scribe to. The following subsection describing the method may help, but getting it right is a matter of practice.
   (i) Because of the high and low spots, scribing is near impossible to do in one go, so do it in a series of steps.
   (ii) First, scribe in one end of the blank, and cut away the waste wood. This will be no more than the top of the most of the high points.
   (iii) Once the end of the blank fits tightly at the end of the area to be repaired, scribe in the other end, and again remove the waste wood.

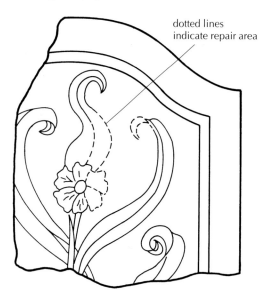

dotted lines indicate repair area

Damage to a relief carving.

position of blanks for recarving

Cutting in blanks to be recarved.

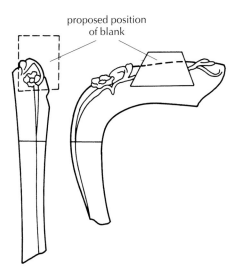

proposed position of blank

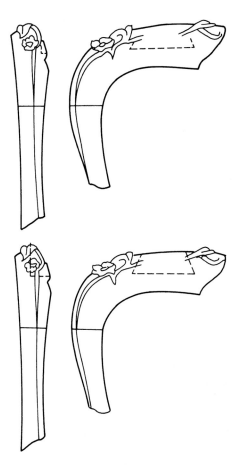

Marking out the repair area from a blank and cutting-in the blank.

(iv) When the blank fits between these two points, any edge of the blank that touches the wood should be scribed and the waste wood removed.

(v) Slowly the blank will drop into position until all its edges are in contact with the wood. Once a seat has been cut for the blank and it sits evenly on it, glue and press it into position, using a cramp if needed.

3. Once the glue is set, shave the top of the blank down to the required contour.

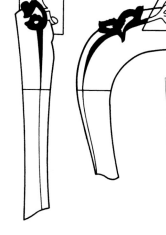

Transferring the design to the blank.

Tips

To make the carving look as if it is part of the old and coming from one hand, don't just copy a flower or leaf from another area and simply place it in your part of the repair: look at the original carving and find similarities within a number of flowers, twigs and leaves. Each leaf or flower will be different, but there will be similar chisel cuts and movements in shape, design and size, and these are the personal signature of each carver. It is this signature that you must try and emulate, continuing the design as he would have done.

4. Roughly draw out the design on the blank, and carve away most of the waste.

5. Now working from the undamaged area of carving, slowly fine down the repair area, moving from each end to the centre until the new carving blends in with the original.

REPAIRING AND REPLACING FEET

This section on repairing feet is specific to chests, chests of drawers and wardrobes. Over the years many have been changed, especially the turned Victorian feet, and it may be felt worthwhile to return them to their original state. Many more have lost their feet altogether, generally to make the piece lower – for example, wardrobes lost theirs to fit into low-ceilinged rooms. Also as furniture went out of fashion it was stored in damp sheds, and the feet simply rotted away. Many more feet wear the scars of ill-treatment, due to dragging over carpet and uneven floorboards; and the culprit for a lot of damage is undoubtedly the vacuum cleaner and its enthusiastic pusher!

Where rot has occurred and no definitive design is left to copy, a little research is necessary, as there is nothing worse than a piece fitted with feet of the wrong period design and proportions, with total disregard to the historical context of the piece; similarly it is often wrongly constructed. To help with this problem there is a small section in the glossary chapter for typical designs and their dating. However, this cannot be held as definitive. A restorer collects books on styles and designs as a chest collects cobwebs, because guessing a design can lead to many mistakes; although even then one is often left to choose between several designs, in which case the proportions and quality of a piece usually answer these conundrums.

Damage due to damp and worm.

To clarify matters I will separate feet into three categories: the turned pillar and post foot, and the bracket, and the foot that is a continuation of the carcase. They form two separate approaches in replacing and repairing, as they pose different structural problems.

BRACKET FEET

Bracket feet come in two categories, although there are many styles to choose from. They can be independent structures that are fixed at each corner and do not actually form any part of the integral structure of the carcase. In this case it is quite usual for the bottom of the carcase to be finished off with a moulding which protrudes from the face of the piece; it is to this mould-ing that the feet are fixed.

The other type of bracket feet are those that are made into a plinth, the moulding being a structural part of the feet. Plinths are normally assumed to be solid without having actual feet, inasmuch as a plinth is a foot in itself; but this is not always the case because many plinths are ornamented, and having bracket feet is just such an ornamentation. The carcase is fitted to the whole unit. This type is used mainly for large pieces, and wardrobes that split into several sections.

So, how can one tell if the feet were inde-pendent or plinth, if all the feet and mouldings are missing? This is usually quite simple, as the method of fixing the two types is very different.

INDEPENDENT BRACKET FEET

These are made of five individual pieces, three being glue-blocks and two the actual feet that are mostly mitred, although those of high quality may have mitred dovetail joints to hold them together. The feet

themselves fit flush with the face of the moulding and are generally no more than ⅞in (22mm) thick. The insides of the feet are strengthened by an upright glue-block, and will leave a tell-tale square glue mark to the underside of the carcase. The other two glue-blocks are placed at right-angles to each other around the upright glue-block, leaving their marks behind, too. The tell-tale marks are further highlighted by the fact that the underside of the carcase will be very dirty, or painted or stained, and this would have happened after the feet and blocks had been fitted.

Where the feet are independent of the carcase, so is the moulding, but there are various ways in which these mouldings will be secured to the carcase. The bottom drawer rail is also part of the base, and the moulding is fixed under this; it is usually stuck to pine or the same wood as the car-case. This basewood for the moulding will first be nailed and glued to the bottom of the chest with the endgrain showing to the sides, and it will be stepped back slightly so that it will not show when the moulding is applied. The moulding will be mitred to

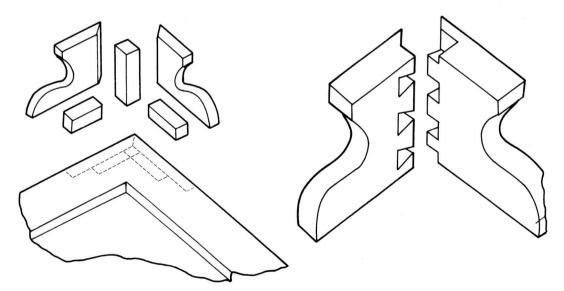

Individual pieces comprising a bracket foot.

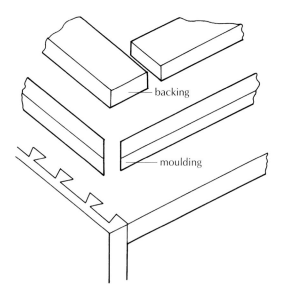

Construction of the base moulding.

give a perfect joint, and then the feet and glue-blocks will be glued.

PLINTH-TYPE BRACKET FEET

The plinth type are part of a complete structure, the whole plinth being generally screwed into position, with possibly four corner-location glue-blocks placed several inches away from the front and sides of the piece. As mentioned above,

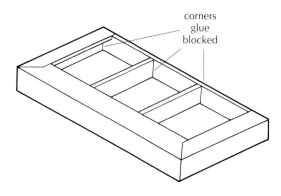

Construction of a plinth for a double or triple wardrobe.

this method is used for very large pieces that come apart to facilitate their being moved. A plinth is a method of holding a two- or three-part wardrobe together, and you will find that the head moulding or pediment is constructed in the same way, to the same end.

Construction of the Plinth
The front, sides and back of the plinth are made of solid planks of wood, and where there are feet these are cut out from these lengths. The front is connected to the sides by a mitred or mitre dovetail joint, and the back is fixed to the sides either by dovetails on the end or a dovetail housing an inch or so from their ends. A central strengthening strut is placed in the middle; this is generally a butt joint and blocked each side. Where a piece is split into more than two sections, there will be more inner struts. These struts will be positioned to carry the load where the sections split, to help tie the whole together.

The moulding is usually part of the capping-board, which is glued on top of the uprights. The whole is then strengthened by glue-blocks, which are pressed in place, using the rubbed-joint method mentioned in chapter 7. When the plinth is set in place, any positioning blocks remaining may not be in the right place. Remove and reposition these, and position any new blocks that are required; these are always in the corners, so that sideways as well as front-to-back positions are attended to simultaneously.

Feet which are a continuation of the carcase are subject to a great deal of wear and tear, from rot to split-out wood, and the problem can be made even more difficult when the piece is veneered. The veneer problem will be covered in a later chapter, the main priority here being repair of the carcase. Let us take the situation for example where one front foot has rotted away and needs to be replaced.

HOW TO DO IT

1. Turn the piece upside-down on the floor. (Be sure to have the top on a carpet, to protect it.)
2. Remove the glue-blocks from around the area, and also the upright block. To do this use a wide chisel: place the blade onto the glue-line and give a sharp tap with a mallet. Do this round all the glue-lines, and the block should pop off.

Front face veneer overlapping side veneer.

3. Once the extent of the damage has been found, draw a faint line showing the area to be cut away. The graft should be in the form of a cut line taking in all the damage and running up to the corner. For this particular exercise, both the front and the side of the foot need replacing; to complicate the matter further, the foot is splayed.
   NOTE: If the foot is solid and not veneered, the join at the corner will be mitred and the wood matched. In the case of a veneered foot, the front wood overlaps the side.
4. Transfer the shapes to be grafted onto the replacement wood, leaving a good overlap to allow for the splay. It is best to stagger the two cut areas and if possible to make the side repair go a little further up the carcase so that it can have a key.
5. Cut blanks, starting with the side first. For a veneered foot, steam and peel back the veneer, then mark onto the carcase with a marking knife.
6. Cut away the waste with a fine-toothed tenon saw.
7. Dry fit the blank to make sure it fits, and adjust if necessary; do not shape the blank yet.
8. Copy steps 5, 6 and 7 to the front.

Using iron and steam to release veneer.

Repair to splay foot awaiting final shaping.

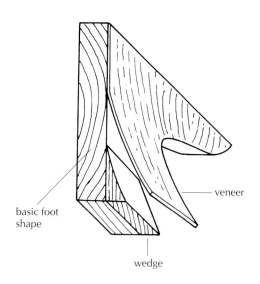

basic foot shape

veneer

wedge

Constructing a veneered splay foot.

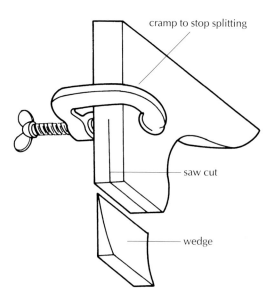

cramp to stop splitting

saw cut

wedge

Constructing a solid-wood splay foot.

Before continuing, it is important to establish how the splayed foot is made, so inspect the good foot to find out. There are two methods: with veneered pieces the first method is generally used, but even so, it is essential to investigate. In method one, first the foot is made and fitted together, then a block is glued to both faces with the front overlapping the side. These are then shaped, and the whole is veneered.

Method two is used on solid wood as opposed to veneer so that no joint can be detected. The base of the foot is cut upwards with the grain the height of the splay, and along the width of the foot, close to the face. A wedge is made to the shape and size of the splay. Two blocks are cramped to the foot, sandwiching the back and front faces.

The front-face block is also shaped to conform to the splay. Glue is applied to both wedge and cut, and then the wedge is tapped home. This forces the front of the wood out into the natural bend of the splay. When dry, the two pieces can be fitted. Remember that with solid wood this must be mitred. If the foot did not have much spare waste you may find it now lacks width at the tip of the mitre.

9. Glue the side section of the foot first. Wait until the glue has set before applying the front section.

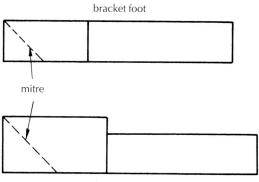

bracket foot

mitre

bracket foot splayed

The extra measurements needed for solid-wood splay foot.

10. Clean up and level. If the area has to be re-veneered, make sure the new wood is below the level of the veneer.

11. If you carried out step 5, the veneer can be held back out of the way by masking tape when just steamed and still flexible. This veneer must be glued back down before you start patching the veneer.

TURNED AND POST OR PILLAR FEET

It is fairly easy to find out if a chest used to have turned feet, as they were always fixed with dowels into the base. Thus bases of chests with holes at the corners, or with circular glue marks, shout loud and clear that at some time turned feet have been replaced. The dowel is an integral part of the turning and if a new foot needs to be turned, this must be taken into consideration when working out the design. Finding the right design can be a problem, since not all feet were made of the same wood as the piece; this is especially the case with Victorian chests which used pine, birch or beech among many woods as well as the same wood as the piece.

POST FEET

The difference between these and turned is only in the shape and fixing. The difference is that the foot is square and may be shaped, and a tenon-stump is used instead of a dowel for fixing. The tenon fits into a mortice cut into the base and wedged.

PILLAR FEET

The Victorians were fond of turnings and put them on corners of chests, and a turned foot would be attached to the bottom as a continuation of the overall design. This type of decoration has earlier roots, since Georgian chests had ropes, flutes and reeded pillars. These can be made off the lathe, and will be covered in the chapter on turning; if you don't have a lathe, however, you will need to have them made for you.

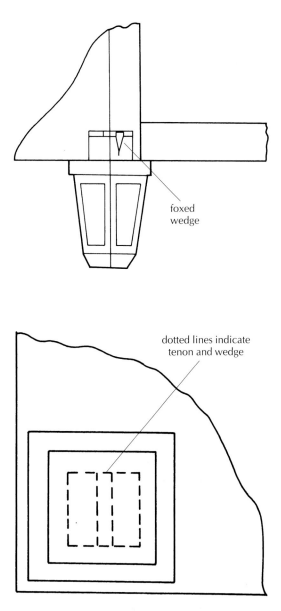

foxed wedge

dotted lines indicate tenon and wedge

Post foot.

nine

REPAIRING SPLITS

This section covers any type of furniture that has a split in it. There are many reasons for a piece to split, and why it does so will sometimes give you the answer as to how to repair it. When growing in its natural environment, wood will have an immense amount of force held within it. A cut plank is not a natural state for a piece of wood to be in, so these forces can be near the surface and may cause problems as the wood ages and shrinks. Furthermore, it may be in contact with other woods whose inherent forces are in conflict with it. Moreover, unless the piece is in a sealed environment, the wood will change with the weather, literally! Modern homes and central heating also play their part.

A table top can split for several reasons, but stress from adjacent woods is not generally the cause. Tops should not be glued to frames, but should be held by screws which can be eased to allow for shrinkage; if this is not done then they could split. Most tops will have an attractively grained wood. However, this very attractiveness generally indicates that the grain has movement in it, and this movement in the grain creates stress which in time can possibly lead to splitting, especially if there is much temperature and humidity change. Knots also cause problems, because they shrink in a different way from the surrounding areas of more normal grain and so the stress around them is greater.

The wood in chests must contend with all of the above problems and a few more besides, largely because differing surfaces are bound together with glue and joints.

Often a chest top will be of superior quality to its sides, and this alone causes stress as the woods may have different shrinking rates: if one piece of wood wants to shrink more than the other, then something will have to give. Moreover tops may be veneered to an inferior substrate (base wood), and this will cause a tremendous amount of stress.

A good way of knowing the quality of a piece is this: a veneered piece where the substrate is of similar density to that of the veneer is of high quality, because less conflicting stress will be caused; for example, rosewood veneered to mahogany is better than rosewood veneered to pine because pine will shrink more than mahogany.

Tops, and especially falls on bureaus, can have cross-battens to stop warping and bowing, and when veneered these will sometimes give problems. Wood shrinks very little along its length as compared to shrinking across the grain, and this fact can have other side-effects when it is jointed and glued across the end.

As well as wood splitting along its grain, where several planks are used to make a face it is quite likely that these may part company. Moreover, a split rarely runs from end to end, but more often in a zigzag fashion, following weaker pathways within the wood. If this were not enough, I have not yet come across a split that was at right-angles to the face, and the angle of the split almost always causes problems when repairing.

Below I have categorized splits into separate sections, dealing with their problems and how to repair them.

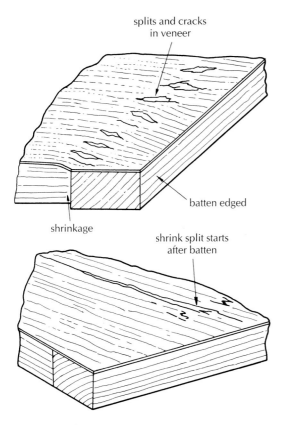

Shrinkage effect caused by longitude battens going across grain.

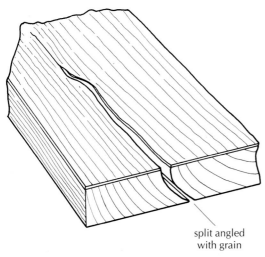

Illustrating peculiarities of split wood.

REPAIRING A SPLIT IN OPEN WOOD

Recognized areas of damage are table tops and other faces that are not jointed or glued to other pieces of wood. The cause may be weakness through age, or where the wood itself is of a wild nature, which although beautiful to look at, has an immense amount of stress locked up inside, which has been released over time and has caused splitting as a result.

HOW TO DO IT

It may be possible to pull together a split in open wood with a sash cramp. However, if it has been split once it is likely to happen again, because the reason why it split in the first place will not have been resolved. There are two alternative ways to deal with this problem:

First Method
This method entails filling the split with a fillet of wood.

1. Using a hacksaw blade or pad saw, clean up the split by sawing its sides. Do not widen the split to a conformed width, let it taper to a blunt point the thickness of

Cleaning out a split with a hacksaw blade.

91

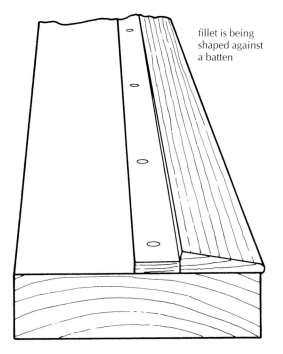

fillet is being
shaped against
a batten

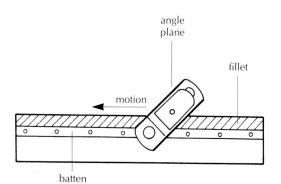

angle
plane

fillet

motion

batten

wedge fillet

Making a fillet for splits.

the blade. (I have a collection of blades, from thin junior hacksaw blades to thick metal machine blades.

2. Select a piece of wood for the fillet that will match the repair area as closely as possible; make sure the grain is going in the same direction.

3. Shape the fillet to match the split, though make it slightly over-size.

4. Using a block-plane, put a slight taper on the fillet to make the cross-section into a blunt wedge. Keep offering it up until it fits, but is proud of the surface.

5. If (as is most likely) the line of the split is not straight, and if the fillet is rather thick and is likely to break when bent to fit, then steam it for an hour or so. Having said that, it is best not to steam, if possible, as you will need to glue it at the same time as fitting it properly, and this can lead to a weaker glue joint.

6. Apply glue to both split and fillet. Press into place, and using a length of wood to cover the length of the fillet, tap down until it is firm. Don't overdo this part, however, as it can force the split to open up further along the wood.

7. When dry, pare flush.

8. Turn over and fit butterfly joints (*see* Chapter 7) across the split. If it is a short split, say 6in (15cm), then one at each end will suffice.

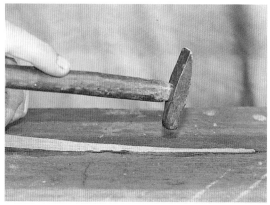

Tapping fillet home.

Paring fillet flush with a chisel.

Second Method

This method may seem drastic, and without the right tool – a wide-throated bandsaw – and the skill, it is one I would advise the beginner not to take on, or at least to practise for some time before attempting. This is because you have only one chance, and if you go wrong it is hard to rectify. You need a true eye, a steady hand and a cool head.

1. Inspect the split bottom and top to find which way it goes through the wood. As mentioned before, a split is rarely at right-angles to the face.

2. On the underneath, tape the split with wide masking tape.

3. Working on the top face and using a soft pencil, start to trace a line starting from where the split finishes. The line must follow along the grain. Also, anywhere along the split itself you may find little bridges of wood that have not broken as the split has zigzagged along the grain; draw a line on these bridges to connect up the split in a smooth line.

4. Before cutting, check the saw and blade. It must be sharp and have no wobble in it; the table must be true and the machine should not be changed until the repair is completed.

5. I always check that anything I may need is at hand, and if the wood is large, that there are roller-props to support it.

6. Place the split end on the cutting table, and at a slow, even speed, feed the piece through the blade. *Do not pause* until you have cut through to the other end. NOTE: When cutting through the split, take a central line until you reach the end of the split, where you will then follow the line you drew on the surface. When coming to the end of the split it will be natural to pause, because from

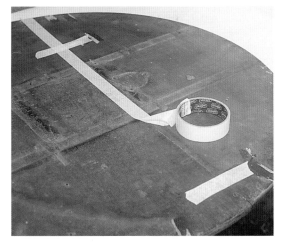

Taping underside of a split prior to cutting.

Cutting through split with a bandsaw blade.

93

this point you cannot return. However, *do not pause.* What you are actually doing is cutting out the split, and the reason for a steady, constant pressure on the blade is that if you slow down or stop, the blade will widen the saw gap in that area. The blade will make the same profile on both sides of its cut even when following a zigzag line, and when butted together the pieces will fit like two jigsaw shapes.

7. Once cut, turn over and gently peel away the tape. On one side or the other will be found pieces of wood that will come away from the split, because of the difference between the angle of the cutting blade and the angle of the split through the wood. These pieces must be glued onto the split side of the wood and held in place with masking tape until set. This only needs to be for an hour or so.

8. Using the procedures set out in the chapter on gluing, glue and cramp the two pieces together. Clean away any sawing 'fur' on the bottom edge of the cut with fine sandpaper: if this fur becomes trapped between the two edges when gluing they will not mate properly. (You will find that the split has closed up a little, so only place cramps across the area that actually comes into contact otherwise you distort the wood throughout the split by creating stress.)

9. When the glue has set and cured, inspect and recut until the split has disappeared. Each time you cut you must stay on the saw line, and each cut must be as accurate as the last.
    NOTE: From the second cut on, it is important to clean off every scrap of glue left on the blade as this can lead to inaccuracies, and can also blunt the blade.

10. Strengthen with butterfly joints underneath.

11. The end product should be a fine glueline, with the grain matching through-

out the piece unless you inspect quite closely; only then will you notice a slight difference in grain change. This is unavoidable, but will not be discernible except by an expert.

This method can only be used when a split is no more than ¼in (6mm) wide, as the grain change will be too noticeable after this amount of wood has been taken out. Also the track of the cut must be carefully plotted so that the cut does not cross the grain. Do not use this method if you have any doubts as regards ruining the authenticity of the piece, and not before you have fully mastered the technique with practice. Lastly, remember you are taking away wood, so things such as circles and lids will be of a different size when finished and may not fit together with the rest of the piece once the repair is done.

Finally, as I said to begin with, you will have to choose which method to use, and my advice is still: if in doubt, leave out!

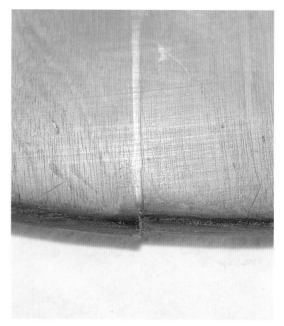

An old repair resulting in the two halves of a round table not matching.

REPAIRING SPLITS ON PLANKED AREAS

When splits occur down a glue-line due to shrinkage at one end, the joint should be split completely and the two faces trued and reglued. This, like the last method described, takes away wood, so be careful to note whether this will affect the fitting of other components of the piece. If this is the case, then a fillet should be added to one side or the other; generally the back end of the piece is the best place for this addition.

REPAIRING A SPLIT ON JOINTED AREAS

This type of split is most likely to happen where two woods are jointed and glued and shrink at different rates, and is commonly found on chests where the side is jointed to the top. In fact the side may be the same species of wood, but of lesser colour and density, it therefore shrinks more than the top, but because it is jointed and glued it obviously cannot decrease in width. When this happens, the wood splits where the grain runs at its weakest down the board; it can actually run from top to bottom. This can be rectified in two ways: by using a fillet as in method one; or by method two. However, method two can only be employed on something like a chest when the drawers don't reach to the back.

HOW TO DO IT

1. Dismantle the carcase. (The sides will be dovetailed top and bottom.)
2. Use the bandsaw method to remove the split.
3. Once the split has been removed and the whole is glued, a misalignment of one part of the jointed section will be found when it is offered up to its mating joints. Always fit back the piece aligning the front part so that the misalignment occurs on the back half. Mark the tails where the pins are now placed.
4. Cut away the waste on the tails for the new position of the pins. (Do *not* cut away the pins with the idea of fitting new pins;

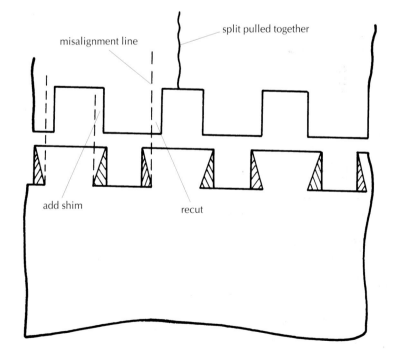

Re-marking position of dovetail.

see the chapter on repairs of joints).

5. Cut a wedge to fill the space left by the pin; glue and cramp.
6. Use a butterfly joint to strengthen.

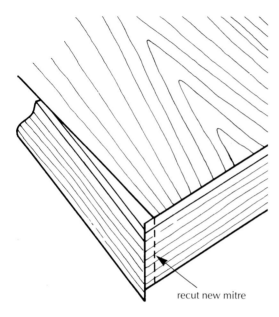

Butt joints.

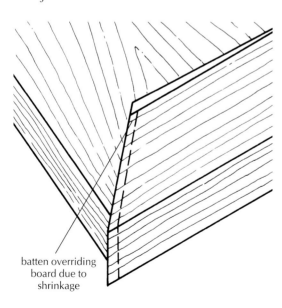

batten overriding board due to shrinkage

Extra tongue-and-groove strengthening on a mitred batten.

SPLITS DUE TO STRENGTHENING BATTEN

As described above, there are several situations where a strengthening batten is used, and these are fixed in several ways. Boxes where the sides go across the grain of the top create the same situation.

Battens and Mouldings
(i) Butt joint: this is rare on battens but not at mouldings, since gluing to end-grain is never satisfactory.
(ii) Tongue and groove: this method is the most typical for battens, and is the strongest way, especially when guarding against warping.
(iii) Dowel: if this type occurs it is generally in furniture made about the turn of this century, and then in lower quality pieces.
(iv) Mitres: on bureau falls and tables the ends will most likely be mitred in, so as not to show endgrain to the front. This mitre can also be tongue and grooved.

Boxes
(i) Tops are generally glued and pinned onto the sides.
(ii) Tops can be rebated into the sides.
(iii) When veneered, the top may be glued inside the sides and then pinned through the sides.

On faces that show a batten or cross-member, as on a box, it will be generally hidden by veneer, *unless* this member is used as a decorative device. This causes two problems: to the main body of the wood, and to the veneer itself, and these problems should be tackled separately. (Where there is no veneer, just leave out the steps in the How To Do It section below, which covers veneer.)

REPAIRING A SPLIT IN A BUREAU FALL

Let us say that the problem is a bureau fall; it could, however, be equated to any other

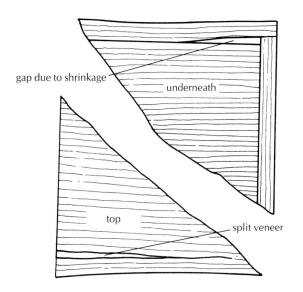

gap due to shrinkage

underneath

top

split veneer

Construction of boxes.

piece of furniture in this situation, down to a small box. The main body of the wood has shrunk, and has split because the cross-member has not shrunk to the same extent and is too well fixed to release the tension. The veneer has also split with the substrate, but where it is glued to the cross-member it has stayed fixed, causing the veneer to break along the glue-line of the substrate and the cross-member.

HOW TO DO IT

1. First, release the veneer from the cross-member and the substrate around the damaged area by steaming and softening the glue (*see* chapter on veneering). Use a thin knife or large kitchen palette knife to lift the veneer. The member may need to be released along its whole length; if this is the case, then the veneer must also be released further than the damaged area.

2. Ascertain the method by which the cross-member is fixed, and release it accordingly:

(i) *End butt glued*: using a thin knife (I have an old ham knife for this purpose) insert the blade at the end of the glue-line and tap gently into it; the cross-member should release itself as you tap along. Check the direction of the grain on the cross-member: if it is running away from the glue-line, then start from the other end if possible. (The knife can run off the glue-line into the member.)

(ii) *Tongue and groove*: place the tip of the knife into the glue-line as deep as the tongue, and tap along it on both sides. Only do a few inches at a time and then do the other side, changing sides every few inches until you reach the end. If this does not release the cross-member – and sadly this will invariably be the case – then use the knife on the whole thickness of the wood and cut through the tongue with the knife, remembering about the direction of the grain.

This method can only be used when the tongue is a part of the cross-member. If the tongue is a part of the substrate, or loose, then the grain will be going across the glue-line and the knife will not be able to cut through. Using the gap created by the knife when running along the glue-line with its tip, saw through the tongue.

(iii) *Dowel or nailed*: use the knife across the whole thickness of the glue-line until you reach the dowel or nail. The knife will cut through the dowel with the help of a sharp tap. Usually nails will release automatically, except for the most stubborn; just cut through these with the knife. An old knife is invariably hard enough to do this, except for large nails, in which case use a hacksaw blade.

Making a rebate with a plough-plane.

3. Once the batten has been released, the split can usually be closed by using a cramp and glue. Then it is a matter of putting back the batten.

Putting Back the Batten

If the batten was simply glued on before, then follow that example; if the piece was dowelled or tongue and grooved, however, a little more work is required.

Dowelled joint: The old dowel holes up to the split will align perfectly. I always start from the front so as to leave any overhang of the batten showing at the back. With dowels that align, remove the old dowels in the same way as described in the chapter on chairs. The other side of the split should be treated as replacing new dowels, and the best method to align these is also found in the chapter on chairs.

Tongue and groove joint: If the joint was released without damaging or destroying the tongue, then simply glue it back. Where the tongue is no longer serviceable, then a replacement loose tongue must be fitted. Proceed as follows:

1. Clean both surfaces flush, removing any unwanted bits of the old tongue.
2. Using a tenon gauge, mark out on the piece requiring a rebate. Take the measurement from the other rebate.
3. Either using a plough-plane or router, cut a new rebate.
4. Cut the loose tongue to size, making the reach of the tongue slightly shorter than the combined rebates to allow for contraction, and glue.
   NOTE: The tongue should be cut across the grain to give maximum strength.
5. Glue and cramp.

ten

REPAIRING AND REPLACING TURNINGS

For those who don't own a lathe and need a turning replaced, it is far easier to get someone to turn it for you. The important thing is to know how to construct an accurate template for your turner because it will not always be possible to take the piece to his workshop, for example if it is attached to a wardrobe.

The only way to achieve quality, accurate work is to prepare well, and in this instance preparation means careful measuring and accurate drawings. Amongst your tools you should have a pair of dividers and calipers. Buy good ones, because a cheap pair can distort under tension, and if your budget allows, screw-adjustable ones are best.

CONSTRUCTING A TEMPLATE

A template is a bit of board or stiff card cut and marked to the external or internal shape of the piece you want to copy. I would produce both, as it is just as easy when cutting out any template.

One other thing to keep in mind when measuring a turning, especially when it is a country piece, is the problem of shrinkage in the piece you are copying. Many turnings are not truly round because they were originally turned from green wood, and after the wood has seasoned and shrunk they will be slightly oval – it can sometimes

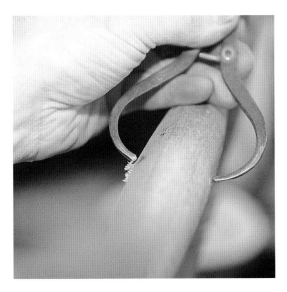

Callipers measuring cross-section of a spindle.

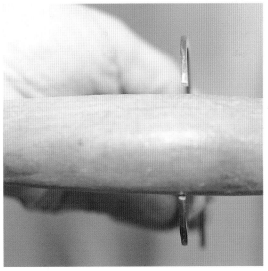

Note the shrinkage of the same spindle making its cross-section oval.

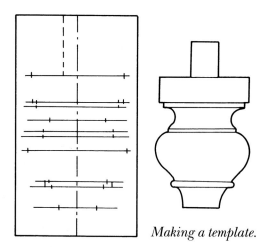

Making a template.

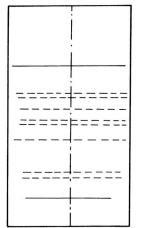

Transposing shape of turning into measurements for the template.

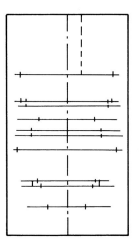

Breaking down diameters into radii.

be quite noticeable. When this occurs, always take your measurements from the largest diameter of the oval.

HOW TO DO IT

1. Using a stiff card larger than the piece to copy, draw a centre line down the middle of the card, and a bottom line across the centre line.
2. Now section the turning into steps by measuring each part of the turning. Start from the top and work down, transposing these measurements onto the centre.
3. These measurement markings are then extended as a line across the card on both sides of the centre line.
4. Referring back to the turning, take the diameters off the different sections you have already set down as lines on your card; remember to divide in two to find the radius.
5. Once these diameters have been registered on the lines of your card, join them up as though you were doing a dot-drawing. You will be left with a series

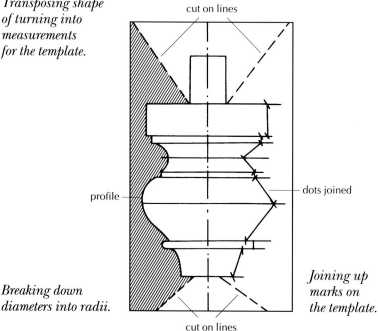

Joining up marks on the template.

of steps that will correspond to the shape of the turning, although not the design, which will be a series of rolls, flutes, squares and bevels.

6. Place the card under the turning with the markings showing, and copy the profile by eye. Where a roll or a flute occurs that is obviously a perfect circle, use a compass.

7. When the profile is completed, mark out the length and diameter of the spigot that will hold the piece in place. When replacing a missing piece, the hole is already there, and unless this hole is damaged, transfer these measurements to your card. If the hole is damaged, either block it in and re-drill, or enlarge it until a satisfactory fixing can be made. If you are replacing a damaged area, then you will need to choose an appropriate size spigot that will be strong but not so large as to weaken the rest of the turning: one third of the total diameter will generally be effective, and a length of 3in (76mm) or more. Do be careful not to end the spigot where the turning narrows, as in this area the ratio will be much less.

8. Using a scalpel knife, cut out the shape. When the shape has been removed you will have the master profile and the external profile, the latter being the card with

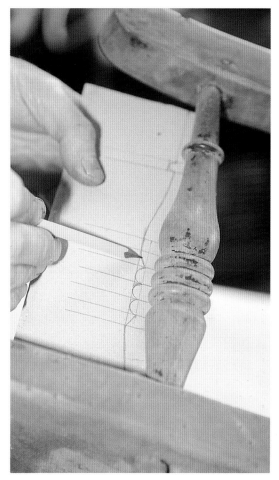

Copying the shape onto a template.

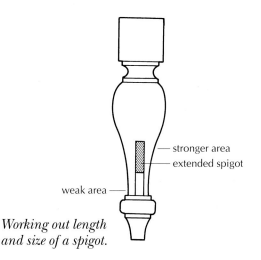

Working out length and size of a spigot.

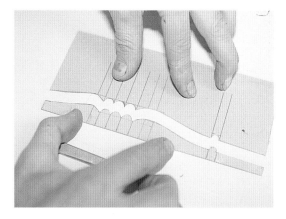

The two parts of the template after being cut.

Shaping a reeded spindle with a chisel.

a hole. This external profile is then halved by cutting down the centre line, and is held against the turning to make sure the contours are correct. The master profile is used to set dividers and calipers.

Where a turning has a lot of ornamentation this method can be used to good effect. Cut off the damaged piece on a turned line so that when it is jointed there will be no obvious joint-lines. The real problem is finding and drilling an accurate hole to receive the spigot.

DRILLING ACCURATELY

Drilling accurately will always be a problem, especially if the hole has to be made by a hand-held drill. Finding the actual centre is the first hurdle to overcome, and there are several tools on the market for finding centres on round objects. But the real test is to drill straight, and here it will be helpful to have an extra pair of eyes to help.

HOW TO DO IT

1. Strap a pair of guide-rules to the leg, adjacent to each other. These rules should stick up above the drilling area, but not so far as to hamper the drill.
2. Line up the drill bit with both rules by eye (this is where you can do with an assistant's eyes). Gently drill the hole, constantly checking. A variable-speed trigger drill is most helpful, and a centre-point drill bit to stay on the mark.

BIRD'S BEAK REPAIR

An obvious type of repair needed is where a foot has rotted and is shorter than its partners; this sort of damage is more frequent in country furniture which sat on flagstones with no dampcourse. This repair can be used on square legs as well. It is known as a bird's beak because of the V-shape of the scarfe. This type of joint needs practice to get perfect, but is worth it as it will be many times stronger than a butt.

HOW TO DO IT

1. Mark out the V-shape as follows: make a mark on the centre line of the leg just above the rot, and from this mark take a line up the leg to each outside edge at about 60°; this makes your V-shape.
2. Once a V-shape is marked on the leg, cut along these lines to give a V-shaped end to the bottom of the leg. Clean up with a plane; for small area use a block plane.
3. Transfer this shape to a prepared piece of wood and cut out the V-shaped waste of wood. This should be cleaned up with a wide chisel.

NOTE: The point of the V where the two saw-cuts meet will be blunt, and this blunt area is difficult to get rid of: the

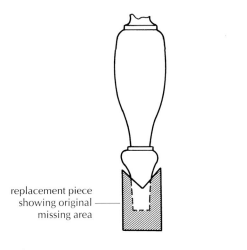

replacement piece showing original missing area

Working out a scarfe or bird's beak joint.

Cutting leg to give a V-shaped end.

Cleaning up the V with a chisel.

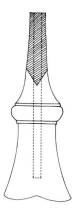

Further strengthening of bird's beak joint by a dowel.

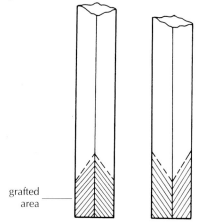

grafted area

Position of scarfe on a square leg.

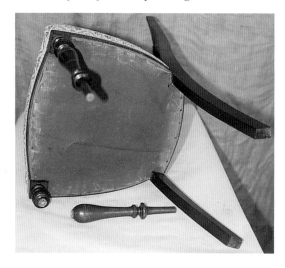

easiest way is to place a flat side of the chisel first on one face of the V and then the other, and slide its blade across the point in a knife-action.

4. Always dry fit to check it fits properly all the way round, before gluing.
5. If the joint is near the end of the leg it can be further strengthened by putting a dowel up through.
6. When the glue is set, shape the replacement part to size. This can be done with a spokeshave, especially if the leg is turned. If the repair is to a square leg, make sure the V-joint runs from corner to corner; this will do away with a cut-line across the grain.

Another way is if the leg can be separated from the piece and repaired by the steps above. Once this joint is set, find the centres of the top and bottom ends of the leg. This again is difficult, and the beginner is apt to turn more than is needed.

BROKEN LEG

Many legs will break just under the joint block, especially with reed-turnings where the leg is quite narrow; it only needs an awkward person to crash into the chair, or the chair to become loose and not reglued. In these cases, it is best if the pieces can be glued back together properly and strengthened; such breaks are never straight, and usually have spikes of wood that will interlock when fitted and glued together.

When the glue has set, drill down through the joint-block with a long drill and strengthen with a dowel. Where the joint-block is visible, however, this can't be done without the repair showing, in which case a hole and dowel must be inserted between the two pieces and these then pulled together. But because of the interlocking

Chair with leg broken at narrow place of turning.

mesh of the wood, drilling without a guide will be virtually impossible; a jig must therefore be made to help you create two holes that when fitted together will not put the leg out of alignment and so inhibit the interlocking of the broken shards.

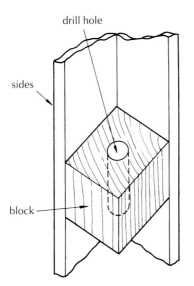

Making a jig to help centre a drill on a turning.

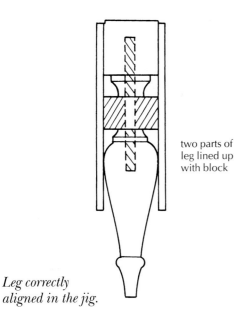

Leg correctly aligned in the jig.

HOW TO DO IT

1. Cut a square block of wood to the diameter of the leg; the block should be at least 1in (25mm) thick. Find its centre, and drill a hole with the drill bit to take the dowel.

2. Cut strips of thin plywood the width of the block and about 4in (10cm) long; glue and pin to the sides of the block, making an open-ended box with the block with the hole at one end.

   NOTE: Because the turning may not be straight within 3in (76mm) of the break, make sure to measure the greater diameter for your block measurement.

3. Place the jig over the end of the leg, and with two cramps secure the sides of the box to the leg.

   NOTE: Where the box is larger than the top of the leg, work out the difference and pack it with spacers.

4. Hold firmly in a vice, and gently feed the drill bit through the hole in the block and subsequently into the top of the leg.

Drilling through the jig into the leg.

Do this to both sides of the break. You may need to make two blocks with sides, as the measurements may differ. This is all right, but do be exact in your measurements. Remember, because of the shrinkage the leg may be a little oval, in which case use some packing.

BROKEN CHIPS FROM TURNINGS

This happens all the time – dogs in particular seem to be partial to knobbly turnings. The simplest method is to cut away the damage back to sound wood, making the face flat to take the repair; then cut a block of matching wood to a similar shape, a little oversize.

Glue the block into position, rubbing it to expel air and surplus glue; then use tape to hold it whilst it dries. Once set, shape it to match the rest.

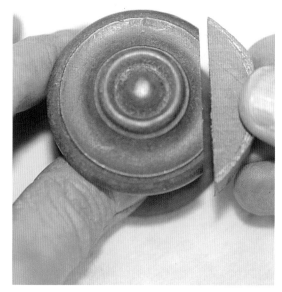

Making a blank to fit to repair a broken turning.

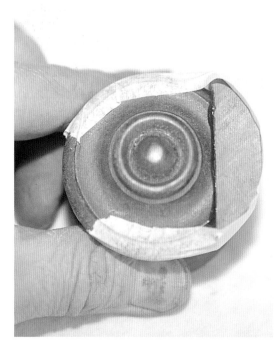

Holding the blank in place with masking tape.

REPAIRING SPINDLES

'Spindles' covers anything as small as decorative turnings on the back of chairs, to turned ornamental or plain chair-stretchers: Wherever possible, repair rather than replace, although the problem is how to drill holes into such a thin piece of wood without the twisting action of the drill doing more damage.

One simple tool will facilitate this delicate operation, and in fact any turning that needs to be drilled where you suspect that the stress of the drilling could cause damage: the simple car hose-clip. Just wrap some paper round the object to protect its surface before tightening the clip. It also acts very well as a clamp to hold a spliced joint to a turned surface while gluing, or where a turning is shattered but all the pieces are complete. Just build up the area and clamp with the appropriate-sized clip.

Using a hose clip to strengthen a spindle whilst drilling.

REEDS, FLUTES, ROPES AND BARLEY TWISTS

These decorations are much simpler if you have a lathe. If you have used the services of a turner already then ask him to complete the job. But just in case he can't or you want to be independent, I shall explain how to carry out these tasks as though you have not got a lathe.

HOW TO DO IT

1. Make an open-top box three times the width of the turning and a few inches longer.
2. Fit a screw through both ends of the box in a central position, but only the radius of the turning from the top edge.
3. With a set-square, draw a line up from the screw hole at each end and then turn onto the top edges of the ends.
4. Drill a hole above and on the centre line to each screw, about ½in (13mm) away or closer if the radius of the turning is smaller. The holes must be the same size

as the round nails you have selected, and are used to stop the turning from rotating.
5. Fit a 3in (76mm) shelf on each side, flush with the top. (This can be used to fit a fence if using a router.)

REEDS AND FLUTES

There are two ways of making these, by hand or by router, the only difference between the two being that one is concave and one is convex. If a router is being used, then it is the cutter that will determine the shape. The simplest method is the router, although the setting up of the machine is critical and will take time to effect.

HOW TO DO IT

First Method: using a router
1. Buy a circular protractor and drill a hole to take a veneer pin dead in its centre.
2. Attach the protractor to one end of the turning with the veneer pin, using the turning centre to position the pin (the

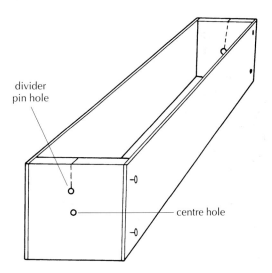

divider pin hole

centre hole

A turning-box.

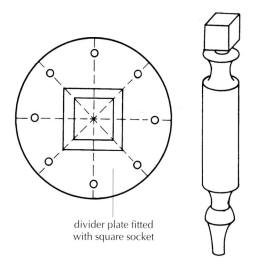

Positioning turnings to make reeds or flutes.

markings on a protractor must be facing the turning).

3. Decide how many divisions you want, and mark them around the turning.

4. Remove the protractor and place the turning in the box. Screw up the screws in the end of the box, making sure they enter the turning points.

5. When the turning is secure, line up one of the divisional marks on the turning with the centre line. Tap in the nails to stop the piece turning.

6. Select the cutter for the job – a core bit for the fluting, or a pointed cove for reeding.

7. Place the router over the turning, with the cutter centred over the line. Either fit the fence provided with the router to run along the outer shelf, or fit a fence to the shelf that the base of the router can run against. Fit a stop at each end to determine the length of cut.

NOTE: If the turning is tapered, you will need to build a ramp on the shelves so that the router base will run parallel with the turning.

8. Adjust the cutter so that it touches the turning, then lower it to the depth required.

9. Turn on the router and make the first cut; then remove the machine, release the stop-nails, and turn one division. Once it is repositioned, cut the next division; and so on.

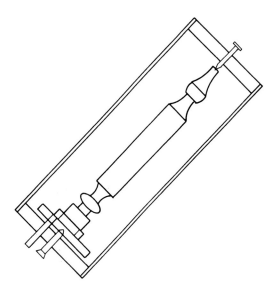

Using protractor and pin to segment a turning.

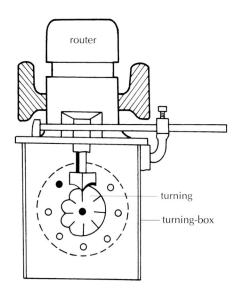

Cutting a turning in a turning-box with a router.

Second Method: by hand
Turning a Reed

1. Follow the instructions given in Method 1 from **step 1** through to **step 5**, then as follows:
6. Draw a line along the turning with a rule, using the centre lines on the ends of the box. Then using a marking knife, mark the line again. Mark out all the lines around the turning.
7. Cramp a straight-edge to one of the shelves, aligning the straight face with the two centre-line marks.
8. Put masking tape along a fine tenon saw, leaving a gap between the edge of

Making a Scratch-stock

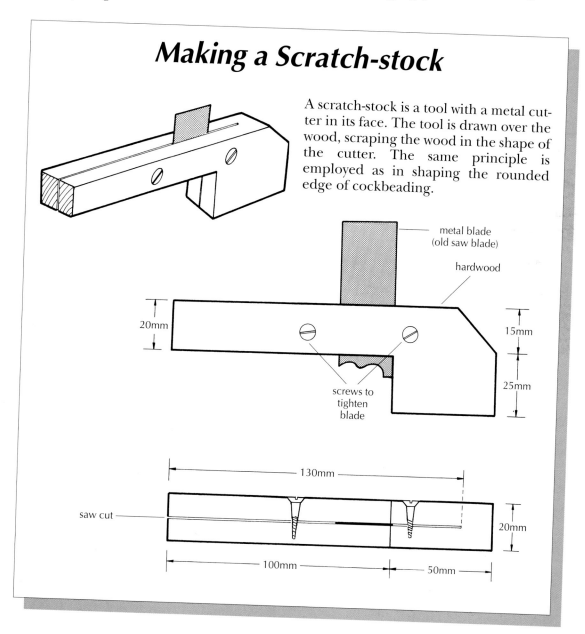

A scratch-stock is a tool with a metal cutter in its face. The tool is drawn over the wood, scraping the wood in the shape of the cutter. The same principle is employed as in shaping the rounded edge of cockbeading.

metal blade (old saw blade)

hardwood

20mm

15mm

25mm

screws to tighten blade

130mm

saw cut

20mm

100mm

50mm

the tape and the teeth of the saw. This gap must be the same measurement as the depth of the reed.

9. Saw the line down to the masking tape; repeat all around the turning.
10. Remove the straight-edge.
11. Draw a centre line between the saw-cuts.
12. With a narrow, long-bladed paring chisel, cut a chamfer from one side of the saw-cut. Repeat on the other side. Continue to cut a chamfer, changing the angle of the chisel until a reed is formed. NOTE: This reed will not be completely round because of the flat, chamfered faces.
13. Make a scratch-stock and blade to correspond to the reed.
14. The scratch-stock can be used freehand or guided by fences. Continue until the turning is done.

Turning a flute: The same principles are used throughout, except that instead of cutting and marking the lines with the marking-knife, the flute is cut freehand with a gouge of the correct size, cutting between the lines and not on them. Again, use a scratch-stock to clean and finish the flutes, using a metal cutter that corresponds to the gouge.

Finishing the Ends
The ends of flutes or reeds are most important, and will have to be finished by hand, even those made by a router. This operation is best done by a chisel of the appropriate shape; the illustrations show the differences you can choose from.

ROPES AND BARLEY TWISTS

These are much more complicated operations, and I would suggest you farm them out, as I do. I use a company that has a lathe

Masking tape on a tenon saw to indicate the depth of cut.

copier, and in all but a few circumstances they always get it right. There was once a piece they could not copy totally: a double barley twist that was open in the middle but not at the ends. To save me time in working out the twists and actually cutting the twists themselves, I got them to do it for me and finished it off by hand. Getting the donkeywork done, and also the set-up on the twist, is half the battle and takes most of morning getting it correct and drawing it out. However, for those who want to be adventurous, here are the steps for the rope and twist.

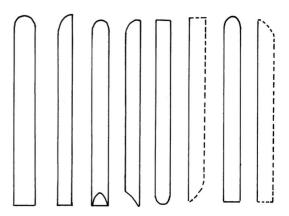

Various ends of reeds and flutes.

HOW TO DO IT

1. Make a turning-box like the one already described, but with the sides low enough to give access to the turning.
2. Draw at least four lines equidistant along the length of the turning using the centre markings on top of the box. (Four lines will do; more will give you a more accurate reading.)
3. Measure the length of each twist: this means the actual 'travel' along the turning it takes for one whole twist around the turning. (This may vary as the twist travels the length of the turning, especially if the turning is tapered.)
4. Transcribe this measurement onto the new turning, marking the start on the first centre line, and then measuring along that same line and marking at the appropriate spot.
5. If there are four dividing lines around the turning, then divide the measurement by three; thus if a complete turn is 4in (10cm), then 4in (10cm) divided by 3in (75mm) = 1.33in (33mm). For example:

    No.1 The starting line marks the start of the twist. Mark this starting line all the way round the turning.

    No.2 From the starting mark on the second line, mark 1.33in (33mm) along the turning's length.

    No.3 From the starting mark on the third line, mark 2.66in (66mm) along the turning's length.

    No.4 On the last line which is a whole turn, this is already marked 4in (10cm) along.

    To keep from confusing yourself, mark the start line and the line denoting a complete turn with another colour. If the twist diminishes in length for a full turn along the turning, then work out the ratio of change and work this into your sums when dividing each complete turn. Join the marks together.

The easiest way to do this is to cut a strip of flexible card, the width taken from the centre point of the twist to the next.

Place the edge of the card-strip on the starting-line and starting mark. Line up the edge of the card to the second line and the 1.33in (33mm) mark. Continue to wrap the strip round the turning until you reach the end, making sure all marks are aligned with the edge of the strip. Secure both its ends. Using the edges of the strip, trace a line on both sides. If it is a twist, then run a centre line between these two lines in another colour. With a rope this is not needed. It becomes more complex when there is more than one twist starting from the starting line. This is always the case with ropes. My advice is to mark out one twist at a time, using different colour markers to define the high and the low spots.

6. Mark your saw-blade in the same way as when cutting reeds, with masking tape.
7. For twists, cut along the centre line from start to end. For ropes, cut on the dividing lines.
8. The task for twists is to remove the waste wood each side of the cut centre line, making the profile of the twist up to the other lines which indicate the high spot of the twist. For a rope, remove the waste each side of the cut divided line, rising to a high-spot centre of the next divided line. (Removal of large sections of waste at this point is best done with a sharp chisel.)
9. Once both twist or rope is formed, take off the rest of the waste with rasps. For a twist you will need a round rasp for the low spots, as well as a flat one to make the curves up to the high spots. For a rope just a flat rasp can be used.
10. Finish with a gooseneck or pointed cabinet scraper, and then sandpaper (*see* Chapter 14 on Preparation for Finishing)

eleven

VENEERS I: SELECTING, STORING AND LAYING

Veneering can be traced as far back as the Egyptians who used slices of wood, ivory and stones on a backing to decorate objects. For our purposes, veneer consists of thinly cut pieces of wood laid onto a backing-wood. Today's veneer is thinly sliced by machine, but previously veneer was cut by hand and is known in the trade as 'saw-cut veneer' against its modern counterpart 'machine-cut'. Machine veneers are cut to a thickness of 0.6–0.9mm.

Because of the demands of restorers, veneer manufacturers are cutting some veneers in varying thicknesses and qualities, so it is wise to check when ordering. There are also 'constructional' veneers which are used solely in the making of plywoods and other man-made boards; these sometimes prove useful when making laminated, pierced sections, for example a rim round a tray.

IDENTIFYING VENEER

The restorer must understand and recognize the difference between saw-cut and machine-cut veneer. Restoring veneers is not the same as laying whole sheets of new veneer onto new pieces, so you need to know what you are dealing with. For example, it would be totally wrong to replace saw-cut with machine-cut if the piece warranted the former. A common trick in patching a

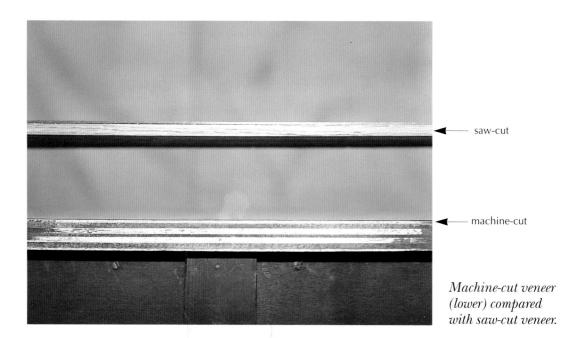

saw-cut

machine-cut

Machine-cut veneer (lower) compared with saw-cut veneer.

saw-cut veneer when no thick veneer is available is to pack out the piece with other veneers and lay the selected one on top. This is never really a success, however, and after a time will show up all too clearly as an improvisation. Thin veneer never seems to have finished quality that a single thick veneer has – even 1.0mm is considered thin for saw-cut.

Acquiring saw-cut veneer is becoming increasingly difficult, but there are two answers: to remove it from old furniture that is beyond redemption; or to cut it with a machine saw, from old wood. There are several ways to recognize saw-cut veneer. One can safely say that furniture before 1860 will be covered with a thick or saw-cut veneer; after this date and as the nineteenth century ends, it slowly becomes more marginal. The thickness of the veneer is also an indication of date, so always check the edges of a piece – though remember that it may have been previously refinished when patina was not so important as we now hold it, so the veneer could have been scraped and sanded down. Finally, the underneath will show up signs of the saw-blade, which would have left sloping, straight saw marks; these may have been scraped down but are hardly ever eliminated.

SELECTING VENEER

When buying veneer do your own selecting: never accept any old dusty package. Some companies put together offcuts of veneer into so-called 'marquetry' and 'restorers' packs and these are useful as stock, but when buying large amounts do the choosing yourself.

There are a few things you need to know about selecting. When cut, veneers are laid down the way they came off the log and stacked in bundles called flitches. When purchasing a number of leaves, there are two places one can take from a flitch, the bottom or the top; *never from the middle!*

Small flitch of mahogany veneer.

In fact the reason is quite logical, because as you move through a flitch you will find that the underside of the top leaf matches the top of the second leaf and so on through the flitch. This is most important when matching veneers, and the Veneer House can only guarantee matching if a flitch is sold in the proper manner. So if the leaf that is perfect for a job is halfway down the flitch, then you buy the veneers before it or beyond it, and an even number at that. This is the accepted code of practice.

STORING VENEER

Veneers are not cheap, so storage is important. Lay them out flat, but before putting them away check for splits, especially at the

113

ends, as these can run and ruin a leaf. If you find splits either within the leaf or on its ends or edges, tape them up. Don't use masking tape because after a time this will dry out and peel off, and even more significantly, it will leave a gum residue that will be hard to remove and can be detrimental if it is on the face to be glued. The proper tape to use is veneer tape. For veneers up to 4ft (1.2m) I use a drawing-office chest; as I lay them, I mark out a piece of tape at their top end and number their sequence 1, 2, 3, and so on.

SUBSTRATES

A substrate is the base on which the veneer is glued, and it can be wood or a composite material. This must be stable, and if wood it is best without knots; in fact the modern composite boards are very good because unless they get damp they are very stable. However, that is all I will say about composite boards as they will have no place in antiques for at least a hundred years!

Before laying any veneer, the substrate must be checked and prepared, to take the glue. The quality of the work depends on how closely the density of veneer and substrate match. Similar density is superior to a hardwood veneer laid on a softwood substrate of dissimilar density. Note, however, that not all hardwoods are dense (balsa wood, for instance), and not all softwoods are soft (as in yew).

When laying veneer onto a substrate, always have both the grains running the

Toothing plane and blades.

same way. The only exception to this rule is when laying burrs, figured veneers, cross-banding and other ornamentation. The surface of the substrate should be finished with a tool called a toothing plane, a special plane that holds the blade at almost right-angles to the surface, and is more of a scraper in its action than a plane. The blade itself is different from normal blades inasmuch as it is toothed and leaves a toothed finish to the surface. This acts as an anchor for the glue as the toothing undercuts into the wood. If laying a thick saw-cut veneer it is advisable to tooth the glue face of this as well (thinner veneer will more likely tear with this treatment). You can make your own tool by using a hacksaw blade, not so good as a toothing iron, but better than nothing at all). The other reason for toothing is that the surface area is increased by the grooves.

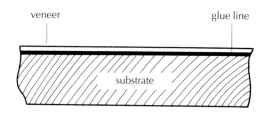

Drawing of veneer and substrate.

PREPARING TO LAY VENEER

Once a choice has been made, lay out the veneer on a flat top, mark roughly to size, and cut. For this use a straight-edge and either a sharp scalpel knife if the veneer is not too hard, or a veneer saw. This saw is specially designed for veneer cutting and is usually set on a cranked handle. The blade edge is semicircular, and swings with the movement of the hand as it is drawn towards the operator. There is no set to the teeth, which are not pitched for cutting either forwards or backwards; on one side of the teeth there is a chamfer making the tips of the teeth like knife blades. When cutting across the grain, use a wide chisel at both sides of the veneer and nick it. This stops tearing when cutting.

There are two sides to a veneer, and it is best to have the good side upwards whenever you can. This is applicable to machine- or knife-cut veneers. Machine veneers are cut with a knife under great pressure and the veneer peels off in a way similar to a shaving in a plane. The front face of the veneer will curl away from the knife and is known as the 'tight side: 'tight' denotes the absence of checks of any depth. The other side is known as the 'knife', or 'loose side'. This side has fractures in it known as checks. It is important to recognize this. The checks are made by the literal tearing of the veneer from the main body of the wood. These checks can be to a depth of 25 per cent of the thickness of the veneer. If the veneer is laid this side up, you will need to scrape and sand down past the checks – otherwise some time after the surface has been finished the checks will appear. If the sides have been muddled, there are two ways of determining which side is which; those who are beardless, gently rub the surface against their cheek; the rough side is the loose side. If you can't decide, hold the veneer by its edges and bend it one way, then the other, and hold it close to your ear: if you have the loose side facing you, it will make a creaking sound.

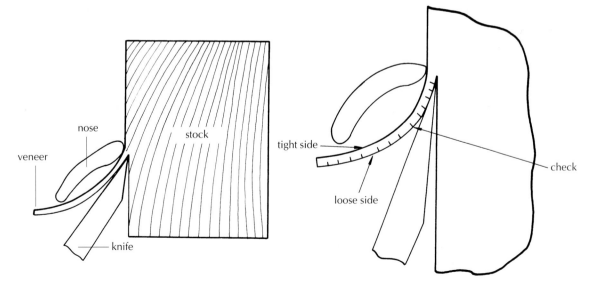

How modern veneers are cut.

The different sides of the veneer.

FLATTENING VENEERS

This is important, especially when the veneer is thick, coarse, or buckled or wavy because of the burrs, figuring or variable grain. Sprinkle water sparingly onto the surface and wipe off with a dry cloth; do not wet too much as this may lead to black spots, a form of mould. I use an atomizer, and don't spray directly at the veneer but actually let the spray drift onto it. Next, lay paper onto each side and press, leaving overnight.
NOTE: Don't use newsprint directly onto the face of the veneer as the ink can migrate, especially on light-coloured veneers.

If the veneer is very brittle, for example with burrs and figures, press in stages, otherwise it may crack.

A home-made press: Use two flat boards (melamine) and battens and squeeze together with cramps or heavy weights. When released, the difference is astounding; the veneer will be flat, supple and easier to cut.

CUTTING VENEER

After the veneer has been flattened you may find the straight lines you had cut are no longer straight. The veneer is now in it's true form. It should be trimmed again, still

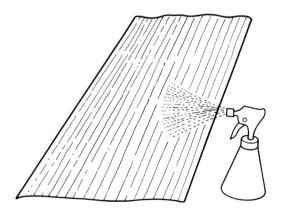

Dampening veneer.

keeping it oversized for the area. If the area to be covered is wider than one leaf, two leaves should be prepared. These can be laid like planks or book-matched. Book-matching and other decorative devices will be covered later; for the moment these veneers will be laid as planks. The butt-joint of the two veneers can be prepared before or after the veneer is laid. I prefer the latter method.

HOW TO DO IT

Joining before Laying: Dry Jointing
1. Lay one leaf on a flat surface and lay a straight-edge along the edge to be trued. The straight-edge must cover the veneer, leaving the edge showing away from the straight-edge.
2. Using a sharp knife to cut through at one stroke, cut the veneer down the edge. The knife should be at an angle of about 15° from upright, making the knife undercut under the straight-edge
   NOTE: Make sure that any splits are removed, or that they are securely taped when cutting, or these areas are liable to move, giving an inaccurate line.
3. Repeat **Step 1** on the second veneer, except this time instead of the straight-edge covering the veneer, have the edge of the veneer covered and the leaf showing.
   NOTE: When the straight-edge is laid over the veneer edge it will tilt back leaving a gap at the cutting edge, because its back edge is not being supported by veneer. The waste cut from the first veneer should be tucked under its rear edge so it will sit flat and firm on the veneer.
4. Repeat **Step 2**.
5. Lay both leaves side by side with their freshly cut edges facing each other. Do not turn either of the leaves over or the cut edges will not match. Have prepared 2in (50mm) lengths of veneer tape at hand: these are called straps. Draw the leaves together so that the joint is tight,

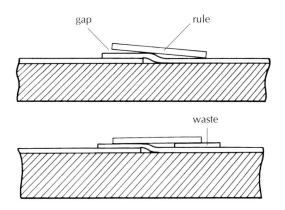

Supporting a straight-edge whilst cutting veneer.

Tools ready for veneering.

and holding both edges with your thumb and forefinger straddling the joint, stick the straps across the joint. Use the base of a spoon to flatten the tape into the veneer. (I moisten both sides of the tape as it seems to adhere better.)

6. After all the straps have been applied – one every 2in or 3in (50mm or 75mm) will do – tape the entire length of the joint.

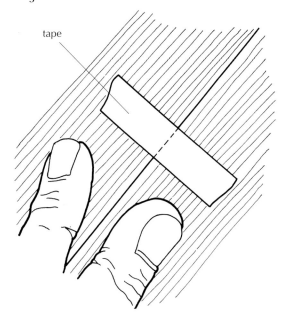

Using veneer tape.

NOTE: If you have to move the veneers, don't fold it as the tape may pull away. Also, don't tape the other side unless you are using *perforated* veneer tape, as this is the glue side and ordinary veneer tape will make an adhesion suspect.

Cutting the veneer after laying will be explained in the next section.

LAYING VENEER

Before laying a veneer, everything must be ready: glue, veneer hammer, knife and straight-edge, cloths, flat iron, artist's palette knife and tape.

Glue: This should be of a thick double-cream consistency, and fresh so that no foreign bodies such as bristles from the gluebrush and suchlike adhere.

Veneer hammer: This is not like an ordinary hammer, but is used to squeeze the surplus glue from underneath the veneer. It has a long handle. Attached to this handle and forming a T-shape is a piece of wood with a brass blade attached to one side

Scalpel knife and straight-edge: The straight-edge should not be of steel: when placed on damp veneer, ordinary steel may tarnish and leave marks. *Stainless* steel is best.

117

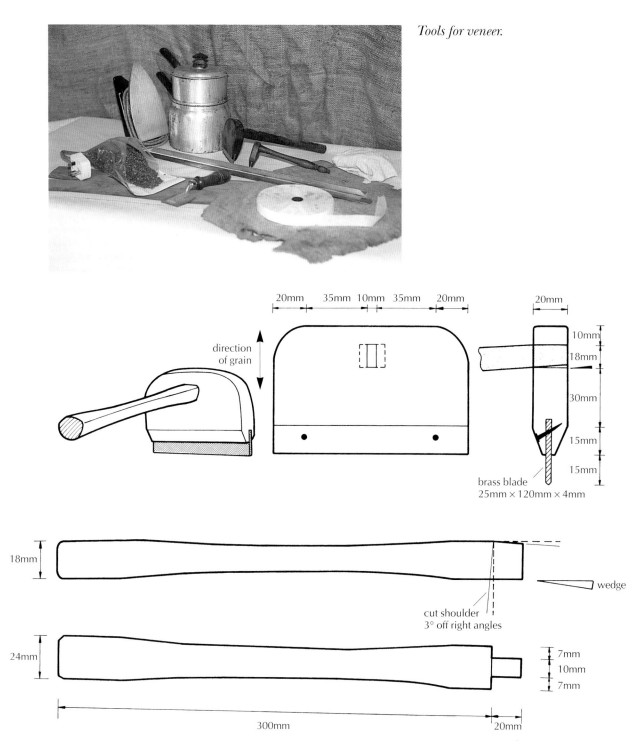

Tools for veneer.

Veneer hammer.

Cloth: This should be lint free, and clean. It is used to wipe any surplus glue off the veneer. It should be damp and used with a bowl of hot water.

Flat Iron: I use an electric iron, set between silk and wool heat. For lifting veneer and applying spots of glue.

Tape: This is necessary for joints and splits.

At the gluing stage, if the atmosphere is cool or the surface to be glued is cold, the glue will chill before it can be spread over the whole surface. If this is the case, try to raise the temperature of the workshop; if this can't be done and the surface is still cold, heat it by going over it with the flat iron.

HOW TO DO IT

1. Apply the glue as evenly and speedily as possible.

2. Lay the veneer, aligning it as best you can. Dip the cloth in hot water and wring it out until it is very damp but not dripping. Smooth the veneer flat, damping all the surface, even any overhang. This will bring the veneer into complete contact with the glue; also, because the glue will add moisture to one side, the veneer will expand on that side tending to make it bow and wrinkle.

3. Hold the handle of the veneer hammer in your right hand and press down on the head with your left (unless you are left-handed). Starting in the centre draw it towards you, wiggling the blade, to the nearest outer edge. Repeat until you have been over the whole surface.

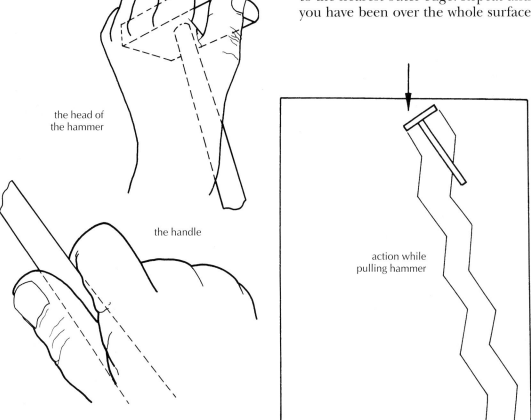

the head of the hammer

the handle

action while pulling hammer

Method for using a veneer hammer.

4. Wipe the surface over with the damp cloth to remove any glue and moisture that was squeezed out of the veneer. Clean up around the edges where the excess glue was forced out. Check the veneer with your fingertips: it should be firm but lumpy with glue that gelled before you could squeeze it out. While the veneer is still damp – and if dry patches appear, go over it again with the damp cloth – lay a piece of paper on the veneer. (I use cheap lining paper.) Pass the warm iron over the paper, warming the veneer but not overheating the glue or drying out the veneer completely. The veneer should slide if pushed.

5. Repeat **Step 3**.

6. Repeat **Steps 3** and **4** until the veneer feels firm and completely flat.

   If there are no more veneers to lay down by the side, tape any splits, lay a piece of paper and a flat board with weights on the veneer, and leave overnight. The following steps will explain how to lay another leaf by its side, and the procedure of cutting after the veneer has been laid (wet cutting).

7. Repeat **Steps 1, 2, 3 and 4**. Once the veneer is flat, and when it overlaps the first veneer by ¼in–⅜in (6mm–9mm) you are nearly ready to cut.

8. Check any overlap, making sure that no thick glue exists. If there is any, warm it up and squeeze out.

9. Lay the straight-edge on the veneer with the cutting edge over the middle of the overlap. The straight-edge should be covering the top veneer leaving the edge showing. Because of the doubling up of veneer, tuck some veneer under the rear edge of the straight-edge.

10. Using the scalpel knife in the same manner as when cutting the veneer dry, cut through both veneers, making sure it slightly undercuts the veneers. NOTE: Undercutting is essential, other-

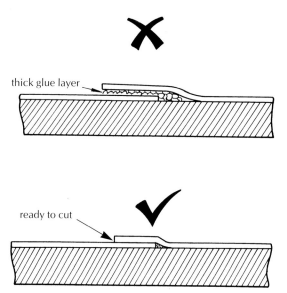

thick glue layer

ready to cut

Cutting a series of veneers to match.

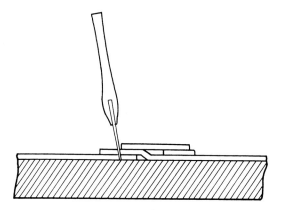

Using a scalpel blade to undercut veneers.

wise the thickness of the knife blade will leave a gap. This is another reason for making sure there is no thickness of glue under the overlap because this would also make your cut inaccurate, leaving the veneers still too long when laid side by side.

*Squeezing out glue
after joint is cut.*

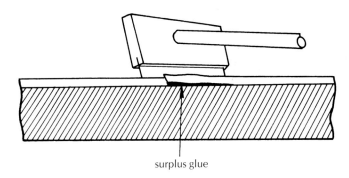

surplus glue

11. Lift away the veneer waste; I use a painter's palette knife because it is thin and supple. Ease it under the waste and, holding the tail of the waste, slide the knife along and lift the waste away. Wipe clean with your damp cloth.

12. At one end, ease the knife under the overlap about twice the depth of the overlap (heat it again only if the veneer is stuck fast), and slide it all the way along, loosening it from the under-veneer and the substrate. Slide the palette knife under the waste of the under-veneer and repeat the same process, making sure no bits of waste are left behind.

13. Using the palette knife, again put fresh glue under the veneer, then press the veneer down flat with the damp cloth, again removing surplus glue.

14. With the veneer hammer angled into the joint, push any surplus glue out, wipe clean and tape the joint, weight down and leave to dry.

    If possible, leave for 48 hours so that the glue is fully cured and there is no risk of shrinkage. Remember, the wetter the veneer the more it will shrink.

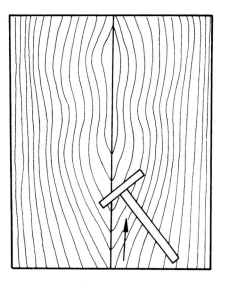

That is why it is so important *never to let water sit on the veneer,* and to use only a damp cloth. Also, as the glue dries it will shrink, and if the joint is not taped it will pull apart. When removing the tape there is a temptation to wet it: *don't.* The cabinet scraper is better, since any dampness at this time could lead to shrinkage.

twelve

VENEERS II: PATCHING AND REPAIRING

There are many problems arising from veneers, from delaminating to actual areas missing. Some of the repairs covered here will also solve similar problems in cases of damage to solid wood surfaces. The following areas will be covered: blisters; missing or 'gouged-out' areas; burns; splits; smashed corners; delamination of curved surfaces.

BLISTERS IN VENEER

Blistering is when a veneer delaminates from its substrate, and it is not always just a small area. It can happen for various reasons, from water damage to an unstable substrate, and it is worth investigating why it should delaminate in this way as it may indicate the method of repair; it is not always because of a breakdown in the glue.

REPAIRING WATER DAMAGE

The usual signs of water damage are a central area of damage to the finish which has gone white or is non-existent, and the veneer wrinkled and split. The only repair possible is to lift this area of veneer if you can and to clean out any old crusty glue and dirt that is there. Then reglue and place a flat board over the area, and press.

HOW TO DO IT

1. Use a palette knife (a large one for big areas) and a scalpel knife. If the veneer is split or open at the edge, then the scalpel knife will not be needed.

2. If there is no split, find an area within the damage where the grain is most coarse, or where the figuring is 'busy'. Put the point of the scalpel knife into the wood at a sharp angle and pierce through the veneer, opening it up a little way so as to slide the palette knife in, and far enough under until it is securely underneath but not stopped by the tightness of the veneer.

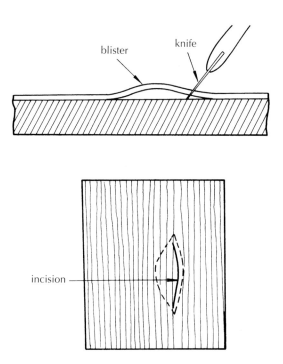

Opening up a bubble.

3. Gently twist the knife until the veneer tears from the cut; release, and move it along and twist again. This must be done in a controlled way so as not to break out the veneer. The reason for tearing the veneer rather than completely cutting it is that when it is re-laid this tear will disappear, whereas a cut, even at an angle, will need to be filled with stopper. Putting the knife in at right-angles would actually create a gap.

4. Once a split has been opened, put a wedge at each end to hold the split open. Then remove any loose dirt.

5. Pushing in a palette knife is *not* the way to scrape out the dirt because you will just force the dirt further into the blister, jamming it in. If the veneer is stable with no loose bits, use a hand vacuum cleaner (a hand one is less powerful and so is less likely to do damage). Alternatively, if the veneer is too damaged, or all the really loose dirt has been cleaned away, dip the palette knife into the glue pot; withdraw, leave for a few seconds, and then wipe with a dry cloth which will leave it sticky. Insert it under the veneer and gently move it about, picking up the dirt; wash it in hot water, and repeat until all the dirt is gone.

6. If there is any glue left and it is not crystallized, leave it; if it is crystallized it will chip away; and animal glue if not crystallized will actually restick.

7. Dip the palette knife into the glue pot and push the glue under the veneer, making sure there is enough glue. Remove the wedges.

8. With the veneer hammer, gently squeeze the glue into areas you could not reach. Use a damp cloth to remove the excess glue and dampen the surface of the wood.

9. With the iron on a low heat, reheat the glue and start to squeeze it back out

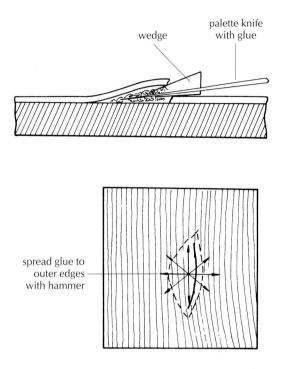

Inserting glue into bubble with a palette-knife.

towards the split; this must be done gently, because if the glue is forced too much as it gels it might split the veneer in other places and damage it further. Remember, the edges of the veneer will be securely held down with glue, and too great a pressure may break the veneer across the grain, making it harder to disguise any damage; moreover shreds of veneer may break off and disappear into the excess glue.

10. Repeat the heating procedure until the veneer lies flat. Do not overheat the glue or veneer, or over-wet it, because the veneer will either shrink, leaving gaps, or it will expand, making the split overlap.

11. Finally, make sure the split goes down in the right sequence. The knife cut was at an angle to ensure that one side

of the split would have an overcut and the other an undercut. The overcut side of the split must go down first, with the undercut laying over the top.

12. Press with a flat board.

EDGE BLISTERS AND SMALL SEALED BLISTERS

Delamination at the edge is dealt with in the same way, except that there will be no need to cut or split the wood. Where the blister is small and not split there should be no dirt underneath. These blisters can sometimes be re-laid by damping the area and using the tip of the iron to reheat the glue, then pressing back; this will damage the polish, but done carefully it need not be too bad. If the blister does not stay flat, insert the point of the knife through the veneer and inject some glue through the knife cut. And if it will *still* not stay flat and is too far away to be clamped, use a pad of wood and a veneer-pin and nail it down.

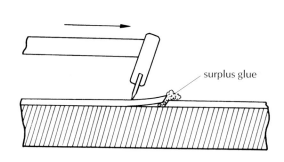

surplus glue

Squeezing glue out of a blister. The overcut edge is laid first.

Put the pin in at an angle and it will not make such a noticeable hole, and when removed it is so small it can be filled

NOTE: Be sure to use a veneer pin and not a panel pin, which is twice as large. Veneer pins are about the same thickness as a dressmaking pin.

Using the tip of an iron and a damp cloth to lay a bubble.

Using veneer pins.

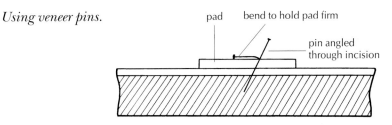

pad bend to hold pad firm

pin angled
through incision

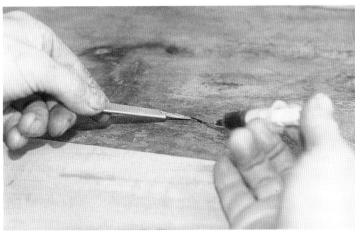

Injecting fresh glue under a veneer bubble.

WOODWORM

Delamination may be due to woodworm attack. This can happen without the wormholes showing on the surface of the wood, especially when the substrate is a softwood covered by a very hard veneer, such as rosewood. When this happens the veneer must be removed and the substrate attended to first.

Woodworm has a great taste for animal glue, and the surface of the substrate can

Releasing a Veneer from a Substrate

Using a medium-hot iron and a damp cloth, heat the surface of the veneer until the glue is soft and a large palette knife can be inserted between the two surfaces. Slowly open up the bond: this can sometimes be frustratingly slow, but just be patient; it will work, and without splitting. Splitting would destroy the finish.

iron

palette
knife

be riddled with galleries where the beasts have been. These galleries must be filled first before the veneer can be re-laid. Remove all the dust from the surface, and any weak wood. Make a putty of animal glue and wood-dust, the finer the better; if you have a bandsaw, its dust is just about right – otherwise go and beg some from a woodwork shop. Not much is needed, and because it will be covered, the wood type will not matter.

HOW TO DO IT

1. Remove the veneer from the area affected; if it is not the whole top, then pull it back and hold it out of the way with masking tape.
2. Make a filler with sawdust and glue; this must be animal glue because you need to stick the veneer back and synthetic glue will not be effective. Make up a thick paste.
3. Use a putty knife and force it into the galleries, then make it level. Leave it to dry hard for at least 24 hours and more if you can; otherwise the heat of the iron will melt and soften the paste, making it impossible to lay the veneer flat.
4. Scrape it level, then re-lay the veneer, and press.

UNSTABLE SUBSTRATE

Where the substrate has split, or where it is made of planks that have become loose, the veneer can delaminate instead of splitting with it. The substrate must therefore be stabilized: release the veneer, attend to the substrate, then re-lay the veneer.

MISSING AREAS

There are many ways a piece of veneer may be missing; note, too, that some of the methods of repair can be used to patch and repair solid wood damage. The most regular parts to be damaged are feet and plinths, as these get kicked and dragged, and are in areas where damp can occur.

PATCHING: HOW TO DO IT

1. Before an area of missing veneer can be replaced, the area around it must be checked and if loose must be glued back in place before cutting in a patch (if the veneer being cut is loose it may actually move during the cutting. Only wait a few hours after it has been glued; this will give it enough time to be firm to work on).
2. Once a piece of veneer has been selected for its compatibility in grain and colour, check as to which way the grain is running. Even if the veneer is thin, the grain will still be running one way or the other, and it is important that the replacement blank has its grain running the same way as the surrounding area. (This can be determined by paring a bit of waste on the piece and on the underneath of the blank. If the blank is put in the wrong way it will show darker one way than the other against the surrounding area, because it will be reversed. This cannot be altered in the finishing stage.)
3. To determine how big to make the blank, draw a line with a ruler on each side of the missing area, as close to it as

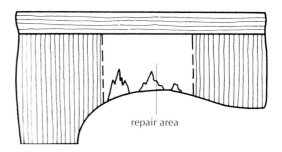

Foot and apron showing crossbanded veneer.

Cutting a veneer blank for patching.

possible; these lines should run across the grain until they meet, making a triangle. Continue with the lines past each other (avoid pressing so hard as to leave an indentation).

NOTE: Where the missing area is wider than it is long, and the two lines converging would make a triangle that nearly takes it across the piece, then a series of pointed fingers are cut into the triangle; this will be explained later. If the piece is a plinth or something of that nature, the grain may be running across its height, like a wide crossbanding. If this is the case, then do not cut a triangle but replace the whole missing crossbanded area.

4. Once the lines are drawn, place the veneer over the damage aligning with the grain. Take a rule and line up with one of the pencil lines that is showing; the rule must be over the veneer. Draw a line on the veneer until it passes over the edge. Repeat with the other pencil line before moving the veneer patch away.

5. The lines on the veneer should make the same shape and size triangle. With the rule on the line but covering the triangle, cut with the knife. Repeat for the other line. (Angle the knife slightly to make an undercut.)

6. When the cutting is finished, you will have a blank in the shape of a triangle just large enough to cover the missing area of veneer, with its edges undercut. Do not trim the back of the blank as this will be useful to hold (like a handle). Place the blank over the missing area, making sure the grain aligns.

    NOTE: If you find it doesn't match, then start again. *Don't turn it over:* even if it does match like that, the grain will be running the wrong way.

7. With the blank held firmly in place, take the knife and with its point put a pinprick at the point of the blank. Then place the rule along one edge of the blank and hold firmly; take away the blank and cut along the rule, starting from the pinprick. (By letting the

Cutting veneer to take a blank.

point rest with only its own weight on the surface, run it along the rule until you feel the point of the blade click into the pinprick.)

8. Still holding the rule against the cut line, replace the blank with its point up to the pinprick. Hold it firmly; remove the rule and place it on the other uncut side of the blank, and after removing the blank, cut along the rule.

9. Once both sides are cut, remove the rule and the waste veneer. Folding a damp cloth into the shape of the blank, place it over the area and heat with the iron. Lift away the waste veneer.

10. Making sure the surface is clean and that the blank fits, apply the glue and fit the blank. Tape it in place and trim roughly then leave until the glue has set.

LARGE AREAS TO BE PATCHED

A large area to be covered may need to be done with a composition of triangles made like a hand with fingers. However, this should only be tackled when you are proficient at doing single blanks, never have the points of the fingers the same length or the valleys between the fingers the same depth. Instead of removing the blank completely,

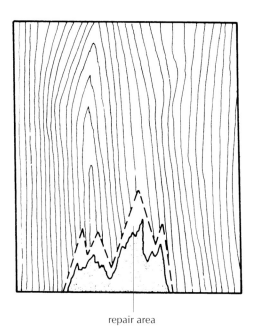

repair area

Patching-in with fingers of veneer.

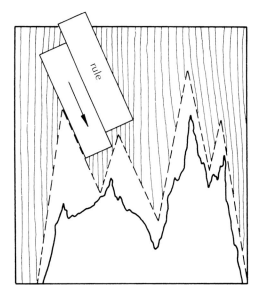

rule

Using two rules to map out the finger configurations.

fix a masking-tape hinge to one side so that when cutting commences the blank can be swung out of the way.

Use two rules, especially when cutting the inside fingers. Your rule will not be able to reach down to the point of the valley, otherwise it will trap the veneer. Place the rule as far as it will go, remove the blank and place the other rule alongside the rule already there. Using the second rule as a guide, slide the first rule along until it covers the whole line.

The technique with rules and the removal and return of blanks is at first tedious and seemingly clumsy, but persist, and practise cutting with both hands, and you will find it to be a fairly foolproof way of being accurate. The method of using the blank itself is not as satisfactory as you may suppose, as the veneer can be cut or lifted from the surface so that the knife slides under the veneer.

GOUGED-OUT AREAS

Whether the gouge is into solid wood or a veneer surface, the hole itself needs to be filled. For a solid wood surface, just make a blank to cover the gouge, thick enough to reach to the bottom of the damage. With a veneer surface, cut your veneer blank and cut out the area to be replaced, removing the waste veneer. Before laying in the blank, fill the hole in the same way as for woodworm damage.

PATCHING AWAY FROM THE EDGES

Where a patch is needed in the centre of a piece, the blank should be in the form of an elongated diamond (two triangles back to back). Where the area is large, the 'fingered' blank is used, except that the fingers are on both ends. For these lone patches, cut and remove the waste veneer from one end first before starting to cut the other end; in this way the blank can be keyed in before starting on the other end, helping accuracy. Where areas are small, a core-plug can be made to cover the damage.

REPAIR TO BURRS AND FIGURED VENEER

Over the years burrs and other highly figured veneers can have problems, ranging from cracking to blistering. In fact, when

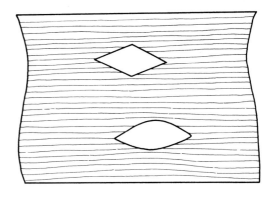

Filling a gouged area before laying veneer.

Double-ended fingered configuration.

such veneers blister they can crack and become detached from the rest of the piece, leaving whole chunks missing.

BURRS

Because they are basically a mass of knots, burrs can 'pop' and disappear. These are easiest to repair if you have veneer of a similar colour and nature. Using a veneer punch (an irregular cutter), clean up the missing area, then use the same punch to cut a blank from a veneer selected to match.

FIGURED

Find something close to a match and cut freehand. Lay this blank over the bad area, and run a knife carefully around its edge. This procedure is more difficult than one might imagine, and I urge you to practise before attempting this particular repair.

Using a veneer-punch to patch a burr.

BURNS

Unless the burn is just a darkened area which can be coloured out, it will need to be patched. To determine which course of action is necessary, several questions need to be answered:

(i)   Is the burn just a scorch mark? If so, a filler will suffice.
(ii) Is the burn deep, in which case is the surface no longer wood, but charcoal?
(iii) Is the surface unstable? (That is, when it is rubbed with a finger, does the charred area come off on your skin?)
(iv) Is there a depression on the surface? If it is a deep burn, as in the last two instances, then you will certainly need to patch. Repair in the same way as the section on gouges. The charred area must be removed as this surface is too weak to hold glue.

SPLITS

Splits may occur in the substrate thus causing the veneer to split too, but veneers will also split of their own accord without the substrate doing the same. If this happens, the area around the split will be loose, so attend to this first. Another kind of split is where the substrate actually shrinks more

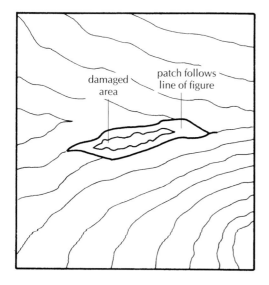

Freehand cutting around a veneer blank.

than the veneer, which loosens from the substrate and ruckles up like a carpet. Sometimes the ruckle can be so severe that the veneer splits and overlaps itself.

SPLITS DUE TO SUBSTRATE SPLITS

We will assume that the substrate has been repaired, the split glued and closed. Now the veneer should also close as well, though one problem preventing it doing so may be the dirt which has collected at the edge of the split. This needs to be totally cleaned out, an operation which may leave a small gap. A thin line can be closed with a filler; otherwise a fillet of veneer will be needed, and as long as the gap is no more than ⅛in (3mm) wide, this is done in the following way:

HOW TO DO IT

1. As most splits are straight, clean along both edges with a knife freehand, and as evenly as possible.
2. Select a piece of veneer to fill the gap. Place a rule on the veneer and cut the edge for the first side, but undercut.
3. By eye, place the rule on the veneer, but over the fillet (remember to place some veneer under the back edge of the rule). Cut the fillet so that it corresponds to the gap closely; the edge must be undercut.
4. The fillet should look like a tail. Lay it over the gap: if the tapered end fits, apply a little glue and gently press it in, though leave it raised above the surface – do not force it home.
5. If the fillet is too large to fit, lay it over the gap and with a knife, cut the edge of the veneer, removing all the waste until the fillet can be pressed in. Glue this length and press it in, until trimming is needed. In this way you will slowly move along the gap until it is all filled. Tap the fillet home, though still leave it raised.

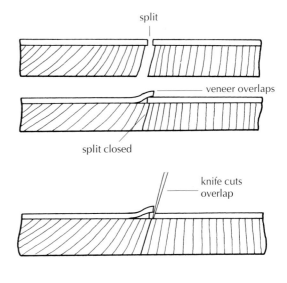

Cutting and re-laying an expanded veneer.

SPLIT DUE TO SUBSTRATE SHRINKAGE

The only option is to cut out the excess. To do this, glue one side of the split first; then with the other side lying on top, knife along the edge, cutting down through the side already glued. Once the waste is removed the other side can be laid and taped. Be aware that most splits will not be at right-angles to the face. The side with the undercut must be laid last. When repairing this fault, cut freehand, following the movement of the grain. When removing waste veneer avoid excessive moisture and heat as these will expand veneers.

SMASHED CORNERS

This is a regular occurrence, and any veneered corners or edges should be built up first. Where the damage is slight the area can be built up with filler, in which case strengthen it by using veneer pins,

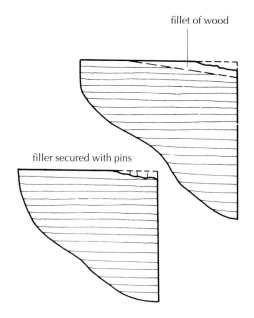

fillet of wood

filler secured with pins

Building up broken corners.

making sure they don't stand proud of the substrate surface. For larger areas of damage a fillet of wood is better.

Once the filler is set, level and prepare the surface for gluing, then veneer over the area as explained in the crossbanding section. Don't try to veneer just part of it and then fill, because any unsupported area of the veneer will bow and you will not be able to get a flat surface.

THE DELAMINATION OF CURVED SURFACES

This problem occurs in many areas, the most usual being the hooped apron of a round or oval table; pillars and veneered mouldings will present similar problems. Generally an apron is made of block-sections of wood cut out and glued together to make a complete hoop, and to give the hoop strength it is built up of two or more

layers. These layers form a brick-type interlocking pattern, and it is here that problems arise because the grain of the wood does not always lie in the same direction. When in the course of time the wood shrinks, the blocks not only delaminate but come to look like uneven stepping stones. The face of the apron on which the veneer is glued therefore becomes uneven and causes the veneer to delaminate and fracture.

As with all circumstances concerning substrate movement, the veneer needs to be lifted and the undermining problem sorted first. Once the apron is ready for veneering, a little time must be taken to consider whether the veneer will lie back without pressing – in other words, with just the use of the veneer hammer. On slow curves, and especially where the apron is crossbanded, this is usually no problem; on tighter curves, and if the grain direction of the veneer is also going round, it may be difficult to hold the veneer in place while the glue sets, particularly if it is thick.

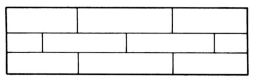

laminated sections for shaped faces

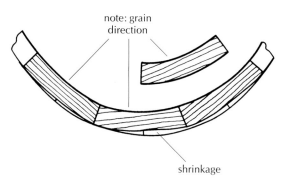

note: grain direction

shrinkage

Splits and delamination due to wood shrinkage.

HOW TO DO IT

1. Cut a strip of thin bendy ply the width of the apron, enough to wrap right around the hoop. If the hoop circumference is too long, then use two pieces.
2. Cut battens to cross the width of the apron; these will need to be spaced every 6in (15cm) or so. Remember to have enough pads for the inside of the apron.
3. Lay the veneer using the veneer hammer and the iron.
4. Once the excess glue has been squeezed out, lay the plywood squarely onto the apron and fix with batten and pad with a clamp.
   NOTE: The end of the plywood should not be over the joint of the veneer.
5. Proceed all the way round the apron until the whole area is covered.
   NOTE: Because this needs speed, instead of laying paper between the veneer and the plywood, which can move about, varnish the plywood. The varnish must be dry. This surface will release easily away from any sticky areas.

VENEERED PILLARS

Pillars are generally veneered when a flashy grain is needed. These veneers will be of a denser wood than the turned substrate, which may even be made of pine. Most of the problem pillars I have worked on have been pine, and over the years they have shrunk across their diameter which causes the circumference measurement to decrease drastically. Added to this, the veneer will not shrink in the same proportion, leaving no alternative but for it to ruckle and split. If it is ruckled all over it will need to be unwrapped, then reglued and rejointed. There are three ways in which this can be done: (i) the string method; (ii) the jubilee-clip method, and (iii) the polystyrene foam method.

HOW TO DO IT

First Method:
1. Remove the veneer and clean the substrate. Make a turning-box (*see* the illustration in the chapter on turning).
2. With the turning between centres, chalk a line on it and mark this on both ends. This is especially important for pillars that are tapered, and where the piece is going to be seen all round and is not up against a face.
3. Apply glue and lay one edge onto the piece butting up against the chalk line. With a veneer hammer squeeze this line home.
4. Now, slowly turning, wrap the veneer around until all is completely covered.
5. Allow the veneer to overlap.
6. Starting from the beginning edge, gently heat with an iron and damp cloth along its length, covering perhaps a quarter of a turn, using a veneer hammer to squeeze out excess glue away from the laid joint.
7. Do this several times until the veneer feels tight against the substrate. Move on to the next quarter, and so on until the whole piece is done.
8. With the joint uppermost, lock into position. Using the marks from the chalkline on both ends, re-mark the line over the veneer.
9. With a rule and knife, cut just inside the line on the top veneer-edge side of the line. The line must be supported at the back to stop sliding and to keep the knife upright. Do not undercut.
10. Remove waste veneer. Heat and lift the edge of the veneer to remove the waste from the other edge. Heat again and lay both edges, making sure they are tight.
11. Tape with straps across, and then tape the length of the joint.
12. Wrap around with paper several times.
13. Use wet cord – this must not be synthetic, because when it dries it must

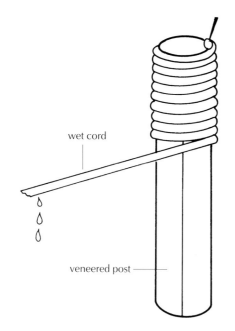

Using dampened cord to hold veneer in position around a pillar whilst the glue sets.

shrink. Tie the cord to one end of the frame, then wrap it tightly round and round the piece until not one bit of the turning is showing. Tie off onto the frame at the other end.

14. Leave it in front of an open window, or in cold weather in front of a low-heat fan-heater until the cord is dry. Leave for 24 hours.

Second Method:

Follow the instructions given in the first method up to and including **step 11**.

12. Wrap in thick pliable waxed card.
13. Put on 'jubilee clips', leaving a little or no space.
14. Tighten up one by one, making sure the screw part of the clip is over the joint, because the clip will pull the joint tight as the band moves through the screw. Don't overtighten as the screw area can leave a mark. Leave for 24 hours.

Third Method:

1. Use a thick piece of polystyrene about the same thickness of the turning; cut two blocks about twice the diameter and the same length.
2. Back these with a solid piece of wood of the same size, and then put on the sides.
3. Before the veneering is started, sandwich the turning between the two blocks and cramp together until the wood sides nearly meet. Leave a ¼in (6mm) gap. Release. You will find that the impression made by the turning will stay.
4. Follow the instructions given in the previous methods from **step 1** to **step 11** inclusive.
5. Replace the foam blocks around the turning and tighten up again, this time making the wood sides meet. Release after 24 hours.

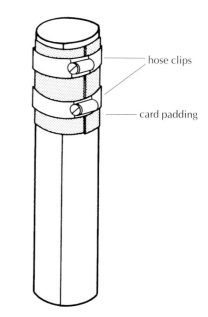

Jubilee clips doing the same job as in the previous figure (above left).

Polystyrene used to hold a curved shape.

NOTE: Make sure the joint is in the least noticeable position; copy where it was before, if the marks are still there.

VENEERED MOULDINGS

Veneered mouldings and other curved shapes are particularly vulnerable to substrate shrinkage, especially over the end-grain areas. There are two ways to hold these under pressure: the one I describe above, using polystyrene foam, or the original way, using a sandbag.

Clean the veneer and substrate of all dirt, apply the glue and lay the veneer back. Use the veneer hammer to squeeze out excess glue, then reheat with an iron and, rolling the cloth into a thick sausage, warm the glue. Press either sandbag or foam into position and secure with a clamp.

NOTE: I have heard that a vacuum bag is very effective in pressing both flat and shaped areas of veneer, but have never worked with one myself. This innovation is quite recent and is used in large and small workshops.

DECORATIVE VENEERING

The repair of decorations – crossbanding, marquetry, parquetry and so on – needs attention as these decorative areas do get

Book-matching

Book-matching is generally found on tops and panels: the easiest way to describe a book-match is to take your mind back to what was said about the stacking of flitches – 'The underneath of the top sheet of veneer matches the top of the second sheet, and so on.' Taking this literally, the top veneer is glued with the underneath uppermost; the second sheet is glued with the top face upwards and where they join, the pattern of the grain and figuring is matched and mirrored. The secret is reliant on accurate measuring and cutting, and a thorough knowledge of veneers and their laying.

damaged. Other decorations, such as book-matching and quartering, are skills that come with experience.

CROSSBANDING

This is a decorative edging that first came to prominence during the reign of William and Mary. It is a strip of edging veneer around a panel of veneer, and as its name implies, the grain runs across the strip; when the strip itself runs with the grain of the panel, the crossbanding shows its full effect. In later periods crossbanding became more sophisticated and borders of inlay were introduced with stringings added in both boxwood and ebony. Not only did the addition of stringing grow, but craftsmen would alternate the different woods; first the wood was the same as the panel, later they used contrasting woods.

Crossbanding is not difficult to make and apply. A cutting board is the main piece of equipment required. This is a composite board with a fence attached, and some veneer pins.

HOW TO DO IT

1. Measure the width of the existing crossbanding. Place the end of the rule against the fence and mark accordingly, both sides of the cutting board.
2. Hammer the veneer pins firmly into these marks. Place the veneer with the grain running into the fence, between the two pins. Place the rule over the top against the veneer, and cut the veneer. NOTE: Not only is the strip the same size as your measurement, but any more strips will be the same. This is important if doing long runs or areas that are inlaid.

Replacing Missing Crossbanding

3. Check all the crossbanding on the piece. Where there are missing bits of banding in front of the piece, replace these with parts taken from the back. (This is an old restorer's trick, as areas replaced at the back are less noticeable than at the front. Also, it is far better to replace one whole strip than to fill in little bits and

Crossbanding with ebony stringing. (Note the directions of grain.)

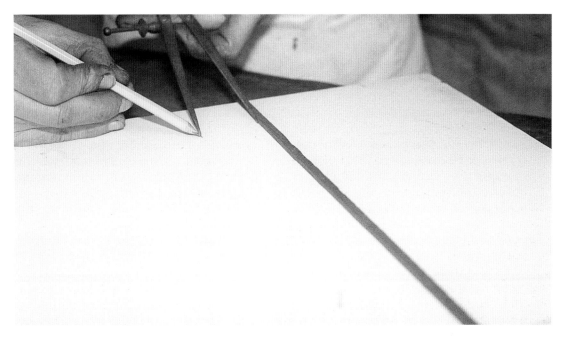

Marking out a veneer cutting board (the brown line is the fence).

pieces all over the place with new wood which will be far more obvious.)

4. Using a cutting board, a small set-square and a wide chisel, first measure the gap to be replaced, and add a little extra so the new piece overlaps the edges of the gap.

5. Cut the replacement piece with a chisel, using the set-square to keep it square. When cutting, angle the chisel slightly to give a slight undercut. Once both sides of the replacement (blank) are cut, offer it up to the gap.
   NOTE: When cutting the sides of either the blank or the gap, always have the flat face of the chisel facing that edge.

6. Holding the blank firmly over the gap, mark with a marking knife. (This should be done with care, as the knife could cut into the blank rendering it useless.)

7. Take the chisel and gently place the blade onto the area to be cut. There are two reasons for marking with a knife:

(i) The fit must be tight, and the knife is a far more accurate instrument.

(ii) When finding the mark, the cutting edge of the chisel will actually drop into the knife mark and can be felt to do so.

8. Using a slight overcut, the same angle as the undercut, true up the sides of the gap. If more than ¼in (6mm) veneer has to be removed, then nibble up the line. The reason for this is that when the chisel cuts through any wood, if the wood on the bevel side of the chisel is substantial it will force the chisel slightly over the marked line causing the gap to be larger than the blank. By nibbling away at the gap you overcome this risk and also loosen these little bits from any adherent glue, making it easier to remove the waste.

9. Test the blank before gluing.

10. Glue and tape into place. If there is a need to clamp, do so.

137

SOME TIPS

(i)   Never have the blank the same thickness as the surrounding area it is being placed in, but always slightly thicker.

(ii) Never be mean with your blank. Cut it in properly on both sides.

(iii) Always take full note of the grain direction of the surrounding area. Although it is called crossbanding, the natural movement of the grain does not always run at right-angles; in fact, in some cases the use of angles is used to give an extra dimension to the banding. When a section is missing in the middle of a piece, and each side of the gap and the sides also show the veneer to be set at angles juxtaposed to each other, this must be followed, finishing the angle-change dead centre of the piece.

(iv) Check the direction of the grain on the blank, and on the area to be replaced.

(v) The corners of banding are most important and should follow what has gone before. If the corner areas are missing, inspect the substrate as generally there are indications left as to how they were fashioned, since corners were usually cut on the piece to make a tight fit. Most will be mitred, although some early pieces have the front-banding cutting across the side bandings. The practice of ornamenting the corners is frequent and various, from squares in another colour to rounded corners.

MAKING CORNERS

There are set procedures to making various types of corner:

1. Fitting half a mitre against a remaining original.
2. Making a full mitre.
3. Fitting a corner lozenge.
4. Making a rounded corner.

HOW TO DO IT

Fitting Half a Mitre against a Remaining Original

1. Have a blank much longer than the gap to be filled. Once the mitre is cut and fitted to the remaining one, then trim back the blank.

2. Because the remaining mitre might not be exactly 45° mark the blank from the piece. Lay the blank over the area and the remaining blank overhanging the end. Mark underneath, and on top of the inner corner of the mitre. If the blank overhangs the edge, mark this as well.

3. Remove the cutting-block and turn on its edge, with the mitre corner marks upward. Mark across the edge to the under surface. Turn over so the under surface is uppermost. Place a wide chisel on both the inner and outer marks and cut, making sure the blade is upright.
   NOTE: The cut should be made with the pressure on the chisel blade, cutting from the outside to the inside mark in a guillotine motion, that is start the cut from one corner of the blade and slowly bring down the whole edge, finishing with the whole cutting edge flat. The reason for this is that if it is cut straight or against the grain, the shortness of the grain will almost certainly produce a pressure that will break off the outside point. Another helpmate in ensuring this does not happen is to attach a piece of gummed tape on the top side of the blank over the mitre area.

4. Place the mitre against the original. If it fits perfectly, then the rest of the problem can be attended to in the manner explained above. If not, a little trimming by eye may be all that is needed.

Making a Full Mitre

1. Glue one of the blanks to the end of the piece, leaving a little overhang.
2. Lay the other blank over the blank that

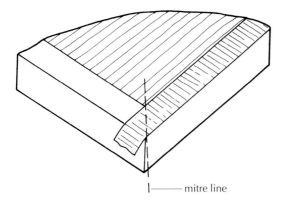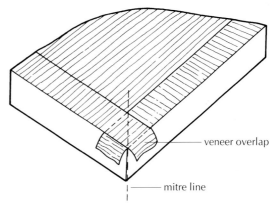

Edge ornamentation.

has just been glued, and mark this one as described in the last set of instructions; then cut.

3. Return the blank to the piece, and where the mitre covers the glued blank, mark with a marking knife.
4. Remove the top blank and cut along the mark with a chisel.
5. Check the fit, and if satisfactory, glue.
6. Tape across the mitre to stop the joint opening.

Fitting a Corner Lozenge
1. Glue one of the blanks to the end of the piece.
2. Line up a rule with the edge of the border to the side and cut across the blank just glued.
3. Repeat **steps 1** and **2**.
4. Cut square, fit, and then glue.
   NOTE: As well as matching the wood of the lozenge, make sure the grain is running the same way as the others; this can be from back to front, from side to side, or from corner to corner.

Making a Rounded Corner
When a crossbanding is carried round a corner with no mitre, then the corner must be attended to first. Look at the remaining corner(s) and you will find that these are

Different directions that grain can be laid.

usually a separate piece of veneer. Measure across the rounded corner to both points where the border straightens out. This measurement indicates the width of the veneer that the crossbanding will be cut from. Cut your veneer a little wider, as this can be trimmed back after it has been glued.

1. Measure the radius of the corner. If the corner is not a true circle, lay a piece of paper over the corner and trace it. This is done by the brass-rubbing technique.

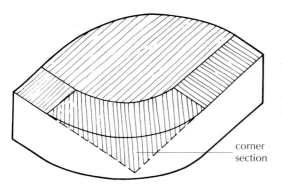

Crossbanding turning a rounded corner.

Tip

To find the radius point, use a set square and take its fence up to the edge of the border, to the actual point where the straight edge touches the circle of the corner. Mark this centre point. Do not actually mark the wood: place a tab of masking tape in the area of the point and mark on that.

2. Take a piece of veneer whose width across the grain is greater than the measurement taken from across the corner of the piece. Find its centre at the end of the veneer. With either a compass or the tracing, mark the veneer across its end.
   NOTE: When drawing out the curve, take it a little way up the veneer.
3. Cut the curve out of the end and offer it up to see if any trimming is needed.
   NOTE: Because the cut line was in from the very edge of the veneer, the curved lines will carry on over the edge of the border on each side. Hold the curved

edge firmly against the border edge and mark where the veneer needs to be trimmed back. While the blank is there, mark the outside edge.

4. Trim the inside corner and then cut the blank away from the veneer.
5. Offer up, and if happy, glue.
6. Using the compass point of the corner radius, line up a rule with this mark and where the corner straightens out, this is the point at which the crossbandings join. The join itself will take a line from the compass point to the outside edge.

Where a bigger curve has to be covered, more than one section of veneer may be needed and the angle of join for these is also worked from this compass point. Thus with two sections the joins will be the centre of the curve and the ends; three will be a third of the curve; and so on.

CROSSBANDING EDGING

Follow the same instructions as for crossbanding. The only thing to mention about crossbanding of the edges is when coming to the corners, where the front-face banding always covers the side-edge banding.

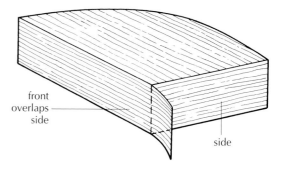

Edge crossbanding.

thirteen

VENEERS III: INLAYS AND STRINGINGS, PARQUETRY AND MARQUETRY

Inlay and stringing might be thought to mean the same thing, but this is not always so: thus, where all stringings are inlay, not all inlays are stringing. A motif, whether it is made of stringing and/or other ornamentation, is inlaid: the stringing is a part of it and so in this context is not thought of as stringing – it is just part of the motif. Stringing augments any area, be it one single strip of wood or a couple of differing colours in a group, or a group of woods set in a geometric pattern bordered by strips of wood. It is separated into five differing categories:

Stringing: Very fine strips cut from any type of veneer, although commonly boxwood, sycamore, and sycamore dyed black. The section is square.

Flat Lines: Also cut from veneer; they come in several widths from $\frac{1}{16}$in–$\frac{1}{4}$in (1mm–6mm), mainly in the veneers mentioned above.

Square Lines: Like the first, these come in square section but are of larger size, generally from $\frac{1}{16}$in–$\frac{1}{4}$in (1mm–6mm).

Purfling: An inlay used mostly by musical instrument makers, but not exclusive to them. The section is square, usually $\frac{1}{8}$in (3mm), and is generally made of three layers of coloured wood making white/black/white or reversed; these are sandwiched and held together by glue. Many different woods are used, as well as mother-of-pearl and, lately, plastics.

Bandings: Of veneer thickness, in widths from $\frac{1}{8}$in (3mm) to 1in (25mm) or more. They are of mixed woods, and comprise at least three layers to a sandwich. There are

Selection of bandings.

also bandings containing crossbanding within the sandwich, sometimes developed to miniature parquetry. However, there are really too many to describe here, besides which most dealers send out catalogues. Marquetry and parquetry motifs come in many sizes and are of veneer thickness; they can be flower centres on a square background of veneer, or arabesques, shells or sunbursts, and may or may not have a stringing around them.

MAKING STRINGINGS

Because there is such a range of all types of stringing you will probably never need to make your own. But even so, there are bound to be times when no match is possible, and you have to make them. More frequent is the problem of matching size, especially with single stringings and lines, although this is much simpler than it seems at first.

HOW TO DO IT

Sizing Lines: 'lines' here refers to single stringings, flats and lines.

The easiest way to adjust the size of a line is to scrape it using a simple tool.

1. Take two pieces of wood, 8in × 3in × 1in (20cm × 7.6cm × 2.5cm) and make a T-section 8in (20cm) in length, gluing and screwing it together.
2. In the upright of the T, cut a 30° angle in the 3in (7.6cm) section, right up to the cross-piece. This cut must be fine, so that a cabinet scraper can be firmly held in the cut.
3. Glue a piece of wood over the cut on one side.
4. Hold it in the vice with one part of the cross-piece, and with the cut uppermost. Slot in the cabinet scraper.
5. Select a line that is close to the size you need, and place it between the scraper and the upper face of the cross-section.

Thinning and stripping with a cabinet scraper.

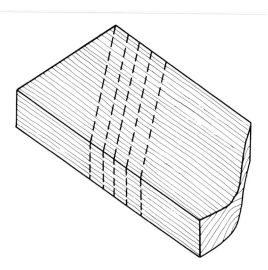

Cutting wood obliquely to produce herringbone blanks.

Position yourself so that the scraper is sloping away from you, and holding the tip of the line firmly, pull the line towards you.

NOTE: The scraper sits squarely on the stop at the base of the cut. With the scraper held and pressing against the line it will produce a simple cut.

Simple Banding

Herringbone banding has many of the steps needed to master the making of most designs. Its name derives from the cloth-weave of the same pattern, where the cross-grain is at 45° with two strips joined and mirroring each other. The body of the banding is in walnut, and these walnut strips are sandwiched between boxwood.

1. Take a piece of walnut 1in (25mm) thick, 3in (76mm) wide and 6in (15cm) long. Cut a 45° cut across the width.
2. Using a fence set at ⅛in (3mm), pass the wood with the 45° cut against the fence, through the saw four times, making ⅛in (3mm) strips of wood with the grain crossing the strip at 45°.
3. Cut two strips of boxwood veneer 1in (25mm) wide and the length of two of the walnut strips joined end to end.
4. Lay one boxwood strip on a flat surface and tape the ends down to prevent the veneer from curling. Apply glue to the top face of the veneer.
5. Lay two of the walnut strips endgrain down and with their ends joined onto the strip of boxwood. Apply glue to the endgrain so that a herringbone pattern is made. Apply more glue and apply the last strip of boxwood. Put under pressure until set.
6. Clean up the edge face of the sandwich, then pass through a saw set to a veneer thickness (I use a bandsaw with a fine tooth blade).

The result of this technique is banding that has a herringbone centre with a white box-wood string on each side.

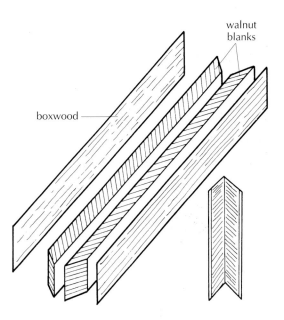

walnut blanks

boxwood

Making herringbone banding.

143

LAYING INLAY LINES

When replacing a missing bit of line, simply clean out the groove the old line used to occupy, then select the same size line, apply glue to three of its faces and press it home. This should be a tight fit and may need a length of wood and a mallet to push it in. Where the new line joins an old line, mitre this joint with the aid of a fine chisel and a scalpel knife. At corners, mitre these also unless the rest of the design indicates not to.

On what would have been classed as cheap furniture of the Victorian and Edwardian period, mitring of inlay did not always happen. This is because it was cheaper not to, so although it is not such a tidy job, copy what happened. Another reason is that when the lines cross each other, it makes it look as though one stringing goes over the other.

Where an area of wood has been replaced and no sign of the line groove is left, a new groove has to be cut. If this is only over a short area, then a rule and knife will do the job. Cut with the rule held outside the line on both sides, otherwise the thickness of the blade will make the groove wider than you anticipated. In between the cuts the wood is cleared and removed by a fine chisel. Where the line is of a length that makes it impracticable to use a rule and knife, a special tool has to be used. This tool is expensive so on the rare occasions this type of a job does occur, another, different tool can be used, although greater care will need to be taken.

HOW TO DO IT

1. Using a knife gauge with the bevel of the blade set away from the fence, set the gauge to the outside of the line; this is the edge of the line closest to the edge.
2. Carefully run the gauge along the piece until the whole line is marked. Do this

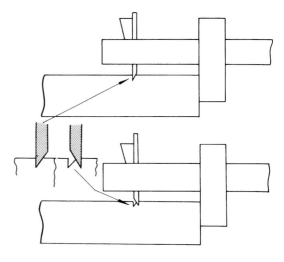

Knifing a line for stringing.

gently so that the blade does not dig in and create a wobble. Pass the gauge over this line several times to create a deep enough cut.
3. Take out the blade of the gauge and turn it around so that the bevel now faces the fence. *Do not adjust the fence.* The blade will be of the same thinness as that of a thin line; if the line is thicker, use spacers to pack the blade away from the fence. A plug and points feeler gauge for a motor engine is a handy tool for this and with the shims of metal cut to the same width as the blade will make accurate spacers.
4. Cut the inside line.
5. Remove the blade from the gauge and replace with a chisel of the same thickness as the line. This is used as a scratch-stock, and is run up and down the line, making the groove. Don't make the groove too deep.

Because the fence is rather small on an ordinary gauge, I have made my own series of different fences. Rounded corners present a problem and these should be worked on separately without the gauge. A set of formers is more accurate.

When replacing crossbanding it is often found that there is a line between the banding and the panel it is bordering. The line should be glued in at the same time as the banding.

An outer-edge line is glued back in place in the old rebate and can be held until set by masking tape. If the edging has been replaced, such as crossbanding, then first attend to the banding and once set, clean up the edge with a plane to make a sharp edge. Then using a knife-gauge set to the thickness of the line, make a rebate with this. Apply the line in the way explained above.

INLAY MOTIFS

These, like bandings and lines, can be bought at a veneer stockist and come in numerous designs. They are backed on paper, and in actual fact the backing is really the top surface: when glued to a piece it is faced upwards and not taken off until the glue has set. These also have to be cut freehand against the edge of the inlay.

HOW TO DO IT

1. Position the inlay exactly and with masking tape straps, tape it to the surface. The paper backing must be uppermost, and the straps 1in (25mm) or so apart. With a thumbnail, press the tape down into the corner where the inlay meets the surface.
2. Make a mark on the edge of the inlay and opposite on the surface of the wood. This is your register mark.
3. With a scalpel knife, cut around the motif at a slight angle. Cut straight through the tapes and after a quarter of the edge has been cut, stop, and replace the straps. Continue cutting until it is finished.
4. Remove the motif, and after heating the cut area, remove the waste veneer.
5. Dry fit the motif using the registration marks. If it fits, glue, and leave a weight on it until the glue has set.

PARQUETRY PRINCIPLES

What is parquetry? A group of veneers cut together to form a geometric patterned mosaic. Most of these patterns are repeating, to make up a whole design – the most familiar to you will be the chessboard. The veneers are cut on cutting-boards with the aid of a fence and stops; it is one craft that demands little in the way of tools. You will need: (i) scalpel knife; (ii) rules; (iii) compass; (iv) set square; (v) protractor; (vi) straight-edge.

The skill of parquetry is in the accuracy of measuring and cutting, and in having a good eye for lining up the grain. The differing designs are all mathematically formulated, and as long as you keep to these principles, you should find your way through the maze.

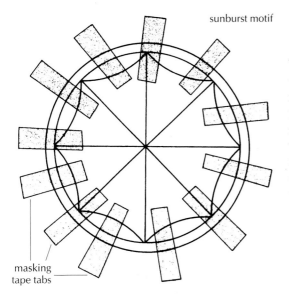

sunburst motif

masking tape tabs

Holding a motif in position for cutting.

So as not to leave you totally high and dry, I have set out below the steps needed to make an accurate chessboard.

HOW TO DO IT

(Chessboard to be 8in (20cm) square with 1in (25mm) squares.)

1. Select two contrasting veneers (say box-wood and rosewood) of a little over 8in × 4in (20cm × 10cm) each after truing up to the adjacent sides.
2. Prepare the cutting board with a fence over 9in (23cm) long. Put in two pins with their outside edges 1in (25mm) from the fence. The gap between the pins must be over 8in (20cm), and the wider the better so that they don't get in the way when cutting.
3. Place one veneer onto the board with one of the trued edges firmly against the fence. Place a straight-edge on the veneer up against the pins, and cut the first strip. Follow on and cut the remainder, then repeat operations with the contrasting veneer.
4. Now, tape the eight strips of veneers together, alternating the colours.
5. True up one edge of the veneer, again across the strips. This must be at right-angles to the sides.
6. Place back on the board with the trued end up against the fence, and between the pins. Lay the straight-edge against the pins and cut this into eight strips.
7. These strips will be made up of 1in blocks. First, lay two strips side by side, then move one strip along a block. Tape these together and you will have a light block against a dark block and vice-versa. Tape the rest of the strips together in the same way until it is completed.
8. On one side of the strip you will have light blocks overhanging and on the other side dark blocks overhanging.

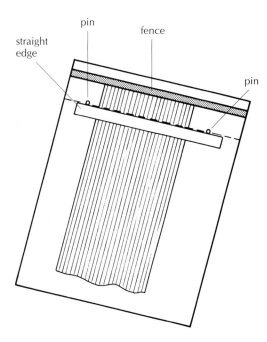

Cutting parquetry on a cutting-board.

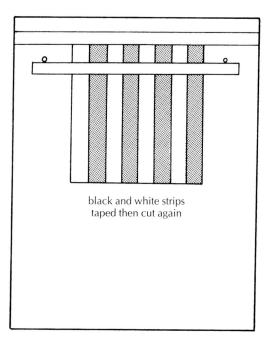

black and white strips
taped then cut again

Positions of strips to make a chessboard.

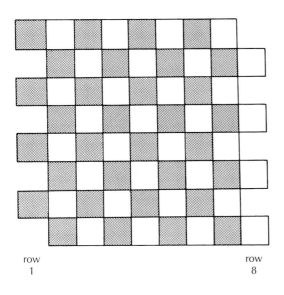

row
1

row
8

Last process to complete a chessboard.

9. Cut away the dark strips and lay them between the light blocks and tape them – and hey presto! a ready-to-glue chess-board.

The chessboard is one of the simpler projects to make, but the principles are the same except that the more complex the pattern, the more complex is the cutting.

REPAIRING MARQUETRY

Marquetry is similar to parquetry except that it is pictorial, meaning flowers, birds and so on, the components jigsawing together to make a picture. Many people avoid furniture that has a little bit of marquetry missing and this is sad, as a bit of ingenuity and patience will reap a harvest. When a piece is missing, the difference between patching this and a veneer is that instead of making the blank first, a master tracing is taken and glued to the veneer selected to fill the hole. As an example, a flower petal is missing: to make it a little

more taxing, this petal has two different coloured bits of veneer to make up the whole petal.

HOW TO DO IT

1. Clean the missing area with a soft-bristled toothbrush and loosen any dirt that has built up against the edges with a knife, otherwise the trace may not be true.
2. Lay a piece of thin paper over the area to be traced and tape down so that it is kept taut. Use a soft lead pencil to make a rubbing, extending further than the edges so that a little of the design comes through. (Use copy paper as this seems to take rubbing well and also glues well to the veneer.)
3. Remove the rubbing and lay it beside the missing area, and referring to this area draw in the line that separates the two missing elements. Still referring to the area, work out the direction of the grain for both pieces and mark this direction with arrows onto the rubbing.
4. After selecting the veneers to be used, cut them into equal squares larger than the area; I would suggest that 2in–3in (50–75mm) is the minimum to work

Taking a rubbing of a missing design.

147

A veneer sandwich ready for marquetry.

with, otherwise they will become too small to hold.

NOTE: If using the knife techniques, go from here to the steps on knife cutting.

5. Take one for your top piece and smear a thin layer of PVA glue onto its surface. Lay the rubbing onto the veneer, taking care to align the grain with the arrow that corresponds to the veneer.

6. Glue a piece of paper to the top face of the next veneer and mark the direction of the grain. Place this one under the first with the paper uppermost, being sure that the grain runs the same way as the second arrow. (The paper is to strengthen the veneer and stop points and little areas breaking off in the cutting process. The paper is always glued to the top face of the veneer.)

7. Lay a thin piece of card of exactly the same size under the veneers, and tape the whole together around the edges with masking tape. This should make a tight little bundle called a sandwich. The rubbing must still be showing. (I use cereal package card. This is used as a backing to stiffen the sandwich and to stop the under-veneer from burring from the saw blade. It also gives extra support when cutting.)

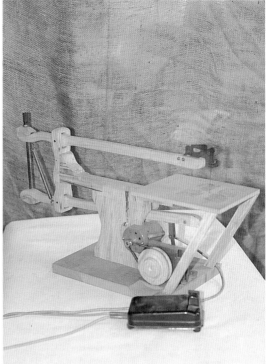

A home-made fretsaw.

NOTE: There are three ways of cutting: the knife cut; the hand fretsaw; and the machine fretsaw.

First Method:

1. Glue paper to the top face of each veneer.
2. Make a cardboard frame for the veneers to fit into tightly. Hinge the rubbing with masking tape to the card frame, with the image directly over the hole where the veneers will fit. Make registration marks so that the rubbing can be located exactly every time.
3. Fit the first veneer into the frame with the grain running in the direction as indicated on the rubbing. Make a mark in the top left-hand corner of the veneer. Lay carbon paper over the veneer and then the rubbing.
4. Trace the line dividing the two pieces of veneer, where the dividing line crosses the outside line of the image, making marks to indicate on the veneer.
5. Remove the veneer from the frame and place it on the cutting board. Before cutting, draw a line from the outside edge to the mark and the line on each side of the veneer.
6. With a sharp scalpel knife, cut from one outside edge to the other end along the line.

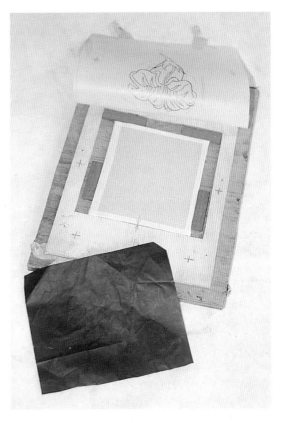

A marquetry frame to hold a sandwich awaiting design.

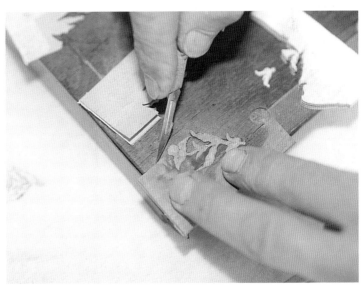

Cutting-in with a knife.

Cutting marquetry with a fretsaw blade.

Glued in place awaiting cleaning up.

7. Put the next veneer into the frame with the grain running according to the rubbing.
8. Place the cut veneer on top, with the corner mark in the right position. (If the required piece of veneer has lost its mark, then still locate it in the position it was in when traced.)
9. Holding the cut veneer firmly, cut along the edge and onto the other veneer.
10. Remove the top piece of veneer and the piece below it, leaving the other bit that is to make up the patch. Replace the top piece and fit it with the other already left, and tape the join.
11. Place the carbon paper and the rubbing over the veneers, and trace the perimeter of the patch.
12. Remove the veneers to the cutting board and cut carefully around the perimeter line. The piece should be ready to fit.

Final cleaning up with a knife around the edges.

Second Method:

This involves the use of a hand fretsaw and a bird's-beak cutting rest. The cut must be on the downstroke (and the sandwich supported over the bird's-beak) with as fine a blade as you can manage (8/0 is the finest, although metal-piercing blades are finer – but these are brittle, and snap easily; they can be tempered by laying in molten lead for a few seconds. Cut as close into the vee as possible at all times. To get a really tight fit, cut at an angle of 10°–15° from the upright. The other tool you will need is a *pricker*, to produce a fine hole for the blade to thread through; a fine sewing-machine needle in a handle will do. Do not drill a hole as this will show after cutting; the hole made by the pricker will close up afterwards.

1. Mount the bird's beak with a 10°–15° incline to the right.
2. Prick a hole through the sandwich on the line going across the area and on the perimeter line of the area.
3. Place the veneer on the saw-rest; thread the blade through the hole, and attach the blade to the saw-frame.
4. Holding the saw upright in the appropriate hand, and placing the finger and thumb on the veneer with the blade between these digits, slowly start cutting along the dividing line until you reach the opposite perimeter line.
5. With the blade fully up, turn the sandwich a quarter of a turn *clockwise* (this is important, because when cutting the perimeter line it must be slightly undercut; if turned anti-clockwise it will be overcut). Draw the blade down and then up again. Twist the sandwich again until the blade lines up with the perimeter line. Draw down the saw again.
6. Continue to saw, entering the perimeter line and cutting around until the blade is back on the opposite side again. Stop. With straps of tape, secure what has just been sawn, both top and bottom. Continue to saw until the job is completed.
7. Release the blade and move the sandwich over to the cutting board; knife the edge of the sandwich and lay out the pieces. Select the pieces and place them together, and tape on the paper-surface side.
8. If everything was accurate, then the pieces are ready to glue into place.

If the piece is a little large, then place it over the area and cut it in with a knife as long as it will not show; otherwise pare down the edges of the patch until it fits.

Third Method:

This is similar to the second method, except that instead of using a hand-held fretsaw, a machine fretsaw is used. This will free both hands to move and hold the veneer, which will make the whole job easier and faster. The table of the saw is angled at 15° to get the undercut.

fourteen

PREPARATION FOR FINISHING

The work described in this chapter is all-important. Doing preparation work on a new piece is easy: you stop when the work is cleaned up and ready to proceed. With antiques there is the same need to do the job well, but you must also take into consideration that the piece doesn't want to look as though it has just come out of a shop. It is important to retain as much of the old patina as possible.

The following sections will guide you through the pitfalls of preparatory work, showing how to meld patches and repairs into the older surrounding areas; how to take out marks and stains and lighten the colour of new areas to match the old; and how to fill small areas with stoppers, and fill the grain.

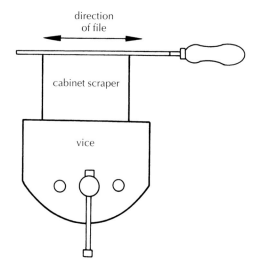

Preparing a cabinet scraper.

THE CABINET SCRAPER

This tool, as already mentioned, is one of the most useful tools for early preparation work and saves a great deal of time and sandpaper. It is also one of the hardest tools to master properly, both in use and in sharpening. However, don't be put off: master it, and the world is your oyster! The cabinet scraper can be bought at any good tool shop and is just a simple sheet of steel. If, like me, you use a saw-sharpening company, ask them if they will let you have an old bit of bandsaw blade: from a 3in–4in (7–10cm) width blade, get them to cut the teeth off, and to make it about 4in (10cm) long, the thinner the better. Then your troubles begin. How to sharpen it?

HOW TO DO IT

1. Place in a vice, and file both long edges square and smooth.
2. Remove from the vice, and smooth further by using an oilstone. Lay flat, remove any burr, and finally smooth the edges again.
   NOTE: Round the corners of the blade with a file.
3. Place back in the vice with 1in (25mm) or so of blade showing. Use an old knife-steel which has been worn smooth, or the edge of a gouge, and run it across the edge of the scraper (a burnishing bar). The angle of the steel is most important: hold each end of the steel angled at about 30° off the horizontal,

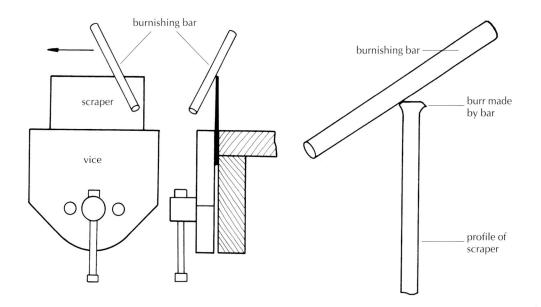

Turning an edge.

Close up of the scraper edge.

with the top hand a little forward of the lower hand. Starting at the furthest end, draw the steel towards you. Repeat on the other side of that edge, then turn over and go through the same motions again.

The edge of the blade should be rounded over, leaving a sharp, even burr along the blade. This edge is pushed over the wood to be removed, and if the angle is correct it will shave the finest sliver off the surface.

Using a cabinet scraper.

HOW TO USE YOUR SCRAPER BLADE

Use of the cabinet scraper is just as difficult to master!

1. Hold the blade with both hands, one on each end of it, with the first two fingers of each hand in front of it, the index finger just above a middle height and the other finger near the bottom edge.
2. The thumbs should be placed close together in the centre back of the blade, just below centre height.
3. Press the thumbs into the blade to give it a slight bow, and angle the top of the blade forwards, between 30° and 40°. NOTE: The angle will vary with the way you held the burnishing bar to sharpen it. Also this angle will vary for the depth of cut, from dust to an actual shaving.

GENERAL TIPS

- Always follow the grain, but angle the blade so that it does not build up a wall in front of its edge.
- If the blade vibrates, bend it slightly to tension it; this should stop the vibration.
- Try never to scrape against the grain. If working with curly grain or other fierce woods, angle back slightly and take a finer cut.
- If a line is to be taken out, make sure the blade cuts across it at an angle.

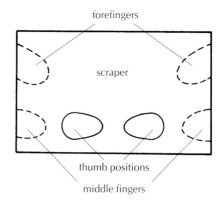

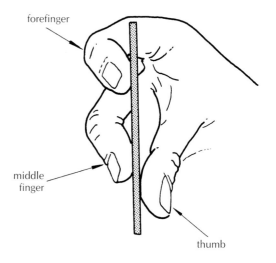

Correct way of holding a cabinet scraper.

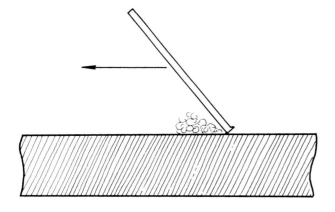

Correct application of the cabinet scraper.

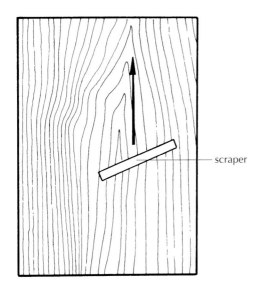

Blade of cabinet scraper slightly angled.

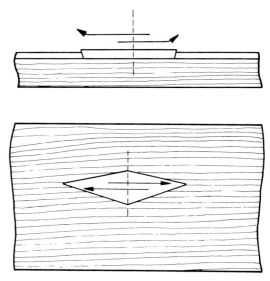

Levelling a small patch.

- When scraping small patches, start just within the patch and work out, then turn around and do the same the opposite way. Make sure that the finishing scrape is with the grain.
- When coming off the edge, turn the wrist so that the blade lifts, otherwise the edge can be torn or if there is a moulding it can be gouged.

SANDING

Whatever am I doing writing about sanding? Well, let me tell you this: one of my teachers was so good at sanding that not only did it not seem a chore, it was also quick and perfect. The reason was that after his other duties as a first-year apprentice, all he did was sand for the whole workshop for a whole year, and although today this would be classed as exploiting a trainee, he has benefited ever since. I'm not proposing you do the same, but understanding the techniques of sanding will help you.

What are you doing when you sand? You are scratching away the surface of the wood with a graded grit. These grades increase in number as the grit becomes finer, although some makes just state 'fine', 'medium', and 'coarse'. I prefer the makes that state a grit size, using about four graduating papers.

TYPES OF PAPER

Coarse: these are from about '80' to '150', and would be used on a very rough surface; however, I prefer to go no lower than '150'. The finish is best brought up by planing and scraping, and then by using medium and fine papers to finish off. The use of varying grades is literally to erase the scratches of the previous grade, until they are so fine that they will not show. Very coarse papers will leave very deep scratches which take quite a bit of moving, even with the next grade up.

Medium: from '180' to '220': if possible it is advisable to start with one of these.

Fine: '240' to '320': there are finer grades, but these are generally used for finishing. Sometimes it may be best to use an even finer finishing paper on close-grain light woods such as boxwood, maple and so on.

There are several different types of paper, from the old-style glass-and-sandpaper, to the modern synthetics; the latter are much finer graded, and although two to three times the cost, they actually last very much longer.

SANDING TECHNIQUE

Always sand *with* the direction of the grain – although there are times when this rule is broken. This is when a crossbanding is involved, when one takes the direction from the major part of the surface; but be wary of using too coarse a paper, because when crossing the grain the scratches will show up for longer. Other types of grain may leave you puzzled, such as burrs and figured woods. The rule of thumb is to sand across your sight-line, for example a burr on a chest of drawers always goes from side to side; one would only go from back to front on a piece such as this when the grain is laid that way. Never go in circles, and stand *behind* your sanding and not to the side, otherwise you are liable to sand with a windscreen-wiper effect, leaving shallow arches all over the surface.

When sanding doors and carcases, always sand first anything that is jointed into the side of another member, as on a door where there are two cross-members and the two stiles (uprights). The cross-members should be done first, enabling you to sand out any scratches that cross the grain on the stile where the cross-member joins that piece.

Use a cork sanding-block most of the time, only using the bare palm on the last finish run. Make shaped blocks to match into mouldings and shaped areas. It is best to purchase a cork block, rather than using a bit of waste wood, because if something gets trapped between either paper and block or paper and the surface it will be absorbed by the softer cork and not mark the surface.
NOTE: *Do not use an orbital or belt sander*: the first will leave small whorl marks that will only appear when the polish is applied; the latter is too fierce and is less controllable, cutting through a veneer in seconds.

Although there is a chapter on finishing, it is relevant to point out now that the

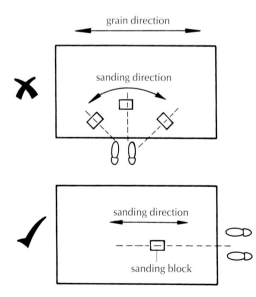

Correct sanding technique.

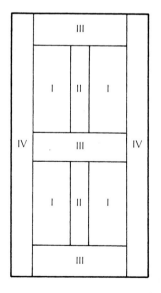

How to sand a door.

merest defect will be magnified by the polish. The attitude of 'that will do' must be *banished* when preparing the surface, because the slightest whisker of a scratch will show as a score under the finish.

When coming to the end of the finish papers, damp the wood and leave to dry; this will raise the grain. Sand smooth, then repeat, and repeat until it stops happening. If this is not done, when you apply a stain the grain will become raised and will then need to be sanded, leaving a patchy surface.

Tip

There is no need to bear down on the sanding block with all your weight; just use a constant, even pressure. Sanding is a relaxing occupation, so enjoy it for what it is: an interlude between phases. It is not a chore, it is a skill.

BLEACHING

It still surprises me how this subject is treated in such a cavalier way even by professionals. Yes, there is a place for bleaching within restoring, but I do not believe one should be blasé about it. First, some of the chemicals used are very caustic, and dangerous to handle. Second, they can be very corrosive, and degenerative to both wood and glue; some can actually destroy the fabric of the wood, literally taking the living breath out of it. So if there is an alternative to using these chemicals, do use it: *bleaching should be thought of as a last resort.*

Instead of taking each chemical individually and explaining what they can be used for, I will work the other way around and take the problems and explain what

chemicals to use and how to use them, starting with the least caustic method. When using any chemical this process of elimination should be used.

INK MARKS

This is a perennial problem, and needless to say is found mostly on and in writing boxes and desks – and because of their purpose be cautious about eliminating these marks completely, as this could be thought of as over-restoring. If a stain is in a very visual area, in a place where stains would not normally occur, or if it is very disfiguring, then yes, try to banish it completely. Otherwise use bleach merely to tone down the mark to a point where it will be acceptable.

HOW TO DO IT

Use oxalic acid; this has never failed to get out the most stubborn of ink stains.

1. Mix a solution of 1 teaspoon of oxalic crystals to ½pt (284ml) of hot water; this

Applying oxalic acid. (Note the pale patch at the right of the hand already treated.)

helps the crystals to dissolve. Wait until they are cold.

2. With a nylon paintbrush, coat the stained area with the solution. If it is a ring, just cover that area carefully – try not to go outside the stain.

   NOTE: The solution may just sit on the stain and not penetrate the wood; if this happens, use a bit of 0000 steel wool to agitate the surface. Let the bleach dry, then inspect. If it is still there, add more solution and agitate the surface with steel wool.

3. When the stain has disappeared you may find that this area is a little lighter, like a halo.

4. Take a rag and wash the whole surface, including the area bleached with the solution; then let it dry.

5. Wash the whole surface again with bicarbonate of soda to neutralize the bleach. Leave until dry.

RUST MARKS

These can occur for many reasons, the most obvious being where steel screws are just below the surface and because of damp have rusted, the rust penetrating through to the surface. Try oxalic acid in the way described above; if after two applications the marks have not started to disappear, use sulphuric acid.

HOW TO DO IT

1. Paint on an 8 per cent solution.

   NOTE: Car battery acid is of this percentage, but if you haven't an old battery you can drain, then purchase the solution from a car DIY store (*not* the distilled water).

2. Use the same method to apply sulphuric acid as for oxalic acid; however *do not wipe over* the whole surface as described with oxalic acid.

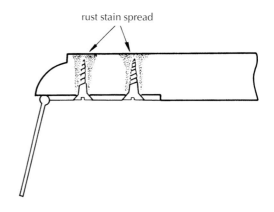

How rust marks appear from screws.

rust stain spread

DARK OR BLACK RINGS ON TABLE TOPS

When water is just spilled onto a top, it generally leaves a white ring; however, if it has penetrated through pottery ware, or where a plant has been watered and the pot was not in a container to stop water from coming into contact with the surface of the furniture, the ring will be dark. This is because this water would have carried with it minerals from either the pot or the earth within the pot, these being fertilizer, sulphates or other minerals. All these will normally darken the wood. Try oxalic acid first, and if this does not work, try sulphuric acid.

COPPER OR BRASS STAINS

This sort of stain happens when fittings corrode and leach into the wood. Remove the fittings responsible, and clean before refitting. Treat the stains with oxalic acid or sulphuric acid.

158

DARKENED WOOD

There are three reasons for an area of wood to look darker:

(i) The area has lost its finish and has absorbed foreign matter that has darkened it.

(ii) It is a patched area and the inserted wood is darker than the wood it replaces.

(iii) The area has lost its finish and has been abraded back to its original colour, whilst the surrounding area has mellowed over the years.

SOLUTION TO (i)

(The area has lost its finish and has absorbed foreign matter.)

There are several other reasons than the ones given above that may cause an area of wood to be darkened, especially if the finish is non-existent. If wood is left bare it can either fade or pick up dirt. The fading can be coloured up with stains (*see* Chapter 15) or washed with water if composed of dirt.

Natural Oils

When handled over a period of time, wood will pick up the grease excreted from the body. However, this can be washed out with methylated spirits, and most natural oils can be extracted from the surface of wood. Soak a rag in meths. and lay it over the area; leave until the rag is dry. The meths will soften the oil and will also evaporate into the atmosphere, drawing the oil into the rag. You may need to do this several times, however; if this is the case, use a new piece of rag for each application. (Make sure you have *plenty of ventilation*.)

Wax

If the discolouration is because of wax, beeswax or candlewax, remove these as follows: lay a sheet of brown paper over the area with the open or rough unpolished surface of the paper downwards. Smooth a warm iron over the surface, the iron being just hot enough to melt the wax; this will heat the wax and draw it into the paper. Lift the paper before it loses its heat. Continue this process until the wax is blotted up, changing the paper as it becomes loaded with the wax.

Mineral Oils and Grease

All chemicals must be used in a ventilated area, and gloves and a mask should be worn; in particular this applies to mineral oils and grease, as discussed here. Wet a clean rag with dry-cleaning fluid and lay it over the area; leave until the rag dries out. Repeat with a clean rag until the oil or grease has gone.

Once the decontaminating of an area has been completed, the area may still be dark: if it is, then a bleach will be needed. First try oxalic acid, using a solution at twice the strength to that recommended for ink spots; if this does not work, then a stronger bleach will be necessary.

'A' & 'B' BLEACH

This is a two-part application bleach, ammonia- and peroxide-based, and can be purchased at any reasonable woodwork and finish supply shop. Never buy more than you need, as it has a short shelf-life – as soon as the 'B' bottle is opened it will degenerate drastically over a few weeks. Follow the instructions on the label closely for best results. This bleach is neutralized by an acid such as malt vinegar.

The problem with this bleach is controlling it; also some woods bleach better than others. This particular product is very much an agent for changing the pigment of the wood, and is not for foreign stains. It is strong enough to turn a medium-coloured mahogany white, and even a wood such as rosewood will be changed out of recognition, taking out all the reds and leaving it grey, with darker grey where the black grain was. I will explain the whole process, and how the depth of the bleaching action can be modified:

HOW TO DO IT

NOTE: These are general instructions: those on the package may differ slightly with each brand, so the instructions given here on how to modify the bleaching action will need to be tested before committing oneself to the piece.

1. Because of the caustic nature of the product, don't use brushes but make swabs. Take two thin sticks about 6in–8in (15cm–20cm) long; make two ribbons of absorbent cloth doubled, 2in (50mm) wide and 8in (20cm) long, wrap one around each stick and then tape to hold in place. Also have ready two clean containers, vinegar and rags, and a pair of rubber gloves.
2. The surface of the wood must be clean and dry. Pour enough solution of 'A' into one of the clean containers and dip the swab into it until it is thoroughly wet. Apply to the surface in straight strokes going *with* the grain, until this, too, is thoroughly wet. Leave for ten minutes: within this time the colour of the wood will actually darken, but don't worry, as this is hoped for – the pigmentation is being drawn to the surface.
3. After ten minutes, pour 'B' solution into the other clean container, and with the other unused swab apply this solution in a likewise manner. After a few minutes a white scum will form; this is nothing to worry about and shows that the chemicals are working.
4. Normally one application is enough to bleach most woods except the really dense ones. If a second application is desired, both 'A' and 'B' need to be applied again. If during the first application it is felt that the desired tone is reached, the bleaching action can be curtailed by neutralizing with vinegar. NOTE: This must be done cautiously, as scum will stay, hiding the true tone of the wood until it has been wiped away with vinegar. There is also the problem of patchy bleaching, as the less dense areas of wood will bleach more quickly than the rest.

Once any bleaching is done, the wood will need sanding, as the grain will be left slightly raised. Although neutralized, you *must* wear a mask, because the dust could contain particles of bleach which escaped neutralization. These particles will reactivate inside the body; because they are corrosive, this could lead to respiratory problems.

SOLUTION TO (ii)

(A patched area, where the inserted wood is darker than the wood it replaces.)
The 'A' & 'B' solution is probably the only way to lighten the tone of the wood, unless the tone is so slight that a strong solution of oxalic acid could do it. The wisest way to do this is to mask around the patch with a couple of coats of shellac; there is bound to be a little bleed under the shellac, but so slight as not to be too worrying. The real point to look out for is the darkening around the edges of the patch. This is caused by the sanding area creeping away from the patch itself when levelling the two surfaces. If so, make sure the shellac mask does not cover this area or there will be a dark area around the patch like a reverse halo.

SOLUTION TO (iii)

(The area has lost its finish and has been abraded back to its original colour, the surrounding area having mellowed over the years.)

This should be treated in the way described in **Solution to (ii)**. When an area has been bleached it is probably lighter than the surrounding wood. This can be adjusted by staining.

LIFTING DENTS

This subject is hard to place, but it is part of the preparation of a surface before finishing; the technique described here can be used whether the surface has a finish on it or not. However, if the surface does have a finish, in the area of the repair it will be damaged if not totally destroyed.

The theory behind the technique described here is that a dent is caused by the compressing together of the fibres of the wood: to release this compression, the fibres need to be swollen by forcing moisture into them. However, this will only be successful providing the fibres have not been broken, such as in a dig in the surface.

HOW TO DO IT

The tool used is a hot iron with a fine point, or a heavy-duty soldering iron, on full heat. The latter is actually better as it is easier to put direct heat to a specific point; and for a surface that is finished, it limits the area of damage to that finish.

1. Using an eye dropper or hypodermic syringe, put a blob of water onto the depression; a screwed-up corner of clean rag dipped in water will do as well.
2. Place the hot-iron point into the water, taking care not to touch the surface of the wood as it can scorch the wood and discolour it. Also it will tend to keep the wood dry and boil the water away into the atmosphere.
3. Continue to apply heat to the water, creating steam. Make sure the water does

not dry up and that the surface of the wood does not dry.

NOTE: If the dent is new, then it should raise quite quickly; old dents will take longer, requiring more patience and several applications.

Tip

If the surface has a finish on it, the heat and steam will have to break down the surface before penetrating the wood. You could remove the finish before application, but I find it better not to for two reasons: first, one tends to remove a larger area of the finish than is needed. Second, the edge where the removing stops will make a step, whereas the damage created by the steam will be smaller and will fade out towards the edges, creating a feathered edge which will be easier to disguise when repairing.

Heating a drop of water above a dent.

4. Leave to dry thoroughly, removing any discolouration with oxalic acid. If you live in a hard-water area use distilled water, and use undyed cloth if you use a rag as an applicator.

STOPPERS AND FILLERS

The difference between the two is this: stoppers are for filling small holes and dents, whereas fillers are more liquid material used to fill the grain prior to staining and polishing.

STOPPERS

There are several types of stopper:

- Wood dust and glue
- Plaster stopper
- Proprietary stoppers
- Shellac stopper
- Wax stopper (beaumontage)

WOOD DUST AND GLUE

The wood dust to be used must be clean and very fine, the type made by a bandsaw. It must also be as pale, if not a little paler in colour than the area to be patched. The glue can be PVA or animal glue, but used sparingly. Remember: most glue will not take a wood stain when dry, and can only be coloured out in polishing. I do not use this type of filler as it can tend to be granular and hard to disguise; also shellac does not readily fix to glue, and can stay dull.

PLASTER STOPPER

There are two types of plaster you can use:
Whiting: Slaked plaster, which when mixed with water will not dry hard and solid like plaster of Paris, and needs to be mixed with glue. Again, PVA or animal glue will do.

Plaster of Paris, or dental plaster: This also needs a certain amount of glue to fix it (though not so much as the whiting), otherwise when a stain is applied to the surface it will 'dish out' and hollow.

Both need to have colour added in order to tone as closely as possible with the surrounding wood. This can be done by adding dry pigment colours once the plaster has been mixed to a thick clotted-cream consistency.

PROPRIETARY STOPPERS

There are many on the market, but I would add a note of caution: choose a water-based stopper and not a cellulose one – the former will take stain, and because of the method of application the stopper will need to cover the indentation and there is no way that you can stop a little from going onto the wood around the hole. Even when rubbed down, the fixer in the cellulose stopper will have penetrated the wood and sealed it, thus leaving a light halo around the filler when you stain.

Because of the shelf life of these stoppers I only buy one colour, normally a creamy one (pine), then add dry pigment colours to my own requirements.

SHELLAC STOPPER

This is a traditional way of stopping: it is made up of shellac and normally comes in stick form, in several colours. You can make your own or buy in. These can be used on bare wood or on an already finished surface. The method is to melt the shellac with a hot soldering iron and let it drip into the hole; when it is hard, you sand it flush.

WAX STOPPER (BEAUMONTAGE)

Like the shellac, wax is also traditional, made of a mixture of waxes and resins. It

Using tip of soldering iron to fill space with shellac.

can be bought in stick form in many colours, and these are soft enough to rub onto the surface over the hole to fill it. They can also be melted and dripped into the hole. This type of stopper is generally used when there is a finish already there, for tasks such as stopping pin-holes on beadings and mouldings, or filling worm-holes. When hard, they are rubbed flush with 0000 steel wool and then burnished, and will take up the shine of the surrounding polish.

This stopper can also be made, and by varying one of its components can be adjusted in hardness, which is useful.

USING STOPPERS

Wood dust and glue and plaster stoppers need little further explanation, but the rest will.

PROPRIETARY STOPPERS

Keeping the lid on, gently heat up by standing in a bowl of hot water for a few minutes; this will make the stopper runny. Scoop out

what you need, then choose an earth pigment colour (*see* Chapter 15 on Staining) that will colour the stopper slightly *lighter* than the surrounding wood, *not darker*. Mix powder into the paste until the right tone is reached. Try not to use water to keep the paste malleable as this will make the paste shrink more when it dries.

I use a putty knife to mix and apply the stopper. When filling the hole, use the tip of the knife to push the stopper into it, and then leave slightly proud. When dry, sand flush with a block and fine sandpaper. If an airhole appears, re-fill and start again. I always make a little more than I need and store the remainder in a plastic film-container; this way it does not dry out and harden.

SHELLAC STOPPER

You can make your own, but really it is far easier to buy these. They come in several colours, from clear, to amber and browns, reds and blacks. Use an electric soldering iron to melt the stick: hold both stick and iron over the hole and drip the shellac into it: then hold the iron gently on the dripped shellac, though guard against touching the bare wood with its tip.

Smooth the shellac into the hole, removing the surplus with a putty knife before it has a chance to harden. Leave the remainder to harden.

After ten minutes, rub the shellac flush to the wood with a block and fine paper. If it seems to drag and pull away, leave it to harden longer. Before the iron becomes cold, wipe off the residue of shellac otherwise it may burn and harden on the tip.

WAX STOPPER (BEAUMONTAGE)

This can also be bought, but I prefer to make my own as it can then be a little harder and is less likely to form a depression. If you use my receipt (*see* below), then the method given above for shellac will work well for applying the wax. Clean up afterwards in the same way, except that after the stopper is flush with the wood, burnish with the *back* of the paper to make it shine.

Receipt:
> 60 per cent beeswax
> 30 per cent carnubia wax
> 10 per cent dumar resin

Heat gently in a tin sitting in a saucepan of water, and melt and mix well. Using pure turpentine, mix a small quantity of earth pigment to a thick creamy consistency and pour into the melted waxes. Stir occasionally, leaving the wax on a gentle heat – just enough keep it molten. Leave on the heat until the smell of the turpentine diminishes (you won't get rid of the smell altogether): the turpentine will keep the wax soft, and only when it has been greatly reduced will the wax harden. Pour into well oiled ice-cube trays, and leave to set. (Leaving the set wax out in the open air will also help to harden it, but this could take weeks and depends on the amount of turpentine used.)

Filler-shrinkage in a polished surface.

I do not mix my colours, but make pure wax colours and mix to the colour I want on the palette knife while filling. This takes practice, but once mastered makes colouring to match more adjustable.

Mixing hot wax.

FILLERS

The reason for filling the grain is to create a flat surface to polish on, and cuts down on the time it takes to fill the grain with polish. Most woods should have their grain filled by the time you have finished polishing, for the simple reason that the open grain will detract from the glory of the wood. As explained before, the grain or open pores of the wood are not the actual figuring and colouring of that wood. If the wood has been polished and the grain still left open, two things will become apparent: the surface may look thin; and the light striking the wood will look diffused, so that instead of seeing the full beauty of the wood, the light will strike the edges of the open grain and reflect back like a mirror.

There are, of course, some exceptions: mainly the large open-grained English deciduous woods such as oak, elm, and ash, besides a few others. This is traditional, and also the grain itself in these woods is a part of their beauty and will not detract from the whole. However, the large open grains of the exotic hardwoods should *not* be treated in this way.

Filling the grain with the polish itself provides the superior finish, but it takes longer and needs more skill. The earlier the piece the more likely that the grain was filled with polish. The difference can be seen quite markedly in late Victorian and even later furniture when it became more of a practice to fill the grain with filler. Furthermore, take a look at a piece of this period and you may find white specks within the grain under the polished surface. This is filler where the colour has leached out, and it is difficult to remove without sacrificing some of the surface of the wood; nor will it take stain. To overcome this problem is difficult, and will be covered in the chapter on polishing. If one finds filler in a piece that is definitely earlier than that of Victorian times then it can

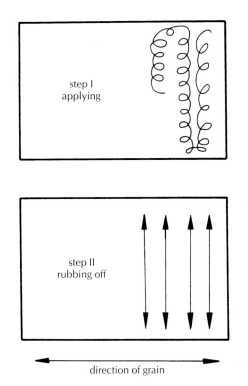

Applying grain filler.

be reasonably assumed that the surface has been refinished since it was made.

There are several proprietary makes that can be purchased, and many receipts to work from. For the former, follow instructions, especially on the drying times.

All fillers need to be worked into the grain, and this is done by applying the filler as a paste, with a coarse piece of damp hessian in a circular motion. This pulls the filler across the grain and fills it in a scrape-like action. The circular motion should continue until the paste begins to dry and the surplus starts to roll off. Once this begins, a clean piece of damp hessian can be used until the wood is clean of the paste, although the surface may have a grubby look. Leave the filler to dry, and then rub smooth with fine finishing paper. The surface should be ready to stain.

Receipt for Grain Filler
2 tablespoons plaster of Paris
1 teaspoon burnt turkey Umber
Mix together dry, and add Van Dyke brown waterstain until a stiff double-cream texture is reached.
Add ½ teaspoon of PVA or animal glue (PVA glue will allow the filler to dry more quickly).

If kept in a sealed plastic container this will store for a couple of weeks, especially if a damp rag is left to cover it before putting on the top. When working with light woods, a paler pigment such as raw sienna can be used, and a diluted form of Van Dyke brown.

DISTRESSING

A pristine repair would look incongruous within a well-lived piece, but it would be equally wrong to do the job with no thought of the surrounding area.

Certain types of ageing happen on different parts of a piece, such as scuffing and bruising of the wood around the feet, or the numerous pit-type scratches around a well-used keyhole. There are many more examples I could give, but this would still not really help you to match this ageing. You must study the surrounding area and try to imagine what shape of implement made the marks, and how.

Distressing must be done in a calculated, scientific way, to blend the new with the original. In no way should you set out to disfigure. Once these wear marks have been made, a stain will settle in them, leaving it a little darker than the rest of the piece. This will also help in the ageing process. As with the old marks it will be found that these 'catch' and have a build-up of dirt.

An assortment of objects and tools can be used to do this, such as a bunch of old keys, ball-pain hammer, and a burnishing-bar. Only repeat marks in areas where repeated similar actions would have occurred, such as around a keyhole, or on a plinth where shoes have scuffed against it. Where there is no cause for a repeat action to take place, like in the middle of the side of a chest, then it is best to keep the marks made with each tool singular. Never overdo it: less rather than more should be the policy.

TOOLS

Burnishing Bar
Use when edges have been replaced. Once prepared, the edges will be sharp and new. These edges can be sandpapered down, but a better way is to burnish the edge, matching the roundness with the remaining old edges. The old edges will have been rounded by pressure and endless years of buffing with a cloth. If the new edges are made with sandpaper then they will have a soft look to them, and not that dense look that comes from pressure.

Hammer
All different types can be used, but be careful of new ones with sharp edges as these will break the surface of the wood and not dent it. Use different parts of the hammer to avoid repetition, and remember not to strike too hard a blow.

Bunch of Keys
These don't necessarily need to be used solely around keyholes.

There are many more implements one may use, but beware of using sharp implements as these will create scars and not bruises.

fifteen

FINISHING: STAINING AND COLOURING

Staining is part and parcel of finishing and can become quite technical, although these days manufacturers try to make it as easy as wiping it on and off. Hey presto! The job is done, now seal it. Dealing with antiques, however, it is not so simple, and there are several factors to take into consideration. What kind of colour would the original have been, and if only a section of the piece is being coloured to match the rest, how was that original colour obtained in the first place? And if the colour you put on is found to be wrong, can you alter it?

Also, what is staining all about? Yes, it is to change the colour of the wood, especially when staining in a patch – but it goes beyond that. although matching to the desired 'look' is paramount when restoring antiques, it should also be kept in mind that originally the reason for staining the wood was not only fashion, but had a deeper meaning: wood, with its grain and figure structure, is a beautiful thing, but finished without a stain it can look rather flat or raw. By staining, parts of the figure can be enhanced, whilst other parts of less interest can be subtly changed, giving the whole surface depth and dimension, like looking into a pool with shifting light. This, I believe, is what staining is all about, and it is an art that so may woodworkers miss: staining can truly make a piece *sing*.

When choosing the right colour and deciding what strength to apply, look on the wood as a graph in the beauty stakes, starting at nought, climbing to ten and dropping back down again to nought: with no stain the wood looks flat – call this nought. As stain is applied the wood is enhanced and in beauty climbs up the scale until it reaches ten, where the stain is helping to display it to its full advantage. After this point the stain will actually start to hide the grain, and becomes more like a paint blanking out the wood itself; from now on the enhancement factor drops until it comes back to nought where the stain dominates the wood and the piece becomes a canvas for the colour. The skill is to reach ten, if the piece does not dictate otherwise.

A word of caution: many people like dark furniture and equate this with richness of

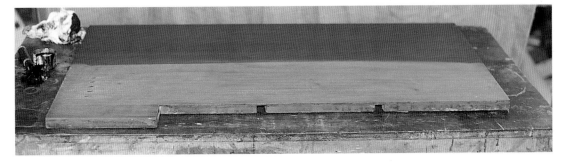

Wood with and half without stain.

colour. Certainly some pieces need to be dark, such as an old oak coffer which can almost look black with light areas of wood showing through on the edges where it has been rubbed over the centuries. Many a time I have had a student start to stain a piece by putting a small test patch in an out-of-the-way place, and then say 'I think a little darker'. But keep in the back of your mind that once the whole piece has been covered with a darkish colour both the colour and the piece will look altogether much darker than you anticipated. Remember, staining can only darken a wood, not lighten it; only bleaching does that.

Lastly, *always wear gloves* even for mixing, not for the obvious reason of keeping your hands lily-white but because some pigments and chemicals are poisonous or can cause dermatitis; also, chemicals such as spirits will be absorbed through the skin and over a period of time can build up and create a reaction within your body.

TYPES OF STAIN

Let's start at the beginning and categorize the different types of stain:

OIL STAINS

These are generally suspended in a naphtha-based oil, and as a product are very good and extremely light-fast. However, this is a problem when applied to antiques where the colour and strength can't be readily tested, because they penetrate deeply into the wood and can be hard to remove if the choice is wrong. On new pieces, however, where the colour can be tested on a scrap of wood, this type of stain would be my first choice.

SPIRIT STAINS

These stains are aniline dyes and are suspended in methylated spirits. They are much less light-resistant than oil stains and can be difficult to apply unless a spray gun is used. The problem here is that the spirit within the stain evaporates so quickly that it is difficult to spread evenly before the stain dries. Sometimes they are useful when strong tone is needed, but this can also be created with this stain after the finish has been applied. More will be written about it in the colouring-up section.

WATER STAINS

These stains are mixed in water and are the basic palette for the restorer; they fall into three distinct categories:

Earth Pigment Colours
These are finely ground earth powders and can be mixed with several different mediums. Their uses are many, from colouring grain filler and stopper, to using them within stains.

These colours can be mixed with many mediums, although turpentine, water and polish are the ones that interest us. When mixed with water, a little size glue is needed to fix the medium; the red or brown powdery colour found on the backs of Victorian chests and the like are done in this way. Polish is also used to fix the medium: pigment can't be mixed with just methylated spirit as it will not dissolve properly; however, adding a little diluted polish to the spirit will be enough as a holding medium.

Water Coating
This is a form of painting and uses a size to fix the pigment. This process hides the natural grain and any other defects and can be classed as a form of distempering for wood.

Pigment and Water-aniline Dyes
Some aniline dyes are made to dissolve in water and these are most useful to the restorer. The principal water stain in my opinion is Van Dyke brown, which comes in

a crystal form and is dissolved by boiling. I call it the cure-all stain as it seems to colour different types of wood to their own various hues. The colour varies according to the strength of the stain, ranging from a light brown to a near blackish-brown, although if the wood has any red in it this will be accentuated by the stain. It can be altered by adding earth colours, although I tend to lay the stains and colours on separately, building up to the desired tone and hue.

CHEMICAL STAINS

These are actual chemicals that may not even look like the desired colour while they are in the bottle. Most notable of these is potassium permanganate crystals, which when dissolved in water turn to a magenta mahogany; this turns to a warm orange colour, a hue common in mahogany furniture of the Victorian period. This change in colour is caused by a chemical reaction within the wood; one of the chemicals present in most, if not all woods to some degree is tannic acid, and it is this and others that make up the structure of the wood and its colours. Another chemical commonly used in the darkening of oak is ammonia, in a process called 'fuming'; if oak is left long enough in ammonia fumes it will actually turn black. (At the end of this chapter is a short list of the different stains and their uses on particular woods.)

HOW TO MIX AND MAKE STAINS AND COLOURS

OIL STAINS

On the whole I would advise the use of proprietary brands, but mediums such as naphtha or pure turpentine can be used. The use of earth colours – siennas, umbers, lakes and so on – are the most useful for this type of stain. One note of caution: if turpentine is used as a base, the finish should not be a wax finish because the turpentine in the wood will dissolve the wax causing dull spots to appear.

Most earth colours come already finely ground and will readily dissolve in these oils. Once the desired colour has been reached the liquid must be strained through a fine muslin cloth: otherwise, once the stain has been applied and dried, the surface will become dusty, and then it would need to be brushed and dusted off; and no trace of dust must be left otherwise when a finish is applied the surface will be bitty, and it will need to be rubbed down and re-coated all over again. Moreover, this rubbing down may cause the stain to become patchy, and this may not be detected before a new coat of finish is put on. So – *strain twice to make sure the mixture is pure.*

SPIRIT STAINS

The aniline dyes that form these stains come in powder or crystal form and dissolve readily in methylated spirits. These stains are very concentrated and are bought by the ounce, and can be mixed and stored in a very concentrated form and then diluted as and when they are needed. They should be kept in a dark cupboard. Half an ounce (14g) to a pint (0.5l) of meths will make a very strong mixture (although some colours are stronger than others). These must also be strained, otherwise when dry, minute granules will be left in the grain of the wood which will be almost impossible to remove completely. When a coat of polish is applied it will dissolve the granules, and the mop or rubber applying the polish will drag these dissolving granules along, leaving streaks of colour over the whole work. This streaking can happen even when great care has been taken over the staining. One way to help eliminate this is by adding a little polish to the mixture, to act as a

Spirit stain granules causing streaking when the polish is applied.

Tip

I always make more than I need of any stain, just in case I need to go over some of the area and patch it. It is notoriously difficult to match colours exactly, and this will save you time.

fixative: 5–10 per cent at most, no more; otherwise other problems can occur, such as uneven patches of colour.

EARTH PIGMENT COLOURS

To reiterate, these come as fine ground powder and are mixed by stirring or shaking them in the medium you have chosen to use.

Mixing with Water (Water-coating Stains)
The stain made with this medium needs to have some sort of size added to it. The size should be made fairly weak – a watered-down animal glue, for example, is very satisfactory. PVA glue can also be used, but be sure to make it very thin otherwise it can form a skin on the surface of the wood. Remember the size is used to fix the pigment, and not glue it to the wood!

Fill a container with water and pour in pigment until you obtain the colour you need. These powders can be mixed together to widen your palette, although never mix more than three because you will then get mud. Add the size and mix thoroughly; then strain through muslin. When coating backs of pieces straining is not necessary, as you will find that the old surface will have a powdery texture to it, and this should be imitated to give it an old appearance.

Mixing with Turpentine and Oils
The process is the same as with water, except that no size is needed; but again, strain after mixing.

Mixing with Polish
This is more a paint than a stain and is used to cover burn marks and other dark patches that can't be bleached out; it can also be used to paint in string-lines and other motifs. The polish in question is shellac, and by preference, bleached or white polish; although button or other shellac polishes can be used, these will add their own tone to the colour you are mixing.

When mixing, the thinner the polish the better: for example, dilute a well bodied polish by at least 70 per cent with methylated spirits. (Meths on its own will not do the job properly.) Because these colours are normally used for just patching or touching up or smaller detailed work, only small quantities need be mixed up at a time. I use clear plastic photographic film containers, and have all my different earth pigments ready mixed; when I need them I simply give them a good shake. These also need to be strained through muslin or coffee filters before use. When two pigments need to be mixed I get another clear container and stir a little of the ready-mixed colours together. If you then leave the mixed colour to stand for a while, the pigment that has not dissolved will lie on the bottom of the container and so needs less straining.

WATER-PIGMENT STAINS AND WATER-ANILINE DYES

The pigments already described are used in water stains, and a few others such as Van Dyke brown crystals and water-aniline dyes can be added to the water-stain palette. The difference between water-coating and water-staining is that in the latter the stain is wiped off before it dries, leaving the surface stained by the pigment; whereas water-coating actually leaves the surface *painted*. In both cases the earth pigments and aniline dyes are mixed with cold water. These colours can be mixed together to form other colours.

Van Dyke brown crystals need to be prepared differently:

1. Put 3–4 tablespoons of the crystals into a tin or small saucepan, pour on ½pint (284ml) of cold water, and stir. When water is added to the crystals you will find that they bind into a sticky mass,

and it is this mass that needs to be dissolved.
2. Place the container inside another saucepan filled with water and gently bring to the boil, stirring occasionally.
3. Allow to simmer for 30 minutes or until the crystals have dissolved.
4. When cooled, decant into a bottle. This solution will be quite concentrated and can be diluted by adding extra water, then shaken. The other colours can be added to the solution. Ammonia can be added, which will help give a deeper tone.

CHEMICAL STAINS

There are many chemical stains, and some come in crystal form; these can be simply mixed with water, and generally do not need to be strained. Be careful that the solution you make is not too concentrated, because it can be difficult to lighten once applied. If the solution does not give a deep enough tone then simply add a second coat. This addition need not wait until the first application has dried, because you are simply adding more chemical to the wood for it to work on.

Making Van Dyke brown stain.

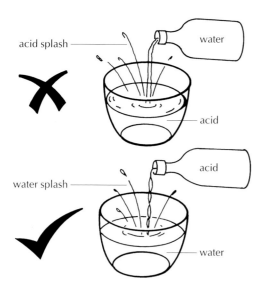

Correct way to dilute acid.

Other chemicals such as nitric acid come as a solution, and if these need to be diluted, proceed very cautiously: fill a container with some distilled water, and pour the acid into the container and not the other way around. There are two reasons for this:

- If there are impurities in the water the acid could react and spit, showering the pourer with concentrated acid!
- Water being poured into acid may create splashes. These splashes will be concentrated acid as the water displaces the acid in the container.

HOW TO APPLY STAIN

Before applying stain to wood it is important to work out which parts of the piece will be stained first, the basic rule being that anything joining into something else should be done to start with. The drawing shows a two-panelled door, and the component parts are taken in order of staining. For the time being don't worry about laying stain evenly or smoothing out; this will be explained later in this section.

1. Panels top and bottom Apply stain with a brush to first one and then the other, by starting in one corner and running with the grain. Cover to the opposite corner. Using the brush along the length of the grain, cover the whole panel. Repeat on the next panel.

2. Mouldings Take a small brush or flitch; load with stain and, starting at the mitre, work all around the moulding covering all the shaped surfaces, taking care not to get any stain onto the panel.

3. Muntin This is the central rail between the two panels, and is done next. Use the end of the bristles to make a straight line at one end of this rail (this is called cutting in). Move down to cover all the rail in stain as you go. As you come to the other end, stop, reverse the brush and 'cut in' the other end of the rail and join up the stain.

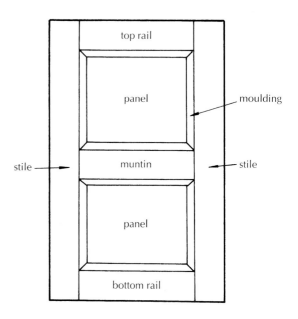

Two-panelled door for staining.

Two-panelled door for staining.

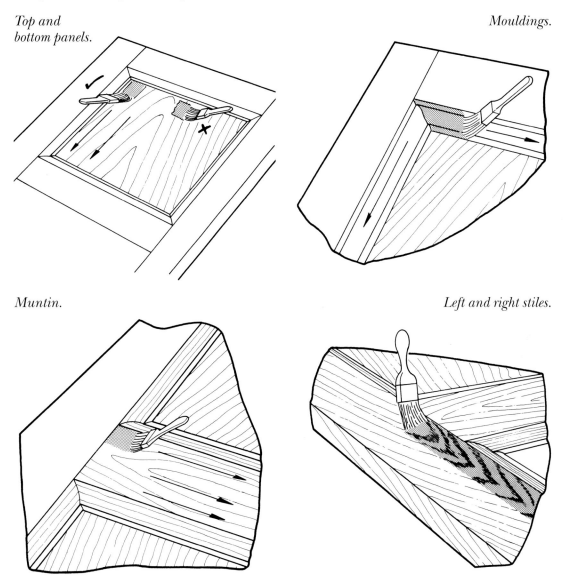

*Top and
bottom panels.*

Mouldings.

Muntin.

Left and right stiles.

4. Top and bottom rail Follow the same method for doing the ends as you did with the muntin.

5. Left stile and right stile These are worked on last, and the stain applied with the grain, starting on the inside first if these rails are larger than the brush. Run straight by the cut-in edge of the bottom and top rail.

When working on any piece, work from the top down. Remove all drawers, and work on these separately. Pieces with tops, such as tables, should be treated a little differently, the tops themselves being stained a tone or so lighter than the legs or bases. (NOTE: This applies to antiques, not new pieces, because over the years the legs or

173

bases would have been exposed to less light than the top.) In fact a little difference of depth and tone will look more natural, and this is one of the tell-tale signs when looking to see if the piece has been restored or not: if the tone conformity is accurate throughout the piece and no fade whatsoever shows on the light open areas, one can normally be sure that it has been refinished at some stage. Of course there are exceptions, but they are rare. Even in new pieces I think it gives a better balance.

APPLYING STAIN

Before applying the stain it is worth practising, as it needs to be done quickly and with a sure hand. Speed is essential, especially as some of the stains are quick-drying. The temperature of the room must also be taken into consideration; too warm, and the stain will dry before you have a chance to smooth it out. Also, how it is laid

Staining in squares leaves a dark line across the grain.

onto the surface is important: never apply it in squares, and always follow the length of the grain where stain joints can be feathered out – if once you make a line across the grain when joining up, there will always be a line: thus the only time you go across the grain is when a piece has crossband decoration.

Where a big table top has to be worked on, I use a large absorbent cloth or sponge instead of a brush. Before starting, lay out everything you need: stain in an open container, brushes of varying sizes, two or three pieces of absorbent cloth, and gloves.

For the sake of clarity I will go through the stains in order of drying time, starting with the fastest and leaving earth pigments in polish and chemical stains until last.

SPIRIT STAINS

These dry almost as fast as one can lay them, and they also dry out very quickly in the applicator (a brush or a rag); I have therefore perfected a technique which seems to offer as easy a solution to applying them as any, apart from spraying on with a spray-gun. Use a wide-mouthed container filled with the stain – a small amount of polish can be added, but no more than 5–10 per cent; I prefer not to use polish for this method. You will also need two absorbent lint-free cloths, and another wide-mouthed container of methylated spirits.

HOW TO DO IT

1. Saturate one of the cloths with the meths and wring it out.
2. Dip the cloth into the stain until it is completely absorbed throughout the cloth, then squeeze it out, leaving it soaking but not dripping everywhere.
3. Apply swiftly to the wood in straight strokes along the grain, backwards and forwards, leaving no area uncovered.

4. Once covered, drop the cloth and pick up the dry cloth, and from where you started applying the stain first, smooth out.

NOTE: If you find the stain is drying too quickly for you, the smoothing cloth can be dampened with meths – not soaking wet otherwise you can create patches.

5. When smoothing out, concentrate on where the stain overlaps, as these are the areas that are likely to appear as dark streaks.

6. Leave to dry for 15–20 minutes, longer if some polish has been put in. Then go over the surface with a clean dry cloth to pick up any stain dust.

NOTE: Generally, if the preparation work has been done well, no grain will have risen. If this is not the case then a light going over with worn finishing paper should cut the raised grain – not too hard though, or this can also make for patches in the stain.

WATER-COATING

You will need the following materials: an open container filled with colour, two wide firm paintbrushes, and flitches if there are small areas to cover. It is best if the areas to be coated can be laid horizontally. Typically, water-coating will be used on backs and bases and other areas not seen, although when an inferior wood is being used, such as pine to look like mahogany or walnut, this coating can be used as a base colour.

HOW TO DO IT

1. Dip the brush into the colour, and squeeze out the excess.
2. Starting at one end, run evenly down the grain, lifting the brush off at the end. (Don't run over the end as the bristles will flick and leave the end uneven.)

Applying a stain to a cross-member.

Finishing off staining across a member.

3. Continue along the surface until finished.
4. If the covering is not sufficient, leave to dry for at least 30 minutes before adding a second coat.
5. Once dry, brush off any dust with a stiffish brush.
   NOTE: I find a wallpaper-hanging brush good for this job as it is fine-haired but just about the right stiffness, and its long bristles seem to lift dust out of the grain and cracks.

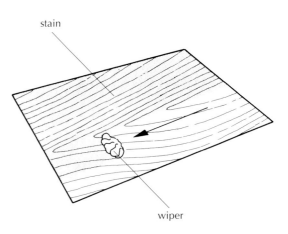

How to apply water pigment and aniline stains.

WATER PIGMENT AND ANILINE STAINS

These stains can be applied with a brush or a cloth (mouldings and fiddly bits are easier with a brush). Three cloths are needed and a container holding the stain. Fold the cloths into even pads.

HOW TO DO IT

1. Saturate the cloth with stain and apply swiftly to the surface in even sweeps with the grain.
2. Once covered, even out the stain using the same cloth, keeping the surface wet all over. The longer you prolong this process the darker it will get until it reaches the darkest that this concentration will allow.
3. Changing to a clean dry cloth, wipe over the surface in straight sweeps with the grain, picking up surplus stain.
4. Turn the pad over to a clean dry side, or pick up another cloth and continue to wipe the surface dry; this time concentrate on the stain overlaps and smears.
5. Leave to dry for at least 30 minutes; another coat can then be added, of the same stain or any other colour. Do not mix mediums, however, such as spirit

and oil. Although chemical stains can be mixed with water, it is best to lay the chemical on before the water stain, as the water in the stain can weaken the first colour.

OIL STAINS

These take the longest to dry and so are easier to apply. Use the same process as with water stains, though remember that the longer you leave these on the surface the darker the wood will get; more stain can be added while you are working, equally you can add more when the first coat is dry.

All the above stains will show their true colour – what they will be like under a transparent finish – as you are wiping them smooth and there is a slight gloss left, just before they are absorbed into the wood and start to dry. This lasts for a few seconds so you need to be watchful. Once dry, the surface can look quite different from what you are expecting, and only when you apply a finish will that hoped-for colour come back – so don't panic and add more stain than you really need.

CHEMICAL STAINS

These come in two distinct forms, the crystals such as potassium permanganate, and liquids such as ammonia and acids. First I will cover the crystalline form, and then the others, because application is quite different. There are several stains which come as crystals, and all of them are applied in the same way.

THE CRYSTALLINE FORM

As already suggested, it is wise to have not too strong a mixture for these stains as they are more controllable when they are weaker. They are applied and wiped dry in the same way as the water and oil stains, and the chemical itself will only work while it is active. It will be neutralized with the tannic acid in the wood, so more solution will be needed to keep the reaction going until the desired colour is reached.

Once it is achieved, wipe dry, quickly smoothing out lines, and the colour change will stop. This is most useful when there are light areas within the surface that you want to even out; you can concentrate on these bringing them in line with the other areas. But a word of warning: don't be too strict on them, otherwise edges can form which are not easy to mask – where light meets dark the join must be feathered to prevent hard edges occurring.

This is done using the brush or cloth with which you applied the stain, but when it has been nearly depleted of it. Before the stain in the surrounding areas has a chance to dry, sweep the cloth or brush lightly over the wet outer edges to blur them, moving diagonally outwards. When they are blurred enough, take the dry cloth and dry out the surface, moving the cloth in the direction of the grain.

AMMONIA

Ammonia darkens all woods and should be used with caution. It can be used on its own, and in conjunction with other water and chemical stains (*see* stain list). It is not advisable to put it directly onto the wood neat, although when mixed with another

A fuming tent. The container in the bottom holds ammonia.

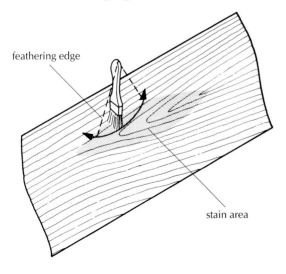

feathering edge

stain area

Feathering out.

stain in a diluted form it can be. When using by itself, this should be either in a very weak solution or via fuming. The latter process always used to be carried out in an enclosed space called a fuming cupboard, though these days the use of plastics makes a cupboard redundant and a simple plastic tent enclosing the piece to be fumed is adequate.

Fuming is a method of staining oak to give it that rich dark brown or blackened look. Although other woods can be given this treatment, it is invariably reserved for oak. The method is to enclose a piece in an airtight area, laying an open tray of ammonia at the base. The ammonia used for the purposes of fuming should be commercial .88; this is full strength and relates to its specific gravity.

The fumes spread throughout the area and slowly turn the wood darker, slow being the operative word; the process usually takes from four to twelve hours. Once the wood has reached the desired darkness, it is released from the enclosure. This is why plastic tents are so useful, because the progress of the change can actually be seen. If the piece has drawers these should be removed and stacked in the tent with the piece; doors should be left open. Sometimes a piece has woods that vary from each other, in which case not all of them will darken at the same speed. When this happens (and chairs are a typical case), remove the piece from the tent as soon as parts of the wood can be seen to have reached the desired colour, and seal these with a couple of coats of polish. When dry, return to the tent and continue to fume.

The cabinet or tent should only be opened when the workshop is well ventilated and a mask is worn. Any ammonia left should be poured back into a sealed bottle. This chemical is harmful to both skin and the respiratory system, and great care must be taken. Also the piece that has been fumed should be left for a day to 'sweeten' because the fumes will hang around the wood.

NITRIC ACID

This chemical is one of the best stain processes, never letting me down, but still surprising me in its results. It can be used in two ways: cold, with or without the 'A' solution of the 'A' & 'B' bleach; or with a hot air gun, because it is heat-sensitive. **Warning**: Nitric acid is very toxic: handle with the utmost care and by an open window. Always have a bowl of saturated salt and a bowl of water close to hand, and wear a plastic apron. If you splash it onto your garment, remove it and then neutralize.

HOW TO DO IT

First Method:
You will need the following materials: nitric acid (20–30 per cent); 'A' solution of the 'A' & 'B' bleach; sodium chloride (saturated salt solution), lukewarm water; plenty of rags (colour-fast); swab sticks (as described in the bleaching section of the previous chapter); rubber gloves; goggles; and mask.

1. Evenly and with the grain, apply the 'A' solution for ten minutes, or until it has darkened.
2. Evenly and with the grain, apply the nitric acid with a swab stick; do not leave puddles of liquid on the wood. Leave to dry.
   NOTE: It may start to smoke, and over an hour, slowly change colour.
3. When the desired colour has been reached (20–40 mins), wash with salt solution and wipe off the surplus. If the colour does not reach the desired tone, apply a second coat after adding the salt solution.
4. Wash over with warm water, and then dry off with rags.
5. If the colour is much brighter than the surrounding area, this can be adjusted by applying a coat of potassium bichromate.

NOTE: It must be realized that the nitric colouring may have to be adjusted by other stains, and as long as the area worked on is lighter than the colour to be matched, this can be done quite easily.

Tips

1. If working on new veneer, make sure the glue is completely cured. I leave it for at least a week, to avoid the acid migrating down to the glue, which it will if there is still some moisture left in the glue and veneer. It will eat animal glue, causing delamination of the veneer.

2. When working on small patches, the surrounding area can be masked with polish (two coats) and the acid can be applied with a small nylon brush.

Second Method:
You will need the following materials: nitric acid, heat gun, saturated salt solution, cloth and swabs, warm water, gloves and goggles.

1. Apply a coat of nitric acid with a swab, evenly and with the grain, until the whole area is moist but not pooling with the solution.

2. Using a preheated hot air gun, start to move the nozzle slowly over the chemical a few inches above the surface. (Do not actually hover over one area because you may scorch the wood.) The colour should change as if by magic, and with practice it is possible to chase the colour-change along the surface of the wood. Once the whole area is completed, if it needs to be lighter, add another coat.

3. This should leave the treated surface slightly brighter than the area to be matched. This brightness will be cooled by the saturated salt solution, and then the wash of warm water.

4. If the colour has too orange a hue, then a saturated solution of oxalic acid should be applied before neutralizing with the salt water, or after neutralizing, add a coat of potassium bichromate.

5. If a cooler look is needed, then a solution of acetic acid and iron can be added; this needs to be made several days before it is usable, but once made, it can be stored in sealed bottle. Prepare it as follows: to one quart of acetic acid (30 per cent), add a handful of clean steel wool, shredded into the liquid; seal, give it a good shake and leave to stand. Check daily, giving it a shake as well until the wire wool dissolves.

6. After applying the solution, use the heat gun in the same way as with the nitric.

7. Use the salt solution to neutralize, and then wash with warm water. Leave to dry.

All this water and acid will tend to raise the grain on both the first and the second methods, so a finish sanding will be needed. Do this with a flow of air moving across the surface and *away* from you, and wear a mask, because the slightest bit of dust with unneutralized acid on it will be reactivated by the moisture in your throat and lungs. *Do not be blasé about these chemicals.*

EARTH PIGMENTS IN POLISH

As mentioned before, these are more of a paint than a stain, and the technique needs a little practice to 'get your eye in' because the colour when dry will be slightly darker. This process can be used either on bare wood after the main staining of the whole

A patch that has been over coloured.

area has been done, or within the polishing sequence. If the whole area is stained first, then a coat of polish is advisable to seal the stain as a little abrasion will be necessary on the paint patches, and an unprotected stained surface will more than likely lighten if sanded, leaving a light-halo around the work.

A scorch mark made by a cigarette is one example. Study a large area around the mark and find the lightest colour within the wood. (If any wood is looked at minutely it will be found to contain many tones and tints of colour.) It is a selection of these tints and tones that will be used to conceal the mark.

Another thing that must be taken into consideration is the direction from which you are looking at a piece when colouring, as wood changes colours and shades according to the direction and angle of view, and also the direction and angle from which the sun is striking the surface. It is important to choose one direction to work from when colouring out, and to stick to that position, because the colour you apply will not change like the wood – take, for example, a chest of drawers you would stand in front of; although a table which may be viewed from all sides is more difficult and a little compromise will be needed.

The drawers of a chest should be worked on in the position they sit, with the face of the drawer being vertical.

To return to the cigarette mark: starting with the lightest colour and using a medium-fine pencil brush, stroke the colour over the mark in the direction of the grain. Don't attempt to colour out the whole mark at this point; also, the coloured strokes should continue a little way past the edges of the mark. Try and reflect the nature of the wood.

TIP: Don't try and copy the wood as though you are imitating wood grain, but imitate the nature or *movement* of it. If you stand back about 18in–24in (45cm–60cm) while painting you will find this much easier to do.

When the first coat is dry, rub it over gently with a worn 400 grade paper, and then with 0000 steel wool. It may happen that some of the colour will be removed, but don't worry: apply some more of the same colour in strokes like the last, and so on until the mark disappears. Try not to overwork the piece or add too much colour at a time,

Colouring-out mark in wood.

as the polish within the colour will tend to build up and leave a raised area that is hard to conceal when finishing. When painting what looks like the black grain pores, don't use a pure black but mix a little colour with it. The only time one can get away with pure black is when ebonizing or painting in a black or ebony line – and even then I would hesitate to use a pure black. By adding a little colour to it you will be surprised at the difference it makes – it makes it live.

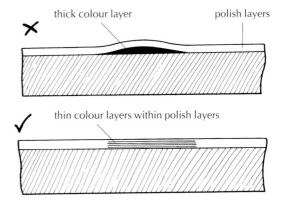

Build-up of colour.

STAINING INVOLVING INLAYS AND MARQUETRY

It is necessary to consider the problems of over-darkening inlays and marquetry with stains, as these decorations are generally of light woods, and the purer their colours can be kept the better. One particular stain is useful for this: bichromate of potash. This leaves a yellow colour until it comes into contact with light (not direct sunlight) but will be found to be slower on the inlays than on other woods surrounding them in shading them darker. On mahoganies this stain will give a richer red to the wood, and even on walnut and oak the colours will darken and become richer.

The problem is that this stain will not cover the variety of colouring that you will need, so another way of protecting the decoration is needed. This is carried out with a steady hand, a pencil brush, and white or bleach polish. Two coats are needed to be sure of a good mask; once the polish has dried, clean up any deformity of line by scraping gently with a sharp chisel. The only type of stain that cannot be used for this process are the spirit stains, as the solution will soften the polish and allow the colour to enter into the body of the polish or even into the wood itself.

Gently rub and smooth down any nibs and imperfections in the polish, before staining. Once the staining has been done and is dry, polishing can commence.

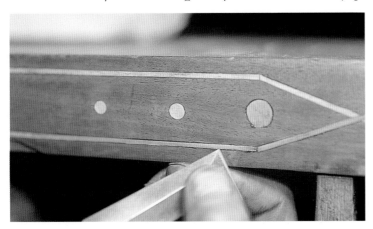

Cleaning edge of stringing after masking with polish.

The table (*below*) constitutes a small guide to the most popular woods. It should not be treated as gospel, because each staining process must be carried out as a small experiment, expecting the colour to do its job properly, but not being surprised should some adjustment be needed.

One last useful colouring procedure: when a piece is stripped back, it loses all the dirt formed on corners, carvings and other out-of-the-way places where the waxing and buffing rags could not reach down through the ages. These darkened areas form an expected part of an antique, and when missing, show up the piece as being repolished.

To re-institute this, after the first coat of polish has been applied and rubbed down ready for the next, apply a stiff concentrate of Van Dyke brown over these areas. Allow to dry a little, and then with a clean rag, rub off. Ball the rag up so that when it goes over the piece it will not go into the out-of-the-way places, only hitting the proud parts. Hey presto! your areas of age are back.

Wood	Colour desired	Stain
Mahogany	Red	*Chem*, bichromate of potash
		Oil stain, red mahogany
		Water stain, mahogany aniline
Mahogany	Orange *(typical Victorian)*	Chem, potassium permanganate
		Water stain, chestnut aniline
		Spirit Stain, Bismark brown and touch of yellow
Mahogany	Chippendale *(rich dark)*	*Chem*, dilute solution of ammonia
		Water stain, Van Dyke brown
		Spirit stain, oak and walnut mixed
		Oil stain, dark mahogany
		Water wash, burnt umber
Walnut	Med/brown *(typical Victorian)*	*Chem*, potassium permanganate with weak ammonia
		Water stain, Van Dyke brown
		Spirit Stain, Walnut
		Oil stain, Walnut stain
Walnut	Golden *(typical on period piece)*	Known as 'God's own colour', *Chem*, nitric acid methods
Oak	Light	*Chem*, potassium permanganate
		Water stain, Van Dyke brown, weak
		Spirit stain, oak, dilute
		Oil stain, light oak
Walnut	Medium	*Chem*, potassium permanganate and dilute ammonia
		Water stain, Van Dyke brown, medium
		Spirit stain, oak, medium
		Oil stain, oak, medium
Walnut	Dark	*Chem*, ammonia (fumed)
		Water stain, Van Dyke brown, and ammonia
		Spirit stain, oak, walnut and Touch of Black
		Oil stain, dark oak

sixteen

FINISHING: POLISHING

TYPES OF FINISH

There are three main finishes that concern polishing antiques. (Furniture from the 1920s onwards – mass-production – generally has other finishes, such as varnishes and synthetic lacquers.) These three finishes are as follows.

OIL FINISH

One of the oldest forms of finishing. Linseed oil is the preferred medium, and an oil finish has two major advantages over a wax or shellac finish. The finish will not crack or blister like shellac finishes, nor will it show marks such as water rings, which are often found in others. So why is it not used more often? Because it is very labour intensive and takes several weeks of daily application to get a good finish; and although this finish is durable, it leaves a dull shine and can never be brought to a gloss like the others. The finish also needs replenishing from time to time. In the words of an old friend 'An oil-finished surface is never finished!' It is a continual job.

WAX FINISH

Wax finishes have been applied to furniture for many centuries, and are the backbone of finishes on country furniture. It is also labour intensive to create a deep gloss finish, and it takes many years to accomplish a finish such as one may come across on refectory tables in some of the great old houses.

SHELLAC FINISH

The best known of the shellac finishes is 'French polish'. This was introduced into English cabinet making at about the end of the 18th century, so to shellac finish a piece dating before this time would be incorrect. Why have I written shellac finish and not French polish? Because French polish is really a technique and not just a medium. When asking for French polish in a shop, you will be sold a form of shellac, but it must be understood that you have not specified the type of shellac you want. *This material comes in many types and quality and can be specific to the piece being worked on.*

What is Shellac?
Shellac is a resin substance from the Far East. This material has been known for about 25 centuries, although it has not been imported into Europe for more than 200 years. The name shellac comes from Lac, an animal-formed substance, and is the only known animal resin. Shellac resin is also used in some old recipes to make many types of varnish.

What is French Polish?
French polish is another type of varnish, the main difference being in the way that it is applied. Generally, varnishes are laid on with a brush, and a high finish is obtained with only a few coats, whereas French polish is applied with a rubber in many thin layers. The application, apart from rubbing down between coats, which both varnish and French polish needs, differs in

that the latter has three main stages to build a proper surface.

HOW TO APPLY AN OIL FINISH

There are two main recognized materials used in this process; either raw or boiled linseed oil, and turpentine. Also, a rag to apply, another to rub it in and off, and plenty of effort.

Some experts advocate raw linseed oil, others boiled, while still others advise a mixture of the two. I believe it is a question of habit. Turpentine is added, and this helps the oil to dry more quickly.

1. Put the required amount of linseed oil into a container and gently simmer for 15–20 mins, making sure the mixture does not boil.
2. Take off the heat and add one eighth of turpentine to the oil, stir in, and allow to cool.
3. Using a small rag, apply the oil to the surface of the wood, but do not leave it to saturate the wood by allowing it to form puddles.
4. Choose a piece of felt or flannel and wrap it around a smooth brick or other suitable heavy block. A brick is useful as this can be heated and will help to dry out the oil.
5. Using the weight of the block, apply pressure and rub continuously over the surface until all the oil has been absorbed into the wood and the surface feels dry.
6. Apply a coat daily every day for several weeks. You will find the wood will absorb all the oil. It takes patience and hard graft to bring it up to a glow.
    NOTE: that an oiled surface will always take more applications, and will only get better. Friction is an aid, and the more you can create without scratching the surface the better. When applying the daily coats, make sure the surface is dusted beforehand, but do not cover after an application. Let it breathe.

HOW TO APPLY A WAX FINISH

This is as simple a process as an oiled finish, and is applied in a similar way. Most restorers seem to have their own recipe, but these

Method of oiling.

do not differ widely. There are several makes on the market that are good and reliable. It is not much cheaper to make your own, but here is a good recipe:

The list of ingredients is short: beeswax, turpentine and, if a colour is needed, earth pigment colours can be used. Resin can be added to harden the wax, but it is better and easier without. The wax with resin added can be used as a first wax coat if any woodworm holes are showing, which will work as a filler and, once hardened, can hide the holes. Then a more malleable wax mixture can be added to bring up the shine. If resin is used, it must be a very small amount or the wax becomes nearly impossible to work.

Another wax that can be added in small amounts is carnuba wax, which is easily obtainable. It does make the working-up process of the wax a little harder but it gives a brilliant gloss to the finish, and is sometimes used by woodturners as a friction wax on its own.

MAKING YOUR OWN WAX

This is a general wax, and the ingredients marked with an asterisk can be added.
If these ingredients are added, the wax may become too stiff, so add a little more turpentine.
8 parts pure turpentine
1 part beeswax
⅛ part carnuba wax*
¹⁄₁₆ part resin* (*If this is added, leave out the carnuba wax*)
Earth pigment colour until the appropriate colour is reached.

There are two ways to make this wax, cold or hot. If carnuba wax or resin is added, the latter is best. When obtaining wax, you might find that there are two choices, pale beeswax or yellow beeswax which can be as dark as ochre. When waxing pale woods, the pale beeswax will not tone the wood, and this can be an asset. On the whole, it does not make much difference. Some people favour white candlewax. Although this is not really a true wax, it is less expensive than pure beeswax, although I find it somewhat inferior.

HOW TO DO IT

Cold Method

1. Have a container divided into nine equal parts, and fill with turpentine eight of the segments.
2. Shred the beeswax finely, and add to the turpentine until the liquid is displaced and fills all nine. Stir and leave to stand overnight.
3. By morning, the wax should be dissolved and colour can then be added, and mixed evenly in with a stick.
4. Put in a sealed container. Turpentine can melt some plastics, so be careful. It is now ready for use.

HOW TO DO IT

Hot Method

1. Measure the beeswax into a metal container and stand it in a pot of water. If any of the ingredients marked with an asterisk are going to be used, add these now. Heat slowly.
2. When it is all melted, take off the heat and pour in the turpentine; stir well with a stick, adding colour if needed at the same time. (Take right away from the hotplate before pouring as turpentine is very inflammable, especially when hot.) Leave to cool and put in a sealed container. It is now ready for use.

HOW TO APPLY WAX

1. Apply with a rag. Do not cover too many surfaces at one time.
2. Remove surplus wax with a clean rag.
3. With another clean rag or soft shoe brush, work the wax into the wood and

buff up. A shoe brush is ideal for this job, as it will pull out most of the wax from the grain which would otherwise remain filled and therefore soft for some time.

4. Finally, use a flannel or felted cloth and buff to a shine. This cloth can be heated before use to give a better shine. Remember that all this buffing is supposed to create friction and, therefore, heat.

5. Leave to harden for a day and repeat the process. This time, apply the wax with 0000 steel wool, instead of a rag. This helps key the coats together and seems to help in keeping the coats as thin as possible, which enhances the look of the wood.

6. Once a body has been built up, wax occasionally (that is, every 3–6 months) although you may buff the wood with a hot rag whenever you want.

   NOTE: You may question the theory of working with thin coats when the advice has been to build up a good body. It is better to have many thin coats than few thick coats because this creates a pool of colour (depth) rather than a thick skin of wax that could be scraped off with a finger nail. This is very apparent with some modern finishes that look as though a sheet of glass has been laid on the wood, so that one can see the finish coating more than the finished wood.

HOW TO APPLY A SHELLAC FINISH

This section deals solely with French polishing. Before getting down to brass tacks, a little background information will be helpful. Shellac is a resin, and therefore exists in a number of qualities and types, and it is also a hard substance, so how is it made into a polish? Most polishes will tone the wood with their colour, and so choosing the correct one for a particular job is most important. We can categorize shellac into several groups:

FRENCH POLISH

This can be thought of as a generic term which applies to all the following polishes. These have certain similar characteristics; only by asking for them by name will you get the ones you need. Some French polishes have additives mixed into them; gums and resins, in order to give a better body and enhance the lustre of the finished work. The colour-tone can vary from a light to mid-brown and can darken a wood considerably.

Button Polish
Also known as orange button polish, the name refers to the original way shellac was processed and shipped. When in the resin form it was in the shape of a large orange button with the stamp of the processors' name embossed in the middle. These days, it is generally ground down, as in this form it takes up less space. It is paler than French polish and more expensive, and held to be of the highest quality. Generally used for yellow and darker woods. As the secondary name implies, it has an orangey-brown tone which it will impart to the finish.

Garnet Polish
The name says it all! This polish is made from garnet shellac. It is more transparent than the first two polishes, although darker. It is used on dark, rich woods and for darkening woods where purity of tone is needed.

Coloured Polish
This can come in many colours, but is generally white or French polish which has been coloured with a spirit stain. This polish can be self-mixed. Remember, unless using a bleach polish, the colour of the polish will

modify the colour you are using, so if purity of colour is essential use bleached polish. Strain polish after mixing in colour.

Transparent Polish

This is used for pale woods. It is clear and transparent, but it is not as long lasting as the white polish (*see* next entry). It works up to a brilliant finish, although some care must be taken as it is liable to become tacky. It has been known to crack with age.

White or Bleached Polish

Where purity of tone is needed, this is the polish. It is superior to the previous polish and is used on white, light and blonde woods, inlays, marquetry and transfers, and imparts no tone of its own. It will work up a little tackier than button polish, but not as much as the transparent polish. This polish takes spirit stain colours well. Makes a good ebonizing polish.

Brush Polish

This polish is similar to French polish except that it can have gums mixed in up to 25 per cent of its resin shellac volume, making it thicker. It is used for fattening or 'bodying up' and is laid on with a polisher's mop. I do not use this polish, but stick with one polish throughout all polishing sequences.

Toppings

This is a form of glaze and is decanted from the clear residue of the white polish after it has been standing for a few days and has separated. It can be used with a brush and will leave a high shine. It is used in places where a rubber can't get in to spirit off, such as carvings and tight corners. I have known it to be used for a finish on a table top where a very bright shine was wanted, but I would not recommend it.

There are several more, but these are the main ones you will come across.

TOOLS AND OTHER MATERIALS

Apart from the tools and materials needed for staining, those needed for polishing are few. Make sure your brushes are of high quality as they will help you produce a better finish. Good brushes are expensive, but looked after properly, they will last for years, and one does not have to have every kind of brush at once.

Tools

A polisher's mop (No.12 will be adequate for beginners) – squirrel hair recommended.
A run of numbered pencil brushes (No.1–No.8).
Flat lacquer-brush, (1in is useful).

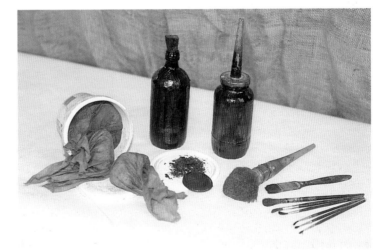

Some equipment for polishing.

Artists' stick. (This is for resting the hand on and can be simply made with 18in–24in (45cm–60cm) length of ⅜in (9mm) dowel with a pad secured to one end.)

A couple of airtight plastic wide-mouthed containers for holding polishing rubbers. (Don't use metal as this will rust due to contact with the meths.)

A rubber can last a long time and if kept in a good condition, will get better as it gets older.

Materials
Polish (white and button).
Methylated spirits.
400 and 500 finishing paper, for rubbing down. One of the oxide types is better than the carborundum wet and dry.
0000 steel wool for matting.
Quantity of clean white linen or lint-free cotton. (Old pillow cases are very good as the hair seems to have an abrasive action on the cotton, leaving it free of lint.)
Wadding. I find cotton wool tends to harden after a time; use upholsterers' unbleached wadding.
Finishing spirit. (This is not essential, and you may find it difficult to obtain.)

POLISHING

Many stories abound about the difficulty of French polishing, and in many respects they are correct. The skill has a fairly steep learning curve on the technical side, but there are other aspects to consider. Humidity and temperature play a vital part, and a dust-free atmosphere is also important. If these are not right then this will be a great handicap to a beginner.

The workshop must be warm, about 60°–70°F (15°–20°C), but not too warm as the polish will tend to get sticky when a 'body' has been built. The humidity should be in the low teens, which can be difficult to obtain in this country, especially in our winters. If the moisture level is too high,

the polish will be sluggish and slow to dry. Cold weather and high moisture-level together is a nightmare, as the polish will tend to go cloudy (Blooming) and this can mean the finish has to be removed and a fresh start made, as the cloudiness denotes moisture being trapped within the polish. There is an alternative method of removing this trapped moisture, but in unskilled hands it is very dangerous, and it should be taught one-to-one.

Dust is best removed by having an extractor fan on continuously while polishing. Don't wear a woolly jumper as this will hold dust and leave particles of fluff in the air. a separate rubbing-down area is useful if it can be managed. When dust gets into the polish, it must be rubbed out immediately once the polish is hard enough. Within the instructions I will set down drying times. These must be taken as variable, because so many factors have to be taken into consideration, and my notes can only be a guideline. The true test of when a polish is hard enough to rub down is when it dusts up under the sanding action, and does not leave polish nodules on the paper.

When a foreign body becomes trapped in the polish, one noticeable thing will happen if the polishing continues. a build-up of polish will be created around this object, and in time this will create a mound of polish (very similar to what happens around the buttress of a bridge when a river is in flood. It collects and seems to stay trapped there). If you drop your mop or brush, wash it out with meths before continuing. If you drop your polishing rubber, replace the skin (cotton cover.) Dust or fluff goes a long way, and before you know it the whole surface will be covered.

Layers and Coats
This may seem somewhat confusing, but there is a difference. Each time you go over an area with the rubber, a layer is laid down. Many layers can be laid before you

need to rub down the surface. Once the surface has been rubbed down, those former layers become one coat. When the polishing continues, another set of layers (coat) is started. This is why it can be difficult to answer a layman when he asks how many coats it will take, as sometimes the number of layers per coat will dictate the actual number of coats needed. I try to lead people away from the idea of counting coats and to introduce the idea that they use their eyes to determine what stage has been reached in the polishing process.

The beginner tends to be timid when rubbing down a surface, and mourn the idea of removing all the polish they have just laid! My answer is 'What must be done must be done', and if the rubbing-down process is not properly done, almost to the point of breaking through the surface, then the finished product will never be as good.

Flattening and Matting

When rubbing down a finish, there are two definite sequences. The first is flattening, and this is done with finishing paper. As the body of the polish is built, areas within the surface will acquire more layers than others, and also pips of dust will arise. So the first concern is to level out or flatten the whole surface. This flattening will consequently smooth the surface as well. This rubbing-down must be done straight with the grain, unless part of the area is cross-banding; then the major part of the surface dictates the direction to be rubbed down. Use the same direction as when finishing the wood.

You could use a block, but I prefer the spread palm of the hand. If a block is used, make sure it is made of cork or felt, and that the edges are rounded and have no sharp corners, as these can scratch the finish. As the paper fills with dust, continuously slap it out, using the flat of the hand.

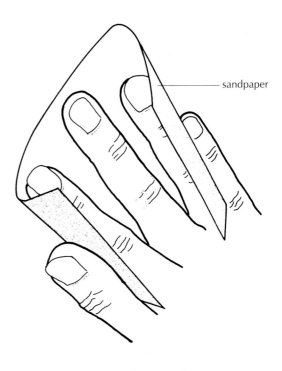

sandpaper

How to hold sandpaper without a block.

If the polish is still too soft, hard lumps of polish will be picked up on the paper. These lumps can score and damage a surface. If this happens, these scores must be rubbed out.

Once the paper has done its job, a matting of the surface is necessary. This is done with 0000 steel wool. Matting is needed for three separate reasons. Although the paper has flattened the surface, there will still be specks of shine where the pores or grain are. These must be matted to create a key for the next coat. The paper removes the finish, leaving fine scratches. These too have to be removed. Finally, the surface is rubbed down, layers will be removed either wholly or in part. Where an edge of a layer is left it must be removed or feathered-out. If left, the edges of the layers will create 'steps' within the polish. These may show only when the light strikes the surface in a particular

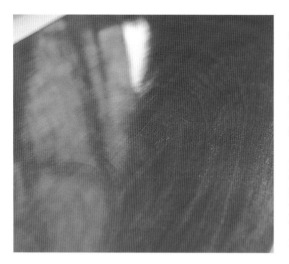

A 'tail' of polish left by a rubber (or 'track').

direction. The matting procedure should leave the surface with a matt-sheen.

NOTE: The importance of good rubbing down cannot be stressed sufficiently. What may seem to be an unnoticeable hairline scratch can become a glaring fault once covered with polish. One of the properties of French polishing is that the finish magnifies the beauty of the wood and simultaneously shows up any faults.

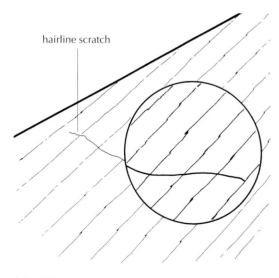

hairline scratch

A hairline scratch.

When rubbing down, position yourself at the end of the work and work down the grain. If you worked from the side, there may be a tendency to create a windscreen-wiper action, and this will leave an arc of scratches on the surface which are difficult to remove with matting and, if neglected, are horribly noticeable.

A quantity of steel wool which covers the palm of your hand should be lightly balled. Once the wool becomes compacted and bitty, throw it away and use a new piece. Don't try and economize on steel wool. The ends of the surface are particularly at risk, so inspect these areas closely.

Raw Linseed Oil (or Clear Polishing Oil)

This is used with the polishing rubber to reduce friction between it and the surface being polished. It is removed at a stage when the surface is being brought up to a shine and is not an additive to the polish. A little is put on the base of the rubber – the word 'little' cannot be overstressed, as too much can cause other problems such as the failure to bring up a shine; sweating, where beads of oil appear after some time; and eventual weakening of the finish, and cracking. Raw linseed oil is frequently used and easy to obtain, although most polishers prefer clear/white polishing oil as this is lighter and is removed more easily.

The Rubber

The importance of a good rubber cannot be overstated. A rubber should be firm but not hard. It must be capable of containing enough polish so that one is not everlastingly refilling it, and its shape must enable the polisher to polish in tight areas. Most importantly, it must be made in such a way as to retain its shape throughout its life. There are two parts to the rubber; the inner wadding that shapes the rubber and acts as a reservoir to hold the polish, and the covering made of linen or lint-free cotton that is the skin. This has several functions; when folded around the wadding in the correct fashion, it will hold the wadding in shape. It is also a smooth barrier between the wadding and the surface finish, but it allows a free flow of polish to be transmitted to the surface from the wadding.

Lastly, it is held together by twisting the ends around each other and creating a form of tourniquet which transmits a light pressure on the wadding and so keeps the polish close to the surface of the rubber. The added pressure when the rubber touches the surface to be polished is enough to draw the polish to the surface of the rubber and so lay it on the surface. When the skin wears, replace it with a new cloth; although the longer the skin can be kept perfect, the better, as this too improves work.

HOW TO MAKE IT

1. Take a piece of sheet wadding about 6in × 6in (15cm × 15cm) and carefully remove the paper.
2. By following the diagrams below and overleaf, gently fold it following the steps.
3. Once formed into a pad, mould the edges into a pear or egg-shaped form. The folded opening of the pad is the top.

Making a rubber (shaping the wadding).

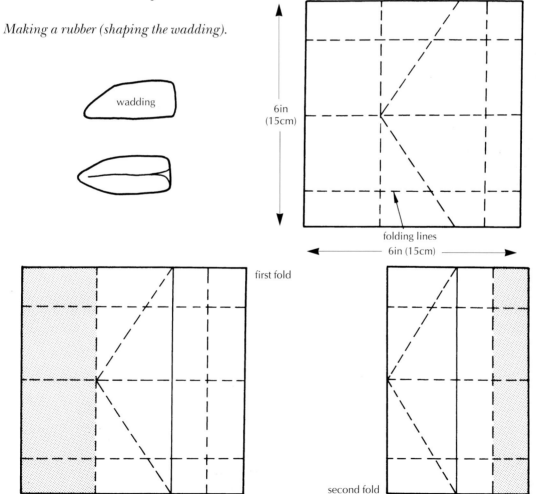

wadding

6in (15cm)

folding lines

6in (15cm)

first fold

second fold

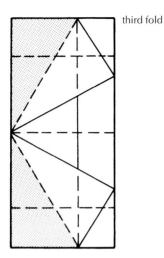

third fold

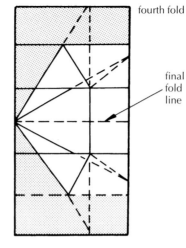

fourth fold

final
fold
line

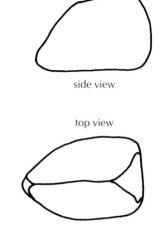

side view

top view

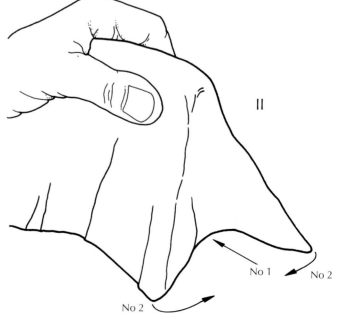

I

wadding

Making a rubber (folding the covering).

4. Take a lint-free piece of cloth about 6in (15cm) square. Place in the centre of the open palm. Place the wadding centrally with the pointed end forward, having two-thirds of the uncovered space of the cloth at the back, leaving one-third in front of the point. (At all times your hands must be clean and dust-free.)

5. Fold the front part of the cloth over the pointed end of the wadding.
6. Hold the folded cloth firmly with your thumb and fold first one side then the other towards the centre of the cloth catching each with the thumb.

II

No 1

No 2

No 2

7. Draw the back end of the cloth up and catch all the loose ends of the cloth with your free fingers, and twist the cloth around itself. The result should look from the side like a shoe with the pointed end of the rubber the toe.

NOTE: The pad, or base, of the rubber must be wrinkle-free, otherwise it will mark the surface and no amount of application will bring up a good finish.

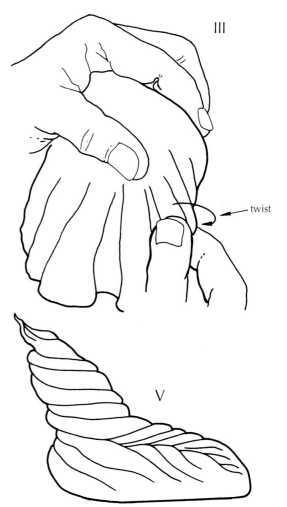

III

twist

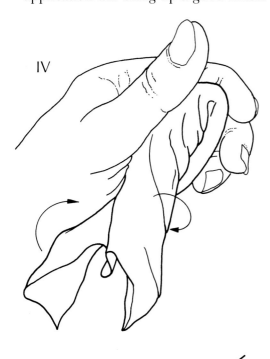

IV

V

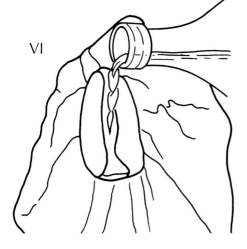

VI

Once rubber is loaded with polish, it will be easier to maintain the shape. This is loaded by untwisting the cloth and pouring the polish onto the wadding. At first, the wadding will need to be massaged, until the polish has penetrated right through it. The rubber should be fully loaded and, once the cloth has been retwisted, the polish should not come dripping out. If it does, hold it over a container and by twisting the cloth a little more, squeeze the excess polish out.

Polisher's Mop

This is a special brush for laying on the first couple of coats. The best quality is made of fine squirrel hair and is round in shape; with a slight dome to the end of the hairs. Because of its shape it can hold a considerable amount of polish without dripping, and releases the polish more slowly than a flat brush.

Great care should be taken of the mop. It should never be left standing in any liquid, but suspended above or in it. To clean shellac polish out, wash the mop thoroughly in meths, holding it at arm's length and swinging it rapidly, causing centrifugal force. Then wash it in lukewarm water with a little soft soap, which must be thoroughly rinsed out. Shake out the excess water. Take a double band of clean paper and wrap carefully around the hairs, making sure you do not trap or twist any of the hairs. Hold the paper band in place with a not too tight-fitting rubber band, and hang upside-down until dry. This will ensure that the mop holds its proper shape when dry.

Storage of a mop.

If the brush has been washed and is still damp with water when needed again, wash for several minutes in meths, shake out and hang. After a little time the meths will have dried the brush.

COMMENCING POLISHING

There are three stages to polishing a surface: bodying-in, bodying-up and spiriting-off.

Bodying-in or 'Fatting up'

This is essentially to seal the wood and fill the grain, and is the foundation for the subsequent stages, and as such it is important to get right. The reason for this stage is twofold: to fill the grain with polish and to create a film on the wood which when dry, can be brought up to a brilliant shine. The polish film should be a thin one, but the pores must all be filled, even if a grain-filler is used. The absorption within the pores will be greater than the surrounding wood, and so when the first couple of light layers are applied there may be a slight sinkage of the polish film into these areas.

To Start: Load the mop with polish and then scrape the excess out of the mop onto the edge of the polish container. Because shellac is not self-levelling like ordinary paints, the way one uses the mop is slightly different from using an ordinary paintbrush. The polish must be laid at once, and not 'worked-out', so it is important that the mop is not too wet. Another reason for not loading the mop too much is that an overloaded mop moving along the surface of the wood creates a mini bow-wave like a boat. This bow-wave will leave ripples of polish along the brushed edge. These lines are called tails or trails. For the same reason, the mop should not be put down on the surface and then brushed, but should be moving as it gently lands on the surface, and, when finishing, should be slowly brought off the surface before stopping.

I always explain the action as being similar to that of an aeroplane landing and taking off, without the bumps. Always work off the edges; this will necessitate starting within the area, and so a light landing of the mop is important, and should be practised. Starting from one side, bring the mop onto the wood about a third of its length away from the end, and cover gently but smartly, running with the grain. As the mop reaches the end, ease the pressure and lift directly off the edge. Bring back the mop and gently land where the mop first started and run it in the opposite direction until it reaches the other end, lifting off as before. Continue across the surface until the whole area is covered. Where the brush misses, only fill in large gaps and do this smartly. If you disturb the surface after the polish becomes tacky, the hairs will have a tendency to stick to the surface, thus damaging it. Leave to dry.

This coat should take about 30 minutes before it can be rubbed down, although it must not be rubbed down until, when sanding, the action makes the surface dusty. This effect is called dusting up and shows that the surface is truly dry. Flatten down with 400 paper, running with the grain with a light pressure. Any lumps, tails or foreign matter must be rubbed out, but try not to go through the surface, as this may lighten the stain, especially a water stain. All faults must be removed, and they will be inevitable until you have mastered the mop. Matte the surface, dust off with a dusting-brush, and wipe over with a clean rag.

If, on close inspection, several areas are through and the stain has lightened, use a diluted form of your chosen stain, and go over these areas again. Wipe off and dry quickly. If spirit stain is used, be careful as a dark edge can form where the stain touches the edge of the polish.

Once the atmosphere is free of dust, a second coat is added. This must be done

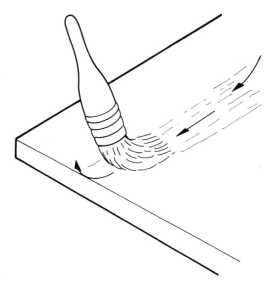

Applying shellac with a mop.

speedily and thoroughly. Leave no area uncovered as this will create problems. The second coat will have softened the undercoat and any patching you have to do will cause the surface to drag. For the same reason, this coat will take a little longer to dry before flattening and matting can take place.

For the third coat, use the rubber well loaded but not to the extent that it will leave tails. Before commencing, take the rubber in your normal working hand and sharply slap the base of the rubber on the clean back of the other hand several times. This will flatten the base of the rubber and broaden the contact surface. Start at one end, using the landing/take-off technique. Cover the surface running straight with the grain. The rubber should be held firmly, but not so much so that the hand and wrist are stiff and inflexible. Contact must be light but sure and the movement along the surface of an even speed. At no time should you stop, leaving the rubber resting on the surface, as when you take it off all the previous layers can be torn away with it. Slightly

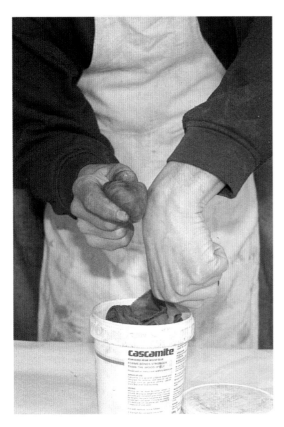

Flattening base of rubber.

overlap each pass with the last, making sure to come off the end lightly. Pressure must be resisted at this point as the whole idea is to lay even, fine layers. Once recovered, start at the beginning and cover the whole area again, repeating until the rubber drags. Then stop! This means the rubber is starting to stick to the surface and will damage all you have done if you continue.

Two or three passes of the rubber should be possible before dragging occurs, depending on the size of the surface. I try and work on two or more pieces of furniture at once and alternate between them; once one drags I step to the next and so on.

After three or four layers have been laid, the action of the rubber should change from straight sweeps with the grain to circular and figure-of-eight action. There are two reasons for this. Firstly, using these movements across the surface will mean that you need only one landing and take-off to cover the whole area. The landing and take-off areas are where most of the faults will appear. This will eliminate most of them at one stroke. Secondly, by doing circular or figure-of-eight motions,

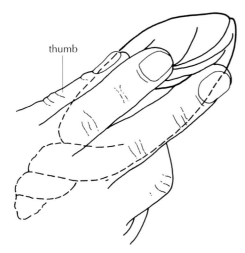

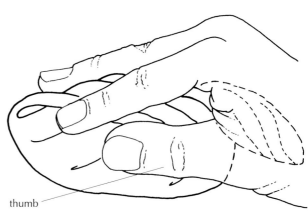

thumb

thumb

Correct way to hold a rubber.

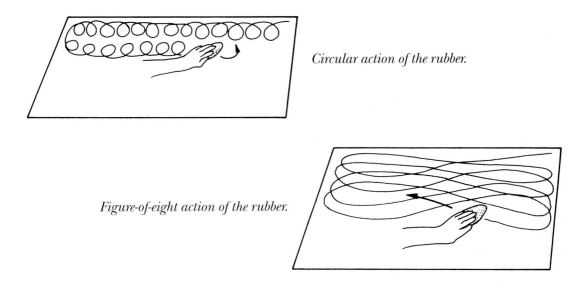

Circular action of the rubber.

Figure-of-eight action of the rubber.

at some point in the circle the rubber passes across the grain and not with it. This greatly helps to fill the grain. When doing circular movements, the tendency is to swivel your hand. This will cause the flat base of the rubber to lift and run on its edge. This will increase the pressure on the rubber, causing more polish to be squeezed out onto the surface, leaving tails. Try to avoid this. The whole base must be kept in contact at all times, and so a conscientious effort must be made to recognize this natural fault.

Carry on laying the polish, stopping and resting when it drags. From time to time, check that the rubber is well loaded with

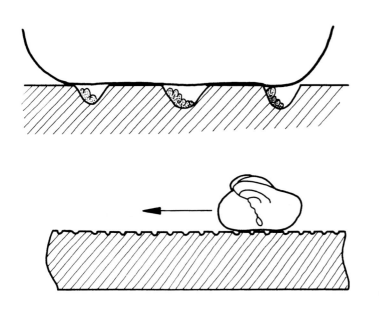

Polish filling grain.

197

polish, by tapping its base on the back of your hand. Do not touch the base or hold the rubber with the base in the palm of your hand even if your hand is clean, as your body oils can be deposited on the surface. When resting the work and not using the rubber, put it away in the sealed container or the base will become hard and scratchy.

When a thick film of polish has built up and no amount of resting seems to stop, drag for more than a moment. Leave it for a couple of hours, and then flatten and matt down. Continue until all of the grain is filled. Once there are no more grain pores open, leave for at least six hours. I prefer to leave overnight, because as the polish hardens it will shrink and settle down into the pores.

NOTE: Before each flattening down, it will seem that headway is slow and the pores are not being filled. This is far from being the case. It seems that way because the area above the pores is also gaining in height. When flattened, the true state will become apparent.

Because of the nature of the wood, some areas of the surface will be made up of more open grain than others. These more open areas will need more concentration if the whole is to be filled evenly.

Before the next part of finishing is started the whole job needs to be flattened and matted to such an extent that the polish film is left thin. The state of the surface should be quite flat and dead, with no specks of shine showing.

Bodying-up

This term describes building up a body of polish which can then be brought to a shine. Take great care at this stage as any faults that are made and left in this section remain for its entire life, trapped like an 'insect in amber'. Dust must be eliminated

Flattening and matting. The right hand edge has a finer sheen and is less scratchy looking; this has been matted.

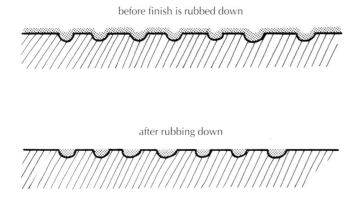

before finish is rubbed down

after rubbing down

How the grain gets filled.

wherever possible. Wear a dust coat for rubbing down and remove it before polishing. Use the same rubber if it is in good condition. The cloth of a new rubber will be too fierce so is less preferable. I use several rubbers at the same time ensuring that at least one is always usable. If the edges of the rubber have become hard, leave overnight with a moist rag of meths in a sealed container, which will soften them and make them pliable.

Before starting, any out-of-the-way areas that won't get touched by the rubber can be coated with toppings. Dip a pencil brush in toppings, scrape off any excess and apply to these areas. Leave to dry for several minutes before using the rubber. This process should be done after every rubbing down until the spiriting off.

Charge the rubber with the same polish as previously used. This time the rubber should be fairly moist but not too wet. A little polish goes a long way so don't over-charge it. It is an assumption of most beginners that the more polish used, the quicker the finish will be obtained. Too wet, and the surface will become ridged and irregular, but too dry and the rubber will drag and pull the surface. This is a matter for experiment and experience, so practise, practise.

When starting, dip your finger into some oil (raw linseed oil or polishing oil) and dab it onto the base of the rubber. Start polishing with light circular and figure-of-eight movements and cover the surface. You will notice that a smeary trail is left behind. Do not be alarmed. This is caused by the oil and will be removed later. When a rubber starts to drag, check that it is not too dry. If it is not, do not add polish but add a drop more oil. Work with the rubber until it becomes dry and then recharge a little and carry on polishing lightly until the finish starts to drag. Stop, leave to dry for a few minutes and then straighten out the strokes, adding the last layer to run with the grain.

Leave for at least 4–6 hours, or overnight, to allow for shrinkage. Using 400 paper that has been rubbed with another piece to take off the bite, gently flatten down and then matte. Dust off and apply another coat in the same way. It should take between three and four of these coats according to the grain. A wood like beech or birch will come up quicker than mahogany, but it very much depends on the discretion of the polisher.

On the last coat there is one alteration. Start with a moist rubber, working as before. When the rubber begins to dry, instead of recharging with polish, add meths to the rubber. This must not be added through the top of the rubber like the polish.

HOW TO DO IT

Do this away from the work.

1. Take a half-full bottle of meths.
2. With the top off, hold upright, and place the front end of the base of the rubber firmly over the neck of the bottle.

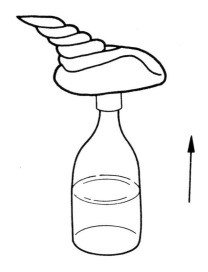

Applying spirit to the rubber.

3. With a swift jerk, shake the bottle upwards forcing the meths up and into the rubber.

4. Repeat, but this time at the rear of the rubber. (Never do this more than twice.)

Work the rubber until dry and repeat this action, making, lazy, long, open fig-ure-of-eights. The last time the rubber is worked, straighten out and work along the grain. This is the last operation before spiriting-off. The work must now stand overnight if possible. It will be noticed that whereas formerly the work was left with smears, the thinning of the polish through the rubber will have taken away a certain amount of the oil which has been burnt off by the spirit. This is preferable, as to leave too much oil sitting on the finish for a long period would make your task more arduous. It also slowly thins the polish in the rubber, making the layers that much thinner. Each time the meths is added to the rub-ber, the coats become thinner. Once the skin on the base goes back to its white cotton state (this takes about three times) you straighten out. This thinning of the layers will help in the spiriting-off.

Colouring-up

Even using prime wood, this is almost always necessary, as differences in tone will now be very apparent. This colouring is done on the lighter areas and the polisher needs a good eye. I do this colouring-up between the last two coats of bodying-up, although another method is to do it after bodying-up.

What is 'coloured-up'? To change or tone in light areas such as sapwood, the colour difference between the top and bot-tom rails of doors and the uprights (stiles). Because of the direction the light strikes on these parts, one or other set will be slightly darker. A section made from a dif-ferent cut of wood will also look different. Be careful not to stain *too* dark.

HOW TO DO IT

My Method:

1. Mix normal polish shellac with meths to 5–10 per cent polish to 90–95 per cent meths. Strain this mixture through a bag containing earth-pigment powders and spirit stains. For a darkish wood, umbers, siennas, and a bit of black. The way the pigments are varied will change the colour. For minute adjustment a little more spirit stain can be added after-wards. The more times the polish is strained through the pigment, the stronger the colour.

2. Put in an open container.

3. Take a 4in (10cm) square piece of lint-free cloth and wet thoroughly with meths, then wring out.

4. Fold, and fold repeatedly, keeping it square until it covers the tips of your three fingers. Where the area to be worked on is smaller still, the cloth can likewise be made so.

5. Dip into the colour and squeeze the colour through the cloth until it is not dripping.

6. When unfolding, it will be found that the inner folds are lighter than the outer ones. Choose the section that suits you. It is better to give two appli-cations than one that is too dark.

7. With a light, sure movement, run the rag over the surface along the grain to be coloured, then leave to dry. Don't go over the colour until the first coat is dry.

8. Rub gently with worn paper to take off any nibs, then brush clean.

9. Use the rubber to seal. The more spirit-stain used the more likely that some of the colour will be removed, Don't worry! Wait 30 seconds or so and go over again with the rubber. The colour will now be sealed.

10. When the polish is dry, more colour can be added if necessary.

11. Now continue with bodying-up.

The Other Method (after bodying up):
1. Mix one part polish to two parts meths.
2. Add colour in the same fashion, and put in an open container.
3. Use a small fine-hair mop or lacquer-brush and dip into the colour.
4. Scrape out excess on edge of container and, moving with the grain, apply colour. Again, use two or more coats to bring up the colour rather than one dark coat. Leave to dry between coats.
5. Rub out any nibs and then seal.
   NOTE: My method is preferable because when using the other method, one can break through the colour and leave it patchy when spiriting-off. Also, when using cloth it is easier to gauge how wet it is, as against a brush.

Other things to be coloured-out like filled holes and small wood patches can be done with fine pencil brushes.

HOW TO DO IT

1. Either use pure spirit stain or a mixture as already explained.
2. Pick correct size brush and load with colour.
3. Scrape off excess and then wipe on absorbent paper.
4. Test colour on the back of your hand. This seems to give a fairly accurate palette board. It also tells you how wet the brush is. Dry the brush until it leaves the spot on the back of your hand cold for a few seconds. Because the wood area will be small, a wet brush will deposit too much at one go and this wetness can **damage** the polish and create an edge.
5. Apply colour carefully, let dry and then seal with the rubber. Add more colour if needed when polish has dried.
6. Then continue with finishing.

Spiriting-off
For the last phase, a new rubber is made, in the same way as the polish rubber, except this time it is covered with a second piece of lint-free cloth. It is best to make this rubber the night before, and then moisten the wadding with methylated spirits. Wring out so that it is damp and leave in a plastic container overnight. A separate one from the polishing rubber is best. The beginner is advised to err on the side of dryness. Spiriting-off removes the surface of oil and removes any rubber marks by burnishing the surface, and at the same time brings up that unmistakable 'French polish' glow.

Making sure the rubber is no more than damp, apply it lightly to the surface in the same manner as in bodying-up. When the rubber starts to dry out, increase the pressure on the rubber and towards the end of this operation change the direction of the rubber so that it runs straight with the grain. It may take several applications of the rubber before the oil and marks start to disappear. Leave the surface to rest between layers and load the rubber by glugging the spirit into the rubber. As the spirit dissipates and the pressure increases you are actually burnishing the surface.

Mellowing a New Finish
The finished article should now look sparkling and bright – *too* bright one may feel for an antique. Here I would agree. If the Van Dyke Brown stain has been applied in corners and indentations of mouldings then we are almost there. But the finish seems too flashy, even brittle, to be that of an antique.

After leaving it for three or four days to harden, longer if you can, apply wax with 0000 steel wool, running straight along the grain. Buff up in the manner already described in the waxing section. Applying with steel wool should have toned down the shine. If it has not done so enough, do it again and again if needs be, until you are satisfied. It is far better to do it several times than to do it too hard with one application.

POLISHING AND PATCHING OLD FINISHES

This is specifically about repairing antiques. All the technical information already covered in this chapter is relevant now, with a little more added.

The cleaning of the finish was covered in Chapter 6, and it is only now with a full background knowledge of how that finish was created that we can proceed fully to repair such a finish.

The piece has been cleaned. If the surface is in very good order then do no more than wax it. But there may be a few badly rubbed areas, or because of crazing the top coats were cut back to get down to sound polish by the gentle application of methylated spirits. This being the case, then where it is only patches rub them smooth with 400 paper and where all the surface was cut down with meths, rub this smooth with paper also. When the patched areas are smooth, matt with steel wool over the complete surface and the other also.

Colour up any areas that have lost colour with your stain. This may even mean painting out with colours. If the patch areas are down to the wood, apply two coats of shellac with a dryish mop, feathering it out where it overlaps old polish. This is most important. When flattened, take great care to remove any steps where the new and old polish meets. If the surface cut down with meths still has its grain filled, proceed immediately to the bodying-up step of polishing and continue as described before, until finished. If the grain is open then go back a further step.

Within the patch, the grain and all this area must be concentrated on first, building up the thickness of finish to match the surrounding area. If the thickness isn't the same, it will be seen as a hollow or depression that can never really be disguised. Only when both finishes are level can the

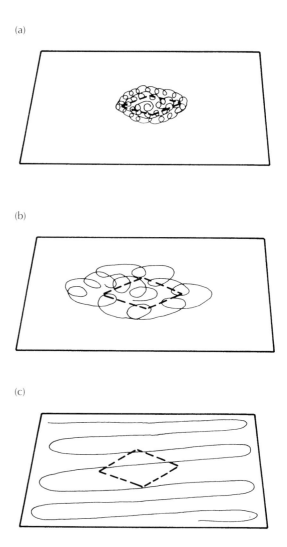

(a)

(b)

(c)

Patching-in.

whole be tackled. When working on the patched area, the edges where new and old overlap must be carefully flattened, otherwise a ridge will form which will be as distracting as a hollow. As the patch is filled, the overlap margin can increase a little. This will help disguise a single edge. Once the whole is being finished, carry on as before until completion.

REMOVAL OF WHITE RINGS

What is a white ring? It is formed when moisture is trapped on the surface of a finish for example either as under a plate of hot food which has been placed directly on the table or with insufficient protection, or if condensation is trapped beneath a plant-pot. This moisture degrades the shellac. The longer moisture is left on the surface, the deeper it goes, until it reaches the wood.

There is an abundance of recipes to remove these ugly white rings from a finish. My feeling is if a method works for you, why change to another? My mother-in-law used to swear by vigorous applications of camphorated oil, but this took a long time and much ferocious energy to work up heat. The following methods are far quicker.

The surface must first be cleaned with my mixture (*see* Cleaning). If the damaged area penetrates down to the wood, the cleaner must not be allowed to reach that patch. You may have to use a lot of elbow-grease, but it is preferable to try this gentle method first. Once cleaned out, treat as in the above section on 'Patching-in'.

The cleaner often clears rings that are not deep, but if this fails, take a spiriting-off rubber, fill it with methylated spirit and go over the area as described in the Spiriting-off section. This will invariably draw it out. If this does not work, cut back the polish with 0000 wire wool and methylated spirit. Once the ring has disappeared, treat the area as for 'Patching-in'.

seventeen

FIXTURES AND FITTINGS

BRASSWORK

Brass furniture will have to be put back on a restored piece, and some may need replacing. Wherever possible this should be done with brasswork that matches the original, and there are several very good companies that will copy pieces that are not readily supplied from a shop. Another thing that must be kept the same wherever possible is when the fitment to be replaced was cast: it should be replaced with one that is cast and not pressed out. For instance – and this is a common fault – don't have mis-matched hinges: even if they are the same size, if one is pressed and the other is cast, then this is wrong.

Always give the brasswork a gentle clean with brass cleaner, and then clean out any sediment with a toothbrush before fitting it back. There is also the question of ageing brass fittings: there is nothing worse in my eyes than over-bright brasswork. Even so, if replacements are needed it is wiser to buy bright brass fittings rather than 'antiqued', because in the latter process a colour and a lacquer has generally been sprayed on (always ask the supplier) and this may not match your originals. It is easy to age brasswork.

HOW TO DO IT

1. Find a tall, wide-mouthed jar with a re-sealable lid. Pierce several small holes in the lid.
2. Thread fine string through the holes and tie the fittings so that they hang from the lid without touching the bottom of the jar.

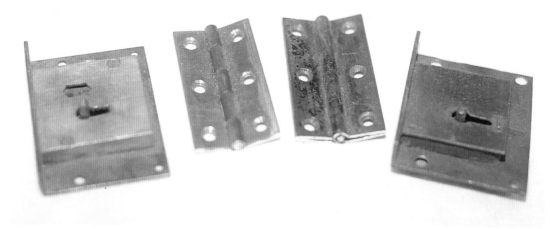

Pressed and solid brass fittings.

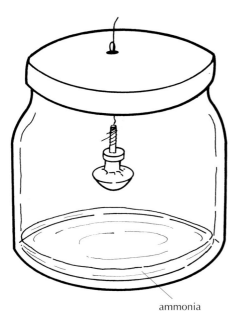

ammonia

Ageing brass.

HINGES

There are two glaring mistakes that can be made when refitting and replacing hinges: first, never use too large a screw for the hinge when it is simply the hole that has been enlarged. Instead, proceed as follows: using a softer wood than the piece, glue a tapered plug into the hole; tap in firmly, but being careful not to spread the hole or the wood may split, leaving a bulge. Offer the hinge up to its site, and tap a hole smaller than the screw.

Second, if the screws to be matched to the original hinge and screw are of a larger head than the new hinge, use a metal countersunk cutter to enlarge the countersink on the new hinge, otherwise the screw will sit proud. If an ordinary drill bit is used, the angle of the countersink will be incorrect and the screw will still sit proud.

NOTE: It is always satisfying to see screw slots aligned, but this is not really necessary unless working on a choice piece.

3. Place a little ammonia in the bottom of the jar and replace the lid with the fittings hanging; *they must not touch the liquid.*
4. It depends on the brass, but normally it changes quite quickly. Leave until the colour matches the darkest areas of the originals before removing.
5. Rinse under the tap, and dry by sponging with an absorbent cloth.
6. Buff up the high spots until you reach a good match.

NOTE: Do not leave brass being treated in this way, especially pressed or delicate work, as the ammonia will eat it away. Once, many years ago, I had to match a brass ball finial on a long-case clock. Despite instructions on how to patinize, being young and clever I decided to leave it in much longer than I had been advised. When I took it out, the piece fell apart in my hand. My boss made me pay for it, and I never did it again.

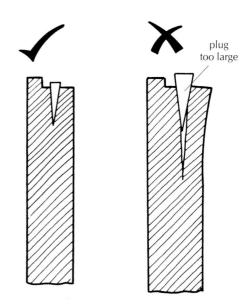

plug too large

Hazards with hinges.

LOCKS

Most pieces have lost their keys, but one doesn't need to be a great engineer to replace them. A set of needle files, and assorted small files and a small metalwork vice, are all the specialist tools you will need for cutting keys. The high-quality cast locks are generally held together with screws, whereas the plate ones are held by tangs that have been riveted over. With the rivets, simply use a small file and file the sides of the tangs until the back plate can be sprung off. There are two main types that you will come across: the back spring lock and the lever lock.

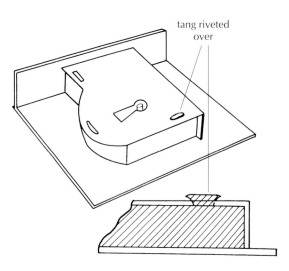

Simple lock.

BACK SPRING LOCK

This is the simplest lock to cut a key for. The lock itself consists of a face plate (a plate of metal with a flange bent up on one side with the bolt gate cut into it), a pin off-centre sticking up, and a flat ring around the pin called a ward. Riveted into the plate is a fence with another gate opposite the bolt gate in the flange. The bolt slides through these gates with an attached spring on the back edge of the bolt, also fitting through the back gate. On the back end of the front edge of the bolt are two notches. When the bolt is forward and sticking through the

front gate, the first notch will be sitting in the rear gate; when it is back, the second notch will sit into the rear gate leaving the front of the bolt flush with the face of the lock. On the same edge but forward of the notches is another, deeper-shaped notch called the talon. The lock mechanism is covered by another plate with a keyhole in it called the cap, or cover.

When cutting a key for a back spring lock make sure the blank fits smoothly onto the pin, without rattling. Next, blacken the key

Two general locks.

Back spring lock.

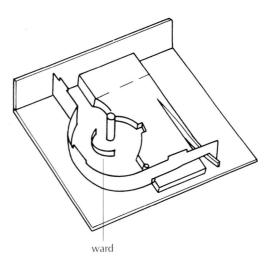

The ward.

by holding it over a candle. Push the blank onto the pin until it touches the ward ring (the little plate ring around the base of the pin). Turn the blank backwards and forwards, then remove it and cut the ward slot in the bottom. Re-carbon the end of the blank and the front edge, then place back on the pin.

With the bolt back as far as it will go, turn the key over the top of the bolt, then slide it completely home on the pin and turn it until it touches the bolt. Use a scriber to mark the edge of the blank where it comes above the bolt. When the key has been removed there will be a mark scribed on the edge of the blank, and on its end where it rode over the bolt the carbon will have been rubbed away.

File away the metal up to the scribed mark on the blank's edge, and down to the carbon on its bottom. Fit the key back into the lock and turn. It should pass smoothly into the apex of the talon of the bolt (the talon is the shaped area of the bolt that takes the key). The key may slide the bolt

forwards, but certainly not without effort. File a rounded edge on the blank where it has just been filed; this will create a rolling contact point to the talon, just like a bearing. The key should then enter the talon and lift the bolt off the back gate and slide the bolt forwards with ease, and vice versa when sliding the bolt back.

LEVER LOCK

This lock is more sophisticated than the back spring lock, having levers that catch the bolt rather than notches. The technique for cutting a key for a lever lock is similar, except that the levers are removed (keep these in order, especially if the key is being made to work several locks). Cut the blank to fit the bolt and get it working smoothly. Replace the first lever and cut the key to fit it, and so on until all the levers work in concert and allow the bolt to slide without catching. When matching a set of locks, each lever must be matched and in sequence throughout the set before cutting the key.

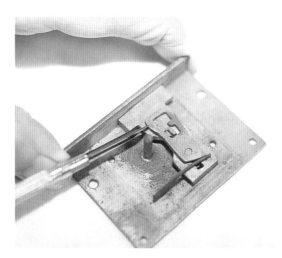

Lever lock.

Filing a lever slot in a key blank.

LEATHERS

Replacing a leather may seem a daunting task, but suppliers have made it simplicity itself; the only criterion is accuracy. Just send measurements of the area to be covered and state the colour and tooling styles desired, and the type of leather needed. There are two thicknesses, called 'leather' or 'skiver', the latter being the thinnest and for most purposes the one generally used. This is most important when restoring a writing slope, for example – it needs to be thin otherwise the box will not fit properly.

FITTING AND GLUING

The old leather should pull off fairly easily unless it has been glued with impact glue, in which case wet the leather with cellulose thinners. This will soften the glue, which will then have to be scraped. An ordinary glue will be happily removed with a hot wet rag. Leather is best glued onto wood with a heavy-duty wallpaper paste: once the surface is dry, brush on a coat of wallpaper paste and let this dry.

Lay the leather on a flat surface. It will probably have gold tooling, and a black tooling line on the outside of that; this black line indicates the actual edge, which must be checked for squareness. A slight difference will not matter as the leather can be manipulated a little.

Using a straight-edged square, cut two sides adjacent to each other. The knife should undercut slightly as on veneers.

Apply more glue evenly to the surface, making sure there are no lumps. Place the cut corner of the leather into one corner. Align one edge, and then the other, without pressing the leather too firmly in contact with the paste. Once the edges are aligned, smooth gently from that corner to the centre with a soft cloth; then from this line of contact smooth out gently to the edges; then go from the centre to the next corner, until all the area is down and there are no air bubbles showing. Using the blunt end of the scalpel knife, run it around the uncut edges, again gently. If the leather is totally aligned, smooth it down firmly with the cloth and then go round the edges again firmly with the blunt end of the knife.

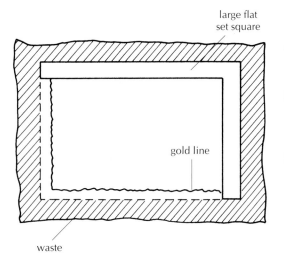

Cutting adjacent edges before laying leather.

If it is not yet aligned and needs to be stretched a little, this can be done by releasing two-thirds of the leather and re-smoothing it down, using a little forward pressure to stretch it. Be careful, however, as once stretched it won't spring back, and it can be stretched quite a bit before actual damage of the surface and distortion of the tooling lines are noticeable.

TRIMMING AND FINISHING

Trimming the rest of the leather must be done accurately.

HOW TO DO IT

1. Before laying leather, lay a straight-edge along one edge, with the tool leaving the border uncovered.
2. Take a 2in (50mm) strip of masking tape at the corner of the leather edge; and fix it to the border with its edge against the straight-edge. Do this to the opposite corner.
3. Go round all four edges, copying **step 2**. When this is done, you should have two tags of masking tape on each corner

going away from the leather area – very much like a printer's alignment marks.

4. Lay the leather as described until you reach the process of cutting the last two edges.
5. On one of the edges of the leather lay the straight-edge down in the same fashion as when putting down the masking-tape tags.
6. Holding the straight-edge firmly, start cutting the leather at one corner with the scalpel knife held at a slight angle, undercutting the leather.

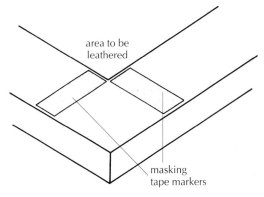

Cutting corners.

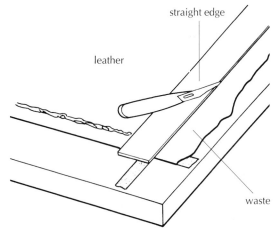

Trimming waste.

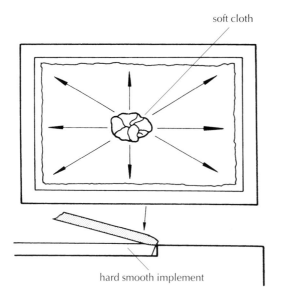

soft cloth

hard smooth implement

7. Copy this on the other uncut edge.
8. Remove the waste, and the straight-edge. With the back of the scalpel knife, press the cut edge of the leather into place, and smooth with a soft rag.
9. With a damp rag, wipe any glue that has squeezed out onto the polished surface, and then wipe dry.

Smoothing-out.

Tips and Wrinkles

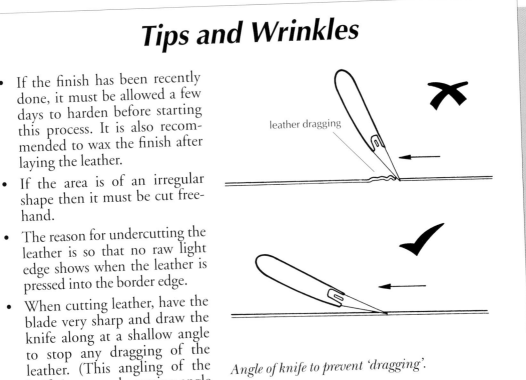

- If the finish has been recently done, it must be allowed a few days to harden before starting this process. It is also recommended to wax the finish after laying the leather.
- If the area is of an irregular shape then it must be cut free-hand.
- The reason for undercutting the leather is so that no raw light edge shows when the leather is pressed into the border edge.
- When cutting leather, have the blade very sharp and draw the knife along at a shallow angle to stop any dragging of the leather. (This angling of the knife is not undercutting angle already mentioned.)

leather dragging

Angle of knife to prevent 'dragging'.

FURNITURE PERIOD CHART

Monarch	Period	Wood	Trade	Some Major Designers	Events and Developments
Henry VIII 1509–1547 Edward VI 1547–1552 Mary 1552–1557 Elizabeth I 1558–1602	Early Tudor Late Tudor/Elizabethan	O A K	Age of the Carpenter	Inigo Jones 1573–1652 Grinling Gibbons 1648–1721	Influence of Renaissance Style
James I 1603–1624 Charles I 1625–1648	Early Stuart Jacobean			Gerriet Jensen c.1700	1642–1648 Civil War in England; Turners become more influential in chair-making.
Commonwealth 1649–1659	Puritan/Commonwealth			William Kent 1686–1748	1666 Great Fire.
Charles II 1660–1684 James II 1685–1688 William & Mary 1689–1694 William III 1695–1701	Restoration Carolean & Late Jacobean William & Mary	W A L N U T	Age of the Cabinet-maker	The Gillow Firm 1731 John Channon 1711–1777 Robert Adam 1728–1792 Thomas Chippendale Senior & Junior 1718–1822	Walnut becomes popular. Veneer and marquetry. Better furniture made by cabinet-makers.
Anne 1702–1713 George I 1714–1726	Queen Anne – Early Georgian			Geo Hepplewhite 172?–1786 Thomas Sheraton 1751–1806	Influence of Baroque style. Mahogany becomes popular.
George II 1727–1759 George III 1760–1819 George IV 1820–1829 William IV 1830–1836	Georgian 1730–1800 Greek Revival/Regency 1800–1820 Late Georgian	Mahogany and other exotics	Age of the Designers	Thomas Hope 1769–1831 Geo Bullock 1782–1818 Augustus Pugin 1812–1852 Ernest Gimson 1864–1931 William Morris 1834–1896	1756–1763 Seven year war with French; Rococo style. 1775–1782 American war of Independence; Neo-classical. 1793–1815 Napoleonic war with France; Greek Revival; French Polish and sprung upholstery introduced.
Victoria 1837–1900	Victorian			E & S Barnsley 1863–1926 Roger Fry 1866–1935 C MacKintosh 1868–1928	1851 Great Exhibition.
Edward VII 1901–1909 George VI 1910–1935	Edwardian New Georgian			Charles Voisey 1857–1941 Sir Ambrose Heal 1872–1959 Hille and Co.	Arts and Crafts 1882. Art Nouveau 1890. Art Deco 1920.

GLOSSARY

Terms Used in this Book and also in the Antiques World

Acanthus Classical, well known leaf decoration of *Acanthus mollis*; very scrolled leaves, as used on capital of Corinthian columns.

Acetic acid See vinegar.

Acroteria Finials or pedestals flanking a pediment, and its apex. Often found on urns and statues.

Ammonia Used in fuming oak, turning the wood dark to black.

Animal glue A hot water glue made from the bones and skin of animals, and used in all early furniture.

Anthemion Stylized honeysuckle ornament, with inward-curling petals. Classical.

Apron Shaped, and sometimes decorated length of wood found beneath bottom framing of drawers, table tops, chair seats etc.

Arabesque Motif decoration, often within strapwork, or symmetrical floral scrolls. Inspired by Middle East. With human figures it is called Grotesque work.

Arcading A series of arches, generally supported on columns.

Arc en arbalète A complex cusped, serpentine edge to a table, tray etc, in the form of a bow.

Architrave The moulding beneath a frieze; mouldings around doorways, mirrors, picture frames etc., sometimes with 'eared' projections at the corners.

Arts and Crafts movement A period of cabinet making from 1882–early 1900s.

Astragal Narrow semicircular moulding, often carved, found in glazing bars, edges of doors, beading.

Back spring lock A form of lock used in furniture.

Bail handling Iron or brass loop handle hanging from either end of a pommel (post).

Ball and claw Common foot-carving on eighteenth century furniture, representing the pearl of wisdom gripped in the talons of a dragon or eagle.

Baluster Turned column in a balustrade, or pillar of a table, swelling out towards the base. When the swelling is at the top it is called an 'inverted baluster'.

Band cramp A cramp that uses a band or belt, used on circular objects.

Banding Ornamental banding, of contrasting, cross-grained wood, or in ivory or brass. Mitred herringbone form was used on walnut from the early eighteenth century.

Bandsaw This is a machine tool which operates a continuous saw blade, in the form of a band.

Barley Twist A sort of turning done in the form of a spiral.

Baroque Originated in Italy and spread throughout Europe in the seventeenth century. Extremely ornate, with swirls and curls; can be overpowering.

Batten A strip of wood used to reinforce another.

Beading Same as astragel, but easily recognized in the moulding of a small, repeated line of beads (called 'pearling').

Bearer Horizontal strut used to support another part, such as the leaves of a table.

Beaumontage *See* Wax stopper.

Bellflower Classical motif of bell-shaped flowers used in chains and swags (can be mistaken for husks).

Bevel Angled edge cut; seen on the glass of mirrors, or in the wood most often edging panels.

Birdcage Support used on four columns to mount a table top on a tripod base, thus allowing circular movement.

Bird's-beak joint A joint with one of its parts resembling a bird's beak, the male part being like a wedge.

Block foot Cubed-shape foot, generally found with square untapered legs.

Blooming When moisture gets into polish and makes it turn cloudy.

Bobbin-turning Repeated ball-turning used on legs and stretchers (typically seventeenth century).

Bodying-in The beginning sequence in French polishing.

Bodying-up The second sequence in polishing.

Boiled linseed oil A vegetable oil extracted from the linseed plant and used in many ways in the work of restoring.

Bole Clay used in the preparation for gilding; mixed with gesso. Colour varies according to period.

Bolecton moulding Bold convex moulding often used to cover joins.

Bombe Describes the bulbous shape of certain chests, commodes etc, typical of Rococo. Often known as 'serpentine'. Favoured by the Dutch.

Bookmatched Where matching leaves of veneer are laid side by side so that their grain makes a pattern.

Boss Carved or grooved ornament, often circular, applied as decoration; often to hide a join.

Boulle (buhl) Figures, flowers and leaves, often the themes for marquetry in turtle- or tortoiseshell, brass, pewter or ivory. Introduced by André-Charles Boulle (1642–1732) in France. With brass ground, it is 'première partie'; when turtleshell, 'contra-partie'.

Bow front Gentle swelling to the front of cabinets, chests etc.; eighteenth century catalogues refer to 'sweep-front'.

Bracket foot A flat, two-piece symmetrical foot, set at a corner, shaped like a bracket at the outer edges.

Braganza foot Seventeenth-century flattened ball foot, fitted by dowel.

Bureau fall The writing flap that comes down to rest horizontally.

Burrs Decorative veneers cut from growths in a log.

Butterfly Or double dovetail, used in holding joints and splits on boards together.

Butt joint Two square plain edges glued together.

Button polish A grade of shellac.

Cabinet scraper A steel blade with its edge burred to create a cutting edge, used to scrape fine shavings.

Cabochon Inspired by a round or oval stone, it is raised ornament found on the knees of cabriole legs. Typical of the mid-eighteenth century.

Cabriole leg Inspired by a goat's leg! Most elegant curved leg, popular in the early eighteenth century but used ever since. Wider convex curve tops narrower concave.

Candle-slide A thin slide to support a candlestick. Found beneath eighteenth-century mirrored doors on cabinets; mirrors reflected light. Also support to table.

Cantilevered legs Can be three- or four-legged around a column. Jointed around it and shaped to lift the column off the ground.

Capital Cap to column; can be carved, scrolled or plain.

Carcase The name given to the body of a piece of furniture.

Carnuba wax A vegetable wax obtained from a South American plant; harder than beeswax.

Cartouche Ornately edged tablet; classically a scroll unrolled to bear a coat of arms or other inscription.

Carver chair Generally denoting a dining chair with arms.

Caryatid Classical female figure appearing to 'hold up' table tops, roofs etc. Male form is named 'Atlantis'.

Casein glue This is a water-proof glue made by mixing a white powder and water.

Caustic soda A chemical favoured by pine strippers; I would advise not to use it on antiques.

Cavetto moulding Concave (hollow) quarter-section, common to cornices.

Cellarette Wine cooler, either part of a sideboard drawer, or free-standing.

Cellulose thinners Used in the mixing with cellulose lacquer, and also used as a cleaner.

Centre-point drill bit A drill bit with a point on its end to help locate a position accurately.

Centre-punch This is similar to a nail punch except it makes a precise indentation to start a drill bit in, and is used on metal.

Chain Hanging pendant (leaves, and/or flowers, fruit, bows etc) 'hanging' from a festoon.

Chamfer Bevelled edge (as in mirrors); usually of 45°, found usually on legs and struts etc. Can carry a further bevel called a 'stop'.

Change to bridle-joint saddled This is an open form of a mortice and tenon.

Chemical Stains Stains which use a chemical reaction to change the colour of the wood.

Chequered inlay Alternate light and dark squares in two or three lines along a length of inlay.

Chinoiserie Designs copied from, or inspired by traditional Chinese furniture and ornament. Very fashionable in the eighteenth- and early nineteenth-century (Regency) periods.

Clearance angle This is the sharpest angle on a chisel, and not the angle on which the cutting is made.

Cleat Like a nautical wedge, but used to describe framing jointed across the ends of a table top to stabilize the 'board'.

Club foot Found particularly on eighteenth-century cabriole legs, or turned, tapered legs which swell to form a flattened ball. There may be a wooden disc beneath.

Cockbead Line of small half-roundels, used as a trim (mostly drawer fronts and doors).

Collar Thin moulding, or banding round a leg for decoration.

Colouring A sequence within polishing for colouring the finish.

Compass An instrument for marking circles.

Composition Resin, whiting and glue size, mixed to make applied decoration.

Console Both the device and the object – a table (generally semicircular) – are attached to the wall, and also the scrolled bracket supporting it.

Constructional veneers A thick-cut veneer for reinforcing or making plywood.

Core-plug A wooden plug that is cut across the grain and inserted into a hole to match the surrounding wood area, to cover countersunk screws.

Corinthian order The range of details comprising classic Greek architecture and ornament (ie fluted columns, acanthus leaves, capitals, scrolls etc).

Cornice Moulded ledge tops to cabinet furniture; often dentil moulding on an underside.

Coved top A flat top, mostly on lids, with a cavetto moulded edge.

Crazed polish This is polish that has cracked in form like a crazy paving.

Cresting Centre-top decoration (chair backs, cabinets, mirrors, bedheads etc).

Cross-section A section cut across an object.

Cross-tongue Inlet of sliver of wood inserted along the grain to join two pieces of wood; may be dovetailed; can be used in mitre joint.

Curvilinear Shaping marked by continuous flowing lines; originally used in Gothic window tracery.

Cusp A recentrant meeting point of two arcs or foils, as seen in Gothic windows.

Cutting angle This is the final angle on a chisel, and is shallower than the clearance angle.

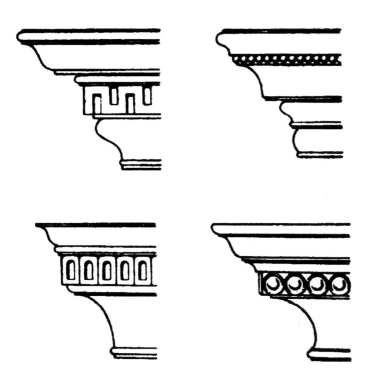

*Cornice mouldings;
Sheraton period (1790–1806).*

Cutting gauge A hand-held tool for making exact and repetitive lines with the edge of a knife blade.

Dentil Small rectangular block, of an equidistant series along a cornice. Source: Ionic and Corinthian ornament.

Diaper Decoration of repeated diamond shapes (in parquetry, or in pierced form, as a lattice).

Dishing Forming a curved depression; as in the seat of a Windsor chair, or a table or tray edge, to prevent objects slipping off.

Distressing Ageing a repaired area.

Domed top Arched top of some seventeenth- and eighteenth-century tea caddies, cabinets etc.

Doric order Earliest Greek 'order' of architecture, copied by furniture makers of the eighteenth century; columns plain or fluted, plain moulded capitals, decorated friezes.

Dovetail Secure and elegant jointing where projecting wedge shape on one piece slots into matched aperture in the other. Half-dovetailing has one side angled and the other straight; a lapped dovetail does not extend all the way through on one surface.

Dovetail template This is a template to mark out dovetails; they can come in several angles.

Dowel small wooden peg used in joinery for securing a mortice and tenon or other joint.

Dowelled joints This is a joint that uses round pegs to joint two surfaces.

Drop-leaf Hinged extension flap to a table, supported when horizontal by a swing leg, or concealed fly-bracket, or a loper.

Dustboard Thin board fixed to the rails between the drawers of a chest.

Earth pigment colours Ground coloured pigments from earth.

Echinus (or egg and dart) Classical repeat decoration, carved representation of above motifs, usually applied to ovolo moulding.

Edwardian A period from 1900–1910, named after Edward VII.

Engaged column Column which is partially attached; not free-standing.

Entablature Found at the top of cabinet furniture, as originally in classical buildings — the beam supported by columns, to carry frieze or cornice, and form part of the architrave.

Escutcheon Essentially an heraldic shield for a coat of arms in furniture, adapted as a pivoting metal keyhole-guard, and keyhole surround. A metal-edge keyhole surround is known as a thread escutcheon.

Fall-front Vertical or slope-fronted flap of cabinet or bureau, hinged at the bottom edge so that with supports, it can form a writing surface.

F cramp A cramp in the form of an 'F'.

Festoon Garland or swag of flowers and foliage, suspended from both ends of a surround.

Fielded panel Wood panel with raised centre and moulded or bevelled surround.

Figure (wood) The name given to striking and irregular colour in a wood. Generally the grain is as wild as the figuring. Excludes burrs, or burles.

Fillet Narrow moulding or flat band between two larger mouldings or flutes.

Finger joint or knuckle joint Wooden hinge with metal pintle. Supports the fly bracket of a drop-leaf table, or swing legs.

Finial The knobs or other ornaments at the very top of posts, domes, or pediments. When hanging from the bottom of posts, they are called pendants.

Finishing The name given to the finished surface material ie wax.

Flare Outward, concave curve (as on a leg). General for flared rim called 'Everted'.

Flattening Process for flattening veneers; a sanding sequence in French polishing.

Flitch A bundle of veneers kept in sequence from the same log; also the name of a brush.

Fluting Half-round grooves as found along the length of pillars, legs, friezes and pilasters. Sometimes filled with wood or brass, when it is called Sto fluting.

Fly bracket Shaped vertical bracket to support a table flap.

French curves These are templates of mathematically formed curves.

French polish A shellac product; also a method of finishing.

Fret Pierced or applied decoration (blind fret). Often used as repeats on bands such as Greek key, Gothic designs etc.

Fuming *See* ammonia.

Furniture (brass) Sometimes used for defining hinges and handles etc.

Gadrooning Carved, decorative edge moulding of convex tapered ribs, resembling frilling or ruffling, but mostly diverging from a central point.

Gateleg A type of leg that moves into position to support a leaf of a table, generally hinged via a knuckle or finger joint.

G cramp A form of cramp in the shape of a G.

Gesso Mixture of whiting and glue size applied to wood for a smooth surface for low-relief carving, or painting, gilding or lacquering.

Gilding Thin sheets of gold laid over either oil size or with water over coloured bole (the latter can be burnished).

Glue block Used to reinforce a joint.

Gooseneck A French, curved, shaped scraper.

Gouge A form of chisel to cut concaved grooves.

Gouging Decoration, typically on oak, where a gouge takes out small semicircles in repeats.

Grain The direction of the fibres of wood.

Grain filler A paste used to fill the open grain before polishing.

Greek key The well known classical repeat pattern, like a winding maze.

Grisaille Monochrome painting, to simulate wood grain or stone – part of trompel'oeil (deceive the eye).

Guilloche Classical frieze decoration of interlaced circles or overlapping discs. Originally plaited ribbon effect.

Herringbone A form of chevron banding used in the seventeenth and eighteenth centuries.

Hipped Shape of a roof with sloping, instead of gabled ends; adapted for some lids, also the term used to describe the extension of the top of cabriole legs, joining to seat-rail; overlapping trim topping some nineteenth-century, round table pillars.

Honing stone A stone, either natural or manufactured, used to create a fine edge to a chisel or other cutting implement.

Husk Decoration sometimes confused with a bellflower; derived from the catkin of *Garrya elliptica*.

Imbrication Carved and painted motif resembling overlapping fish scales.

Impact glue A glue applied to both surfaces that bonds immediately once these are placed together.

Indo furniture Furniture from India and its surrounding areas with an Eastern influence in its design or decoration.

Inlay (including marquetry). Decorative patterns or figures set into contrasting wood.

Inscrolled foot Typically seventeenth to eighteenth century, sometimes called 'Spanish foot' because it is carved to curl down and underneath the leg, as opposed to the later 'French' outcurving foot.

Ionic order Classic Greek style: moulded base. Fluted columns, volute, capital, plain frieze.

Japanning Imitation oriental lacquer, from seventeenth century onwards; of spirit and oil varnishes.

Joint spreader An implement for pushing joints apart by means of a screw thread.

Keeled Like the sharp keel of a boat, some cabriole legs have sharp-edged corners.

Kerf The gap left in wood by a saw blade.

Kerfing Bending wood by cutting a series of deep, close-set parallel slits into one side of the flat.

Kicker A 'stop' fixed into a carcase just above each side of a drawer, to stop it sliding right out when pulled.

Lac The base material from which shellac comes.

Laccifer lac The beetle which forms the lac.

Lacquer Japanese or Chinese painted top surface; delicately painted figures, trees, mountains, pagodas, mostly on black or red ground built up with the sap of the lac tree.

Laminated Several leaves of wood glued together, the grain of each layer usually placed to run in the opposite direction to the layer it lies next to so as to add strength.

Lappet Rounded flap shape employed in decorative carving.

Lathe The machine used in turning wood.

Lever lock A form of lock that uses levers within its mechanism.

Linenfold Carved 'folded cloth' effect found in fine oak panelling from the early sixteenth century.

Linseed oil An oil extracted from linseed.

Lipping A strip of superior wood added to a board of inferior quality, placed where it is most visible.

Loose side The side of a machine-cut veneer which has knife checks running into the thickness of the veneer to 25 per cent.

Loper The bar that is pulled out of a slot to support a bureau front.

Lotus Stylized waterlily flower, often found in card tables. 1810–1840; inspired by ancient Egyptian finds.

Lunette Decorative semicircle, carved mostly in oak furniture; intersected, or in repeat bands.

Machine cut Used to describe machine-cut veneers.

Marking knife A knife used in marking out joints before cutting.

Marquetry Pictures in inlaid wood; in furniture, motifs, mostly of figures or flowers, laid on or into a wooden surface.

Matting The last sequence in rubbing down a finish using steel wool.

Methylated spirits Used in the making of French polish; can also be used as a cleaner.

Mitre Generally the corner join, as found in picture frames.

Mitre cramp A cramp used to hold mitres together.

Mortice The female part of a mortice and tenon joint: the square or oblong hole cut into the legs and other members.

Mortice and tenon Common joint, where a 'tab' extending from one piece of wood fits into a matching slot in the other. Through-tenon: the mortice cuts right through the wood.

Mortice gauge A marking gauge with two marking points to create parallel lines.

Motif A design or emblem set on or in an area for decoration.

Moulding a shaped piece of wood used round panels, or as a finishing edge.

Moulding template Template made of numerous small pins that when pressed against an object will take up its exact shape.

Muntin Main vertical or horizontal framing member of a stile.

Nail-punch An implement for sinking nails below the surface of the wood, used with a hammer.

Naphtha A mineral-based spirit.

Neo-classic Architectural and decorative style simulating the ancient Greek; highly fashionable in the eighteenth century (Nash, Adam, Allen etc).

Nitric acid Used in staining wood.

Octangular Elongated octagon (like a rectangle with chamfered corners).

Ogee Gothic influenced moulding of a concave above a convex arc. Also eighteenth-century feet in this style, found on clock cases and cabinets.

Oil finish A form of finish done with linseed oil.

Oil stains An oil-based stain.

Ormolu Cast brass or bronze elaborate ornament with fire (mercury) gilt surface; Louis Quinze to Victorian credenzas.

Outset corner Circular or square projection at corner of table (*see also* Architrave).

Ovolo moulding Sunken convex moulding of quadrant profile, used mostly at corners of panels.

Oxalic acid A natural product, used as a gentle bleach to remove ink spots etc.

Oysters Veneers cut across the grain of small branches; walnut, olive, laburnum especially, and laid in decorative manner. 1700.

Pad foot Club foot resting on a disc.

Palmette Classical ornament depicting palm leaf with outcurved fronds.

Papier mâché Tough, malleable material made from paper or cardboard and glue size, popular in the eighteenth and nineteenth centuries for furniture, fire-screens, boxes; often inlaid with mother of pearl.

Parcel gilt Partially gilded surface; highlighted effect on features.

Parchemin Sixteenth-century relief-carved motif on panelling.

Parquetry Like marquetry, veneered inset decoration of contrasting woods, but geometric or architectural patterns.

Patera A slightly dished circular or oval classical ornament, sometimes containing flowerhead or fan motif.

Patina The ageing effect on both the wood surface and the finish.

Pedestal Tall block, often on a base, used to support statue, vase or table top. Also cupboards flanking a serving table in the dining room.

Pediment Classical gable of low pitch (as on the Parthenon), topping mirrors or cabinets; triangular, can be segmental, broken, scrolled, swan-necked.

Peg foot Slender, turned foot used on cabinet furniture; late eighteenth, early nineteenth century.

Pendant Drop finial, or repeated pendants beneath a rail; or a chain.

Piecrust Shaped, moulded edge of a circular table top or a tray. Mid-eighteenth century. Copies the curves and curls found on silver salvers.

Pierced work Also known as fretwork, an open lattice or other design cut through a piece of wood.

Pilaster Flat column, used decoratively in low relief.

Pins through the joint This is a wooden securing pin that is driven through a mortice joint, used on early furniture and woods of an oily nature that do not glue well.

Pitched top Generally on boxes where four steep pitches stop to form a flat top. If they continue to a point the top is called 'Pyramidal'.

Plaster of Paris Used in fillers (*see* Whiting).

Plinth Low, square block support to column, or solid board supporting case furniture instead of feet.

Polisher's mop A brush for applying French polish.

Polishing oil A light vegetable oil to stop dragging when polishing.

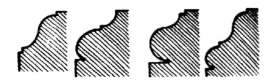

Plinth mouldings;
Hepplewhite period (1760–1790).

Pommel A bolt with a rounded or decorative head passed through a drawer or door front to secure a bail handle.

Potassium bichromate Chemical stain.

Potassium permanganate A chemical stain which turns mahogany an orangey-brown.

Pot board Low shelf under a buffet on which flagons and pots were kept.

Pounced Granular or sanded ground found on early eighteenth-century gesso furniture, for texture; not to be confused with 'punched' or 'pitted' ground.

Putto Winged cherub; also known as Amorini.

PVA glues A polyester-based glue, ready to use.

Quadrant hinge Hinge with two long arms rotating on a short pintle, often used at the top and bottom of cabinet doors, card-table flap, or fall.

Quadrant stay Sliding piece of metal of quarter-circle circumference used to support a fall-front (bureau, secretaire etc).

Quartering Four matching figured sheets of veneer laid to produce an 'ink-fold' design; particularly walnut.

Quarter-sawn The cutting of a log radially to achieve maximum figure and stability.

Queen Anne type A style from the early 1700s which takes its name from the monarch of that period.

Rabbit glue An animal glue used mainly by gilders in the making of gesso.

Rail Horizontal framing member (chair-rail, back-rail, bed-rail etc).

Rake Degree of slope from the vertical, as found on a chair-back.

Rebate Right-angled recess cut into the edge of wood, or formed of two pieces, one set back to form a support for a mirror, panel or drop-in seat.

Rebates and tongues Also known as tongue and groove, used in joining boards together.

Reeding Repeated concave mouldings (channels); often round pillars, legs, and sometimes in flutes.

Renaissance Fifteenth century Italian revival of classical styles, which spread throughout Europe in the sixteenth century.

Riband back Typical Chippendale chairs in which carved ribands (ribbons) are a feature.

Ribbing Repeat-decoration of small-scale reeds, generally found in panels or bands.

Ribbon ornament Carved and/or painted decoration used in rococo design.

Rinceaux Repeat classical decoration of acanthus leaves curling in alternative directions.

Rococo Early eighteenth-century architectural and decorative style developed in France which superseded the heavier baroque.

Rope a form of turning done in the form of a rope.

Roundel Applied circular decorative motif.

Router A machine for cutting mouldings and grooves.

Rubbed joint A glued joint that is rubbed together to form a suction, and where no cramping is used.

Rubber A pad for applying polish.

Rule joint Stopped, hinged joint used on table leaves, press doors etc. Long ovolo moulding which leaves no gap.

Runners These are members on which drawers slide; they are also used for moving members on an expanding table.

Rust marks Black marks in wood formed by rust.

Sabot French-style cast brass or ormolu foot mount.

Sandwich A sandwich of veneers held together while cutting marquetry.

Sash-cramp A cramp with an adjustable end so that it can be extended further than its screw-thread, used for cramping chairs etc.

Saw-cut veneer A veneer cut by hand which is at least ⅛in (3mm) thick. Used on furniture up to the late 1800s.

Scagliola Coloured composition of plaster and marble chips, pictorially or to imitate marble, especially on seventeenth-century Italian table tops.

Scalloped Shape of a scallop shell, with lobed or foiled edge.

Scotch pearl glue An animal glue used in antique furniture.

Scratch-stock A tool for holding a shaped scraper blade to shape mouldings and grooves.

Seaweed marquetry Seventeenth century. Depicts feathery fronds, utilizing the natural grains in veneer.

Serpentine Convex curve flanked by two concave curves to produce a sinuous shape popular on chest fronts. Early eighteenth century and later.

Sheer strength The name given to the sheering power of an object when it breaks across its grain.

Shellac finish French polish.

Shellac stopper A form of shellac used in filling small holes.

Shells, sunbursts Forms of motifs.

Shoe Shaped horizontal bar (as in chairs, fitted round the bottom of a splat, over upholstery and tacked into a back rail. Eighteenth century.

Skiver A thin leather.

Sliding bevel Similar to a set-square, except that the blade can be moved to make different angles.

Sodium chloride Salt solution used to neutralize acids.

Spade foot Square, tapered or 'thermed' foot, generally used on a tapered leg. Eighteenth century.

Spandrel Triangular space formed between the curve of an arch and its square framing. Without the arch, the shape is called 'Bracket'.

Speed cramp A form of fast-action F cramp.

Spider A metal plate to secure the underneath of cantilever legs by holding them together.

Spindle Slender, turned baluster, often used in rows.

Spiral twist Turning of leg or column like a screw thread.

Spirit stains Stains in a spirit, or methylated-spirit base.

Spiriting-off The last sequence in polishing.

Splay Originally of a window recess, or reveal. The angled taper of the sides. Called 'flared' when curved.

Splayed foot The outward curve of a foot on certain periods of furniture.

Splice A butt joint cut in at an angle across the grain.

Splint Vertical board, usually flat with shaped sides, often pierced or carved, inserted into a chair-back between the top and the seat rails.

Spokeshave A tool used by chair makers for shaping a stave etc; named because it was used in the shaping of spokes by wheelwrights.

Spoonback Name given to a particular shape of Victorian chair, usually open and in the form of a spoon-shaped hoop.

Staining The use of stains to colour wood.

Steel wool Strands of steel so fine as to look like wool, used in smoothing finishes. It comes in many grades from fine through to coarse.

Stiff leaf Carved motif of curled acanthus leaves. Gothic.

Stile Vertical framing member in joinery. Subsidiary of muntin.

Stopper A paste used to fill small holes.

Straight-front Completely flat front of cabinet or chest.

Strapwork Symmetrical ornament of flat interlaced bands or ribbons.

Stretcher Horizontal rail connecting and bracing legs; can be arched, or cross-stretchers employed for decorative purposes.

Stringing Thin, decorative inlaid line of brass or contrasting wood, almost always veneer.

Stripper A chemical for dissolving a finish prior to removal.

Substrate The base on which a veneer is laid.

Sulphuric acid Used to remove rust marks.

Swag Ornamental garland or festoon, carved or applied, featuring flowers, fruit, foliage or drapery, suspended from both ends (of chain).

Table clip or fork Two-pronged, generally brass clip which slides into sockets to link two table leaves.

Tally sticks Used in aligning.

Tannic acid A chemical within wood that reacts with chemical stains.

Template a template is an exact copy of an object that the maker wants to copy.

Tenon The male part to a mortice-and-tenon joint, a tongue that fits tightly into the mortice hole.

Term A pedestal or pilaster tapered to its base, the top formed as a human figure (as of caryatid).

Tester Flat canopy, as in tester bed.

Tight side The side of the veneer that has little or no knife checks.

Tongue and groove Joint obtained by cutting a groove in the centre of the edge of one board to house the tongue rebated in an adjoining board.

Tooling Either black or gold decorative lines on leather.

Toothing plane The iron is toothed, and is used in making a keyed surface for veneers.

Toppings a form of glaze.

Tracery Pierced or blind decoration, as seen in Gothic windows.

Trefoil Gothic motif of three cuspid arcs or lobes (three-leaf clover).

Trifid foot Three-part division on a club foot, often with foliate decoration. Common on cabriole legs.

Trophy Classical motif often employed for military pieces; trumpets, drums, crossed guns etc. Marquetry, brass, painted.

Try-square Used to ascertain right-angles, either for checking or marking out.

Tunbridge work Small-scale mosaic of various coloured woods, used pictorially or geometrically. Started at Tunbridge Wells in the early nineteenth century.

Turned, and post or pillar feet Turned foot for chest of drawers etc.

Turning The name given to an ornamental round object, ie a round leg.

Turpentine Pure spirit taken from 'pitch pine', used as a solvent, mixed with paint, stains and in the making of wax.

Tuscan order Classical style similar to Doric, but with plain, *un*fluted columns, moulded bases and plain friezes.

Upholstery The covered padding on a seat or chair.

Van Dyke brown crystals A pigment used in water stain.

Variable grain Where the grain in the wood changes direction many times. This gives shading to the wood like a fiddle-back.

Veneer Thinly cut wood, laid on another wood, usually of more expensive or exotic nature than the base wood.

Veneer hammer A tool for squeezing out the glue between substrate and veneer.

Veneer pins Especially thin pins for holding down veneers while the glue dries.

Veneer punch A cutter to stamp out shaped veneers to patch with.

Veneer saw A saw with a crank handle, the blade edge being a shallow curve, and the teeth having no set.

Veneer tape A gummed tape used in veneering.

Vernis Martin A form of translucent japanning: French, early eighteenth century. Introduced by Martin bros.

Victorian The period covering Victoria's reign, 1837–1900.

Vinegar Used in cleaning and neutralizing alkalines.

Vitruvian scroll Repeated classical scrolled-wave decoration. Derivation: Marcus Vitruvius Pollio, a famous Ancient Roman architect.

Voluté Ram's-horn scroll, as seen on Ionic capitals.

Wainscot Fine, straight-grained, quarter-cut oak imported from the Baltic. Its name derives from its original use which was for wagon shafts.

Ward A steel ring at the base of the pin in a lock that allows only the correct key to engage.

Warped a twisted board.

Water-aniline dyes Aniline dyes suspended.

Water-coating A form of staining with earth pigments.

Waterleaf Motif based on waterlily foliage, often found carved into mouldings circa 1810–1840.

Water stains Water-based stains.

Wave moulding Alternate curves produce a wave effect on a length of moulding.

Wax finish A form of finish using beeswax.

Wax stopper (beaumontage) A mixture of waxes and resins for filling in small holes.

Wedge A sharp, triangular piece of wood used to tighten or force things apart. A folding wedge is where two wedges are used.

Wedge cramp a cramp using wedges to apply pressure.

Wheatsheaf back Chippendale chair in which the splat resembles a wheatsheaf.

Wheelback Hepplewhite chairs where the splats radiate from a central carved boss.

White or bleached polish A bleached form of button polish, used on marquetry.

Winding *See* Warped.

Windlass A means of tightening a cord by using a rod that twists the cord around itself. Also known as a 'tourniquet'.

Woodworm The grub of the woodworm beetle, which eats wood and leaves hollowed tunnels in it.

INDEX

bleach, 'A' and 'B' 159
bleaching 157
brasswork (including aging) 204–5

cabinet scraper 152–5
calipers (for measuring) 99
carving:
    matching design 83
    repairing solid carving 82
    replacing missing pieces 83
    restoring sections 80
caustic soda 43
chair frames, circular 69–70
chair rails 71–4
chairs, hoop-backed 71
cleaning 39–40
cleaning recipe 39
cockbeading 79
copper or brass stains 158
cramping 71–4
    blocks 71
    boards 74
    dovetail drawer 71
cramps 62–6

dark or black rings 158
darkened wood 159
darker patched areas 160
dents, lifting 161
distressing 166
    tools 166
dovetails 32, 53–9
dowels 50–2

feet, repairing, replacing 84
    bracket type 185–6
finish:
    recognition of 39
    'lost' 160–1
finishing, preparation for 152

glues 36–9, 61–2

hinges 205

ink marks 157
insertions, butterfly 74–5

joints 28–32

kerf (as in bird's-beak) 9

leathers, laying 208–10
locks 206–7

marquetry, repairing 147–52
    using fretsaw in 148
mellowing a new finish 201
methylated spirits 40
mineral oil and grease 159
missing pieces, making up 76
mitre dovetail 85
mitre-blocks, making 80
mortice 47–8
mouldings 78–9

natural oils 159

oxalic acid 157

paring 50
parquetry:
    principles of 145–6
    making a chessboard 146–7
plinths, construction of 86
polishing (French polishing) 183–4, 186–7
    bodying-up 198–200
    colouring-up 200–1
    mop 194
    rubber 190–3
    rubbing down, matting 189–90
shellac 183, 186, 187

spiriting-off 201
polishing and patching old finishes 202
    oil finish 183–4, 190
    wax: making and applying 183, 185–6
polishing methods 188–90, 194–201
polishing tools 187–8

rubbed joint 75
rust marks 158

sand papers 155–6
sanding 155–7
sanding technique 156–7
screws 21
shims 67
splice 49
splits:
    bandsaw method to remove 93–4
    in bureau fall 96–7
    in dowelled joint 98
    in jointed areas 95
    on planked areas 95
staining: 167–90
    ammonia 177–8
    application 172, 174
    chemical 171–7
    earth pigments 168–70, 179
    for inlay and marquetry 181
    method, all pieces 172–3
    nitric acid 172, 178–9
    oil-based 168–70
    shellac mix 170
    spirit-based 168–9, 174–5
    staining a door 172–3
    to cover scorch-marks 180
    turpentine mix 170
    types of 168

Van Dyke brown crystals 171
    water-based 168–71
    by water-coating 175–6
    water-pigment and aniline 176
staining chart 182
stoppers and fillers: 162
    dental plaster 162
    grain-fillers 165
    plaster 162
    plaster of Paris 162
    proprietary 162
    shellac 162
    wax (beaumontage) 162–3
    wood dust and glue 162
stripping 40

template (how to make) 99
template for turning 99
tenons 45–7
tools 9
    chisels 10
    cutting angle 13
    drawing instruments 12
    grinding angle 13
    grinding stones 14
    hammers and mallets 12
    Japanese 9
    lathe 99
    miscellaneous 13
    planes 10
    pliers 12
    power 14
    punches and screwdrivers 12

saws 11
scratch stock 109
second-hand 9
sharpening 13
tube drill 24
turned posts and pillars 89
turnings:
    'bird's-beak' repair (skarf) 102
    blanks, making 106
    broken chips from 106
    broken leg 104
    leg (drilling leg) 104–5
    measuring for 100
    reeds, flutes, ropes, barley-twists 107
    reeds and flutes by hand 109–10
    repairing spindles 106–8
    ropes and barley-twists by hand 110–11
turning-box 107–33

veneers 16
    blisters on 122
    book-matching 135
    burns in 130
    crossbanding 136–8
        fitting mitres in 138
        making corners in 138
    cutting 116–7
    delamination of curved surfaces 132–3
    filler in 131–2
    flattening 116
    gouged-out areas 129

    herringbone bands, making 143
    identifying 112
    inlay lines, laying 144
    inlay motifs 145
    laying 117–21
        preparation for 115
    missing areas 126
    missing pieces 87
    mitres, making full 138
    patching 126–8
    releasing from substrate 125
    repairs to burrs and figured veneer 129–30
    saw-cut 113
    selecting and purchasing 113
    splits in 130–1
    splits in wood 90–4
    storing 113–14
    stringing, making 142
    substrates 114
        unstable 126
    water-damage, repairing 122–4
    woodworm damage in 125
    patching away from edges 129
veneered mouldings 135
veneered pillars 133–4
veneering (decorative) 135–6
    splayed feet 87–9

wax 159
white rings, removal of 203
wood 15